PSYCHIATRIC
TALES

DARRYL CUNNINGHAM

Blank Slate, London
2010

Slate 8

Psychiatric Tales

First published 2010 by Blank Slate, London

Publisher: Kenny Penman
Editor: Isobel Rips
Book Design: Duncan Bullimore

Hardcover
ISBN 9781906653088

Discover more about Blank Slate at
www.blankslatebooks.co.uk

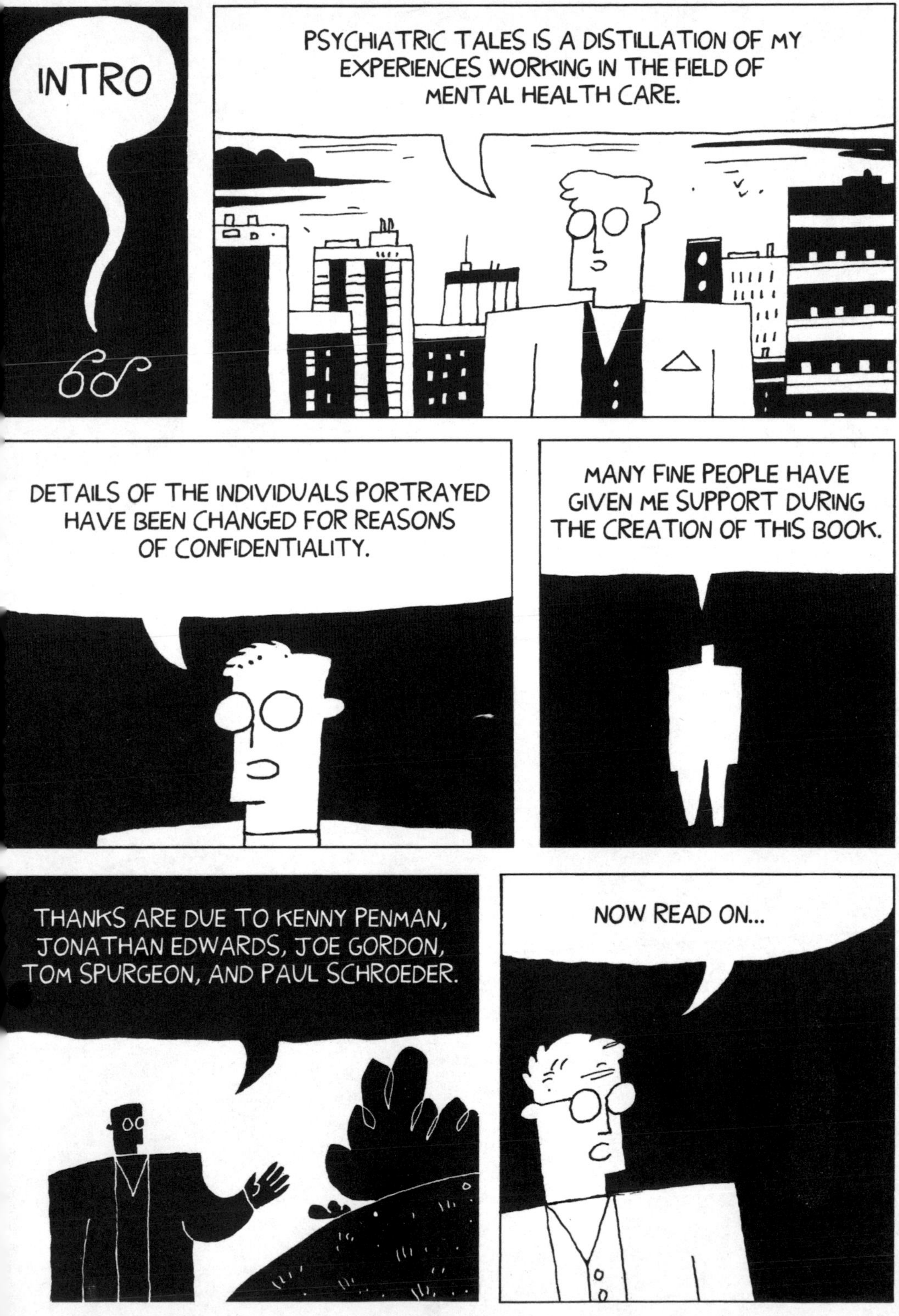
INTRO
PSYCHIATRIC TALES IS A DISTILLATION OF MY EXPERIENCES WORKING IN THE FIELD OF MENTAL HEALTH CARE.
DETAILS OF THE INDIVIDUALS PORTRAYED HAVE BEEN CHANGED FOR REASONS OF CONFIDENTIALITY.
MANY FINE PEOPLE HAVE GIVEN ME SUPPORT DURING THE CREATION OF THIS BOOK.
THANKS ARE DUE TO KENNY PENMAN, JONATHAN EDWARDS, JOE GORDON, TOM SPURGEON, AND PAUL SCHROEDER.
NOW READ ON...

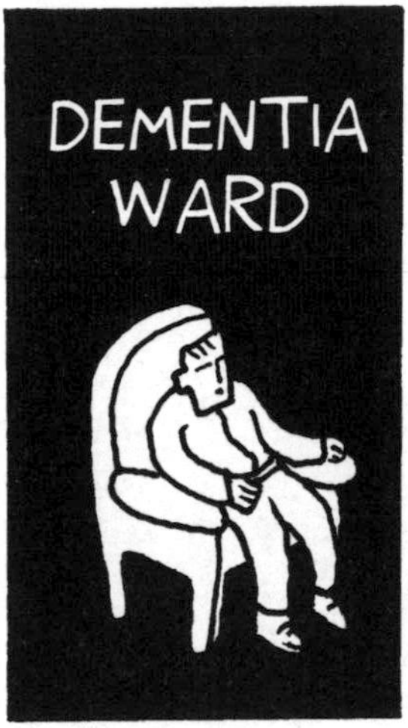
DEMENTIA
WARD

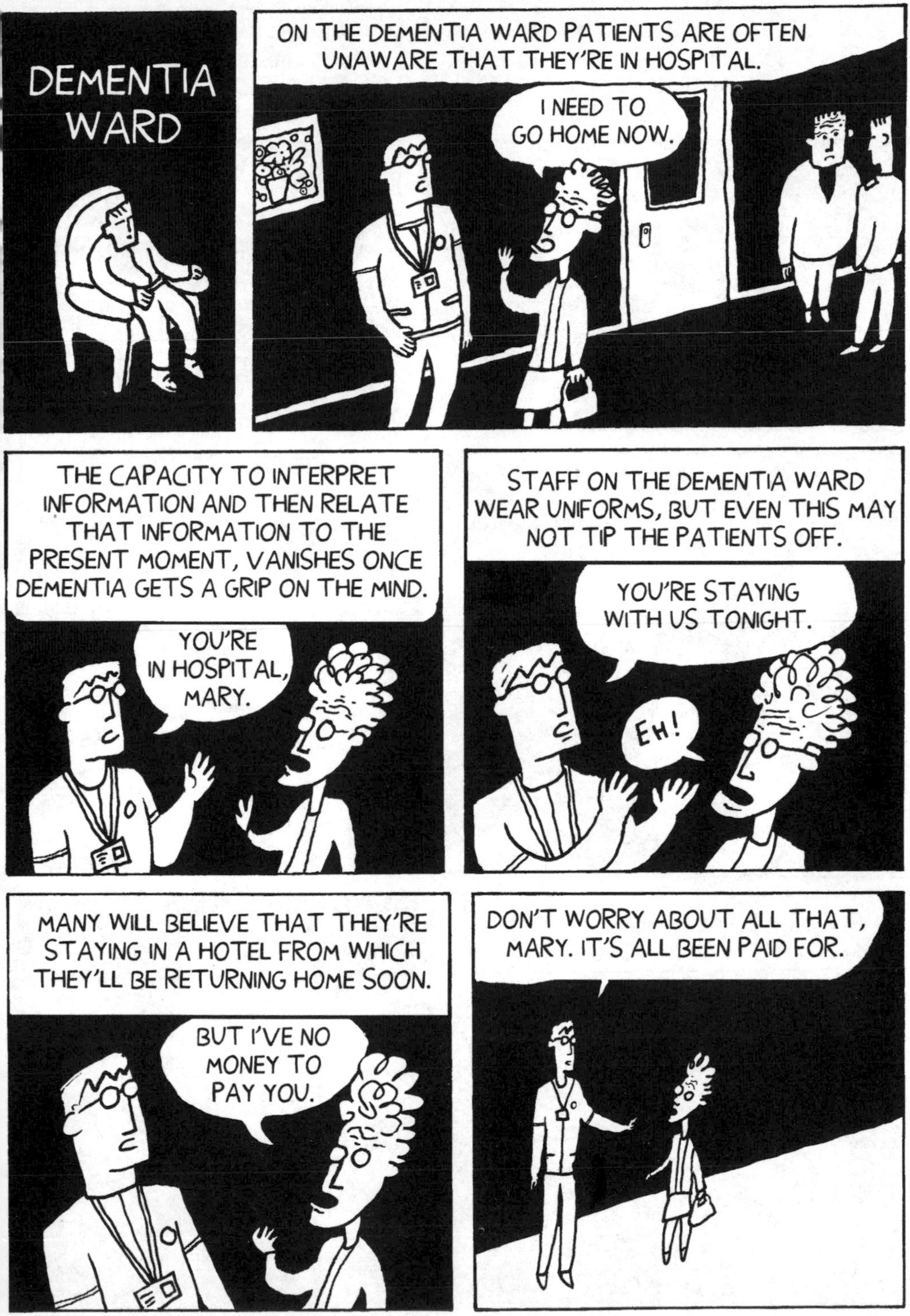
DEMENTIA WARD
ON THE DEMENTIA WARD PATIENTS ARE OFTEN UNAWARE THAT THEY'RE IN HOSPITAL.
I NEED TO GO HOME NOW.
THE CAPACITY TO INTERPRET INFORMATION AND THEN RELATE THAT INFORMATION TO THE PRESENT MOMENT, VANISHES ONCE DEMENTIA GETS A GRIP ON THE MIND.
YOU'RE IN HOSPITAL, MARY.
STAFF ON THE DEMENTIA WARD WEAR UNIFORMS, BUT EVEN THIS MAY NOT TIP THE PATIENTS OFF.
YOU'RE STAYING WITH US TONIGHT.
EH!
MANY WILL BELIEVE THAT THEY'RE STAYING IN A HOTEL FROM WHICH THEY'LL BE RETURNING HOME SOON.
BUT I'VE NO MONEY TO PAY YOU.
DON'T WORRY ABOUT ALL THAT, MARY. IT'S ALL BEEN PAID FOR.

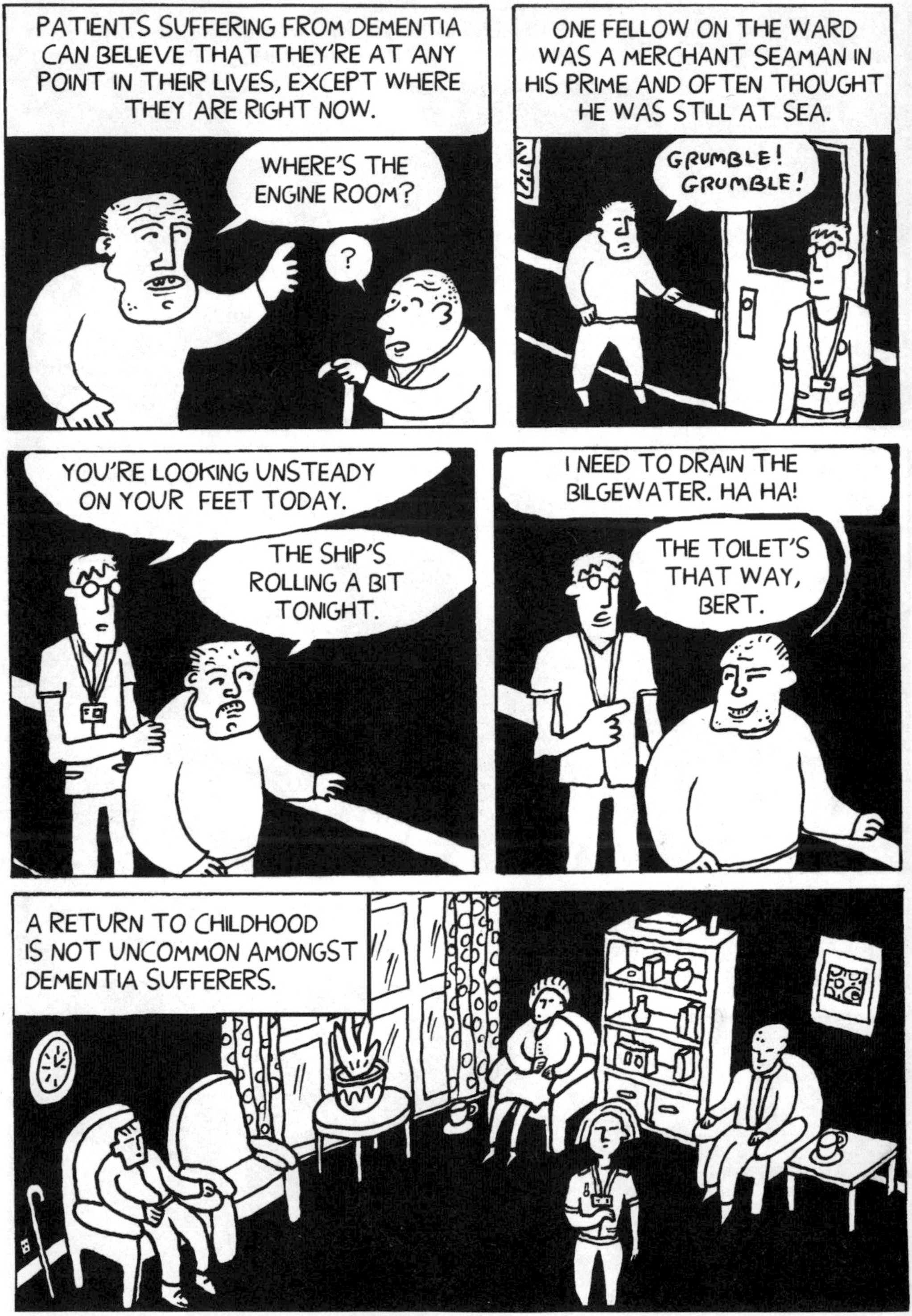
PATIENTS SUFFERING FROM DEMENTIA CAN BELIEVE THAT THEY'RE AT ANY POINT IN THEIR LIVES, EXCEPT WHERE THEY ARE RIGHT NOW.
WHERE'S THE ENGINE ROOM?
?
ONE FELLOW ON THE WARD WAS A MERCHANT SEAMAN IN HIS PRIME AND OFTEN THOUGHT HE WAS STILL AT SEA.
GRUMBLE! GRUMBLE!
YOU'RE LOOKING UNSTEADY ON YOUR FEET TODAY.
THE SHIP'S ROLLING A BIT TONIGHT.
I NEED TO DRAIN THE BILGEWATER. HA HA!
THE TOILET'S THAT WAY, BERT.
A RETURN TO CHILDHOOD IS NOT UNCOMMON AMONGST DEMENTIA SUFFERERS.

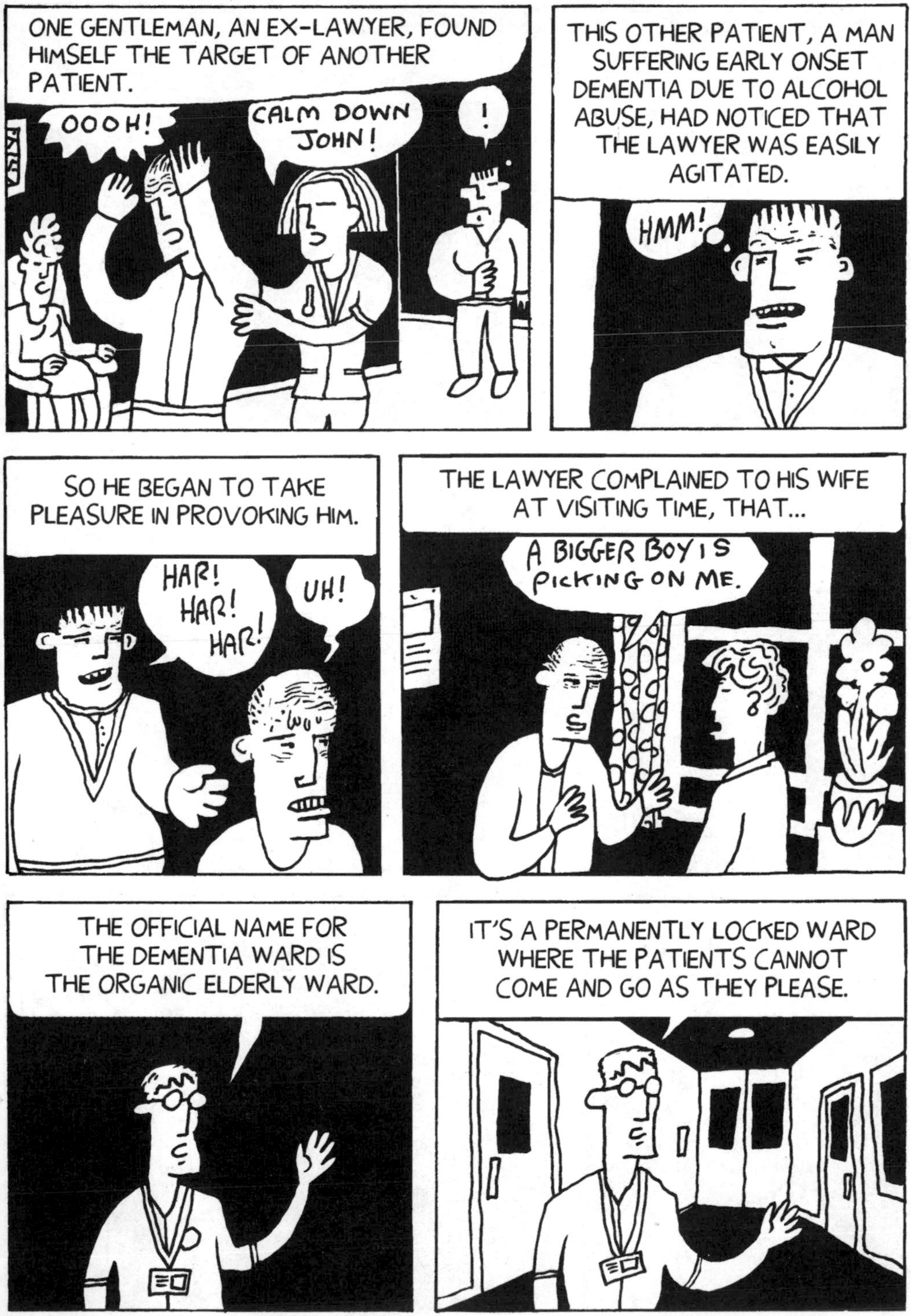
ONE GENTLEMAN, AN EX-LAWYER, FOUND HIMSELF THE TARGET OF ANOTHER PATIENT.
OOOH!
CALM DOWN JOHN!
!
THIS OTHER PATIENT, A MAN SUFFERING EARLY ONSET DEMENTIA DUE TO ALCOHOL ABUSE, HAD NOTICED THAT THE LAWYER WAS EASILY AGITATED.
HMM!
SO HE BEGAN TO TAKE PLEASURE IN PROVOKING HIM.
HAR! HAR! HAR!
UH!
THE LAWYER COMPLAINED TO HIS WIFE AT VISITING TIME, THAT...
A BIGGER BOY IS PICKING ON ME.
THE OFFICIAL NAME FOR THE DEMENTIA WARD IS THE ORGANIC ELDERLY WARD.
IT'S A PERMANENTLY LOCKED WARD WHERE THE PATIENTS CANNOT COME AND GO AS THEY PLEASE.

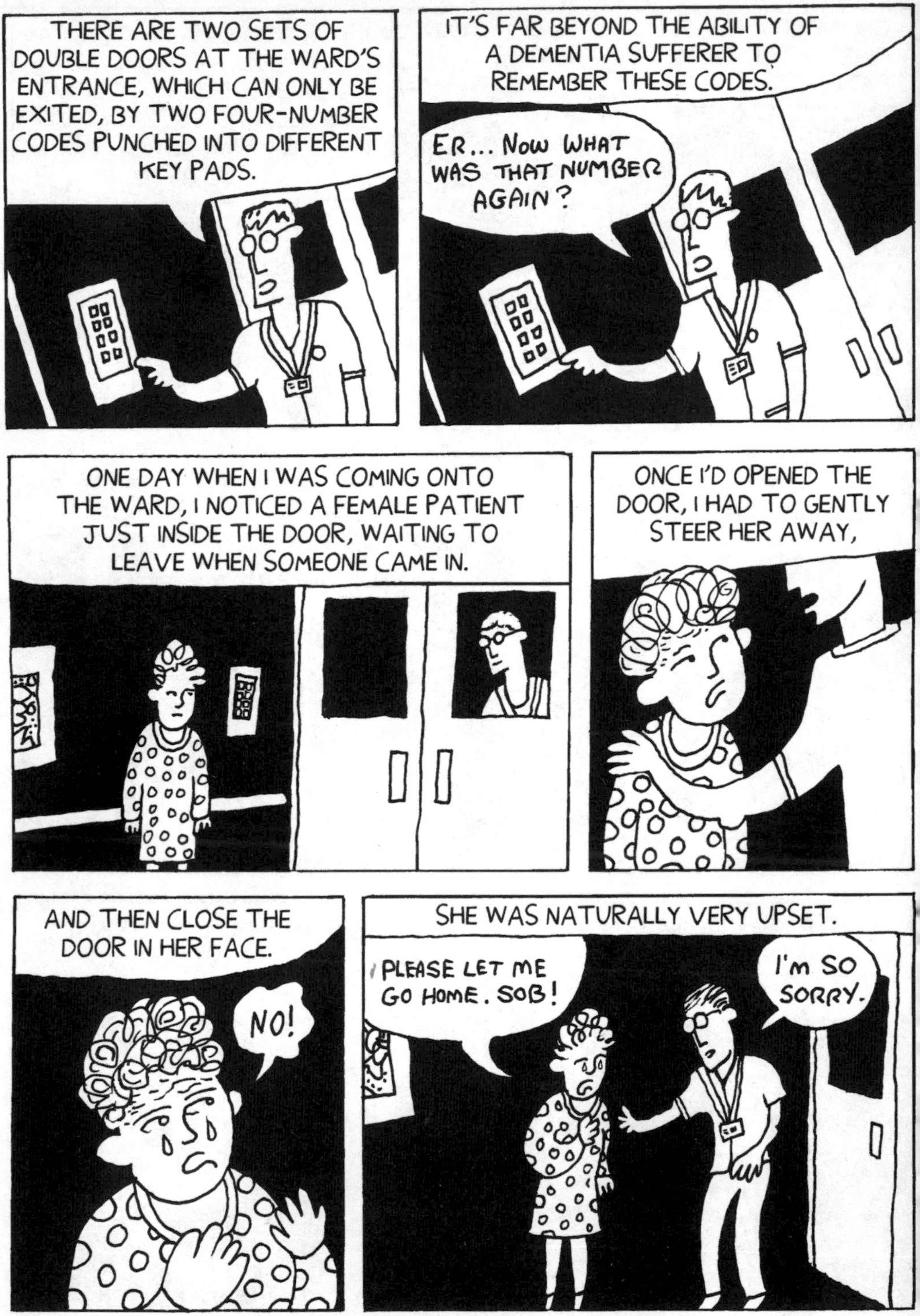
THERE ARE TWO SETS OF DOUBLE DOORS AT THE WARD'S ENTRANCE, WHICH CAN ONLY BE EXITED, BY TWO FOUR-NUMBER CODES PUNCHED INTO DIFFERENT KEY PADS.
IT'S FAR BEYOND THE ABILITY OF A DEMENTIA SUFFERER TO REMEMBER THESE CODES.
ER... NOW WHAT WAS THAT NUMBER AGAIN?
ONE DAY WHEN I WAS COMING ONTO THE WARD, I NOTICED A FEMALE PATIENT JUST INSIDE THE DOOR, WAITING TO LEAVE WHEN SOMEONE CAME IN.
ONCE I'D OPENED THE DOOR, I HAD TO GENTLY STEER HER AWAY,
AND THEN CLOSE THE DOOR IN HER FACE.
NO!
SHE WAS NATURALLY VERY UPSET.
PLEASE LET ME GO HOME. SOB!
I'M SO SORRY.

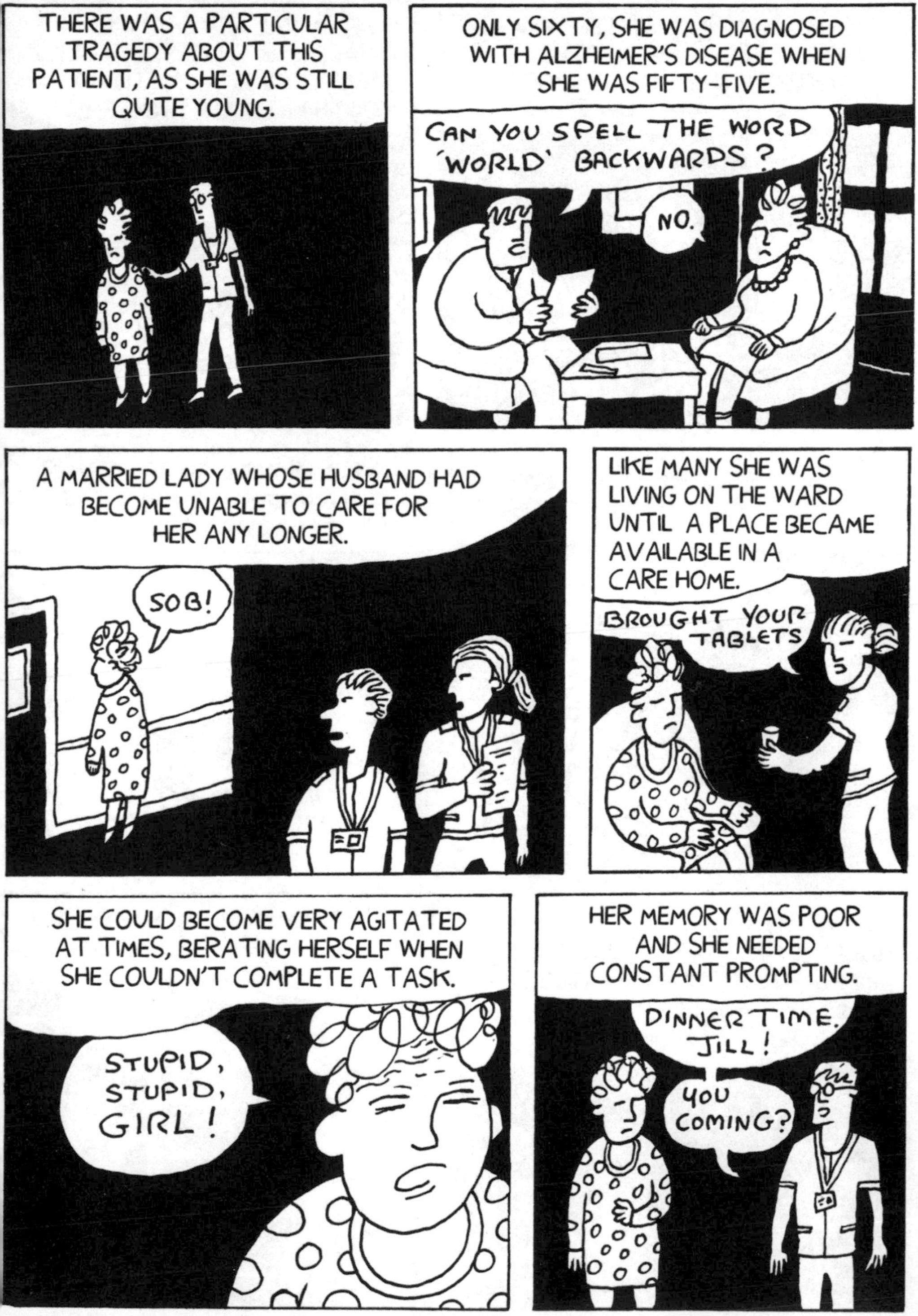
THERE WAS A PARTICULAR TRAGEDY ABOUT THIS PATIENT, AS SHE WAS STILL QUITE YOUNG.
ONLY SIXTY, SHE WAS DIAGNOSED WITH ALZHEIMER'S DISEASE WHEN SHE WAS FIFTY-FIVE.
CAN YOU SPELL THE WORD 'WORLD' BACKWARDS?
NO.
A MARRIED LADY WHOSE HUSBAND HAD BECOME UNABLE TO CARE FOR HER ANY LONGER.
SOB!
LIKE MANY SHE WAS LIVING ON THE WARD UNTIL A PLACE BECAME AVAILABLE IN A CARE HOME.
BROUGHT YOUR TABLETS
SHE COULD BECOME VERY AGITATED AT TIMES, BERATING HERSELF WHEN SHE COULDN'T COMPLETE A TASK.
STUPID, STUPID, GIRL!
HER MEMORY WAS POOR AND SHE NEEDED CONSTANT PROMPTING.
DINNER TIME. JILL!
YOU COMING?

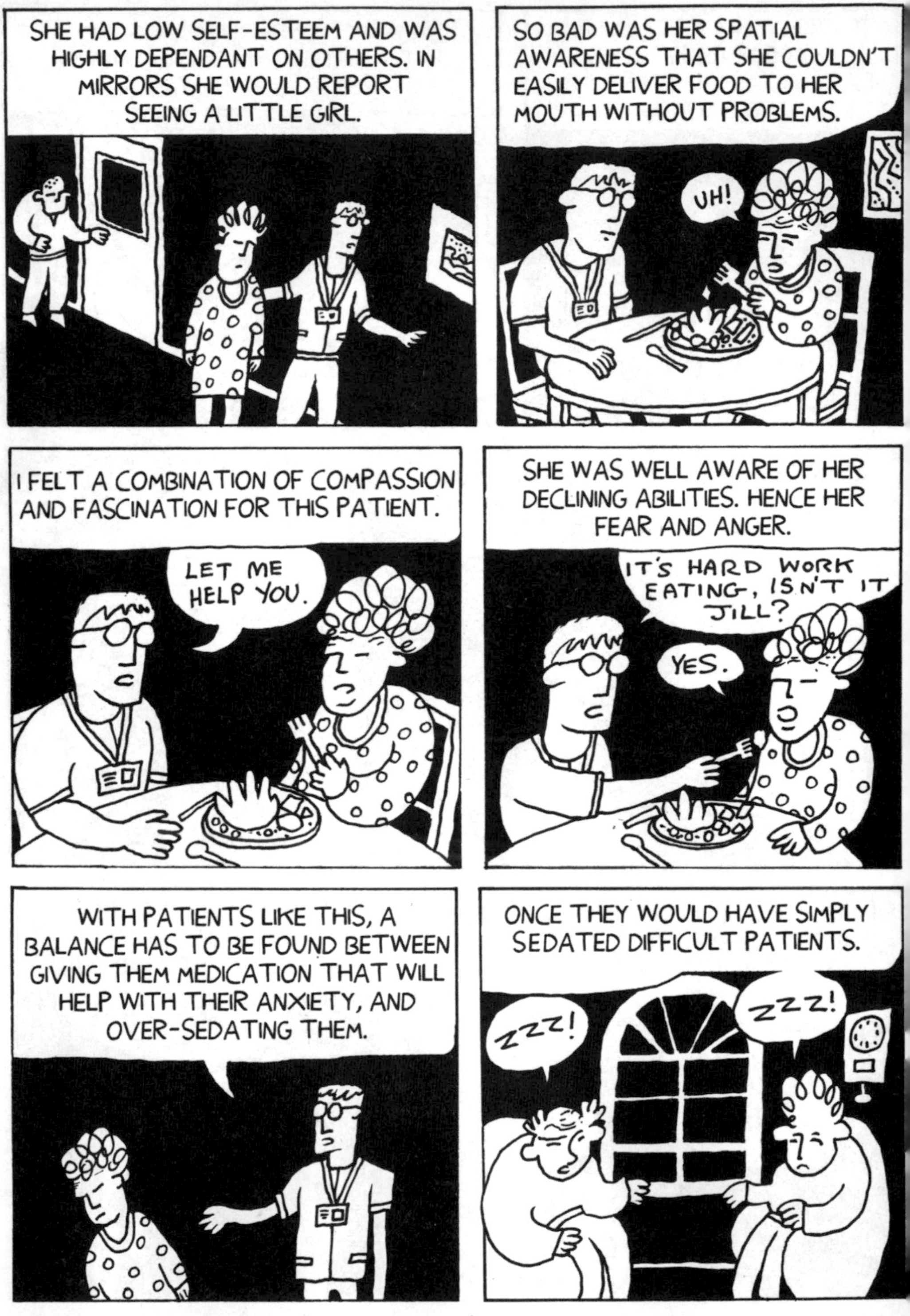
SHE HAD LOW SELF-ESTEEM AND WAS HIGHLY DEPENDANT ON OTHERS. IN MIRRORS SHE WOULD REPORT SEEING A LITTLE GIRL.
SO BAD WAS HER SPATIAL AWARENESS THAT SHE COULDN'T EASILY DELIVER FOOD TO HER MOUTH WITHOUT PROBLEMS.
UH!
I FELT A COMBINATION OF COMPASSION AND FASCINATION FOR THIS PATIENT.
LET ME HELP YOU.
SHE WAS WELL AWARE OF HER DECLINING ABILITIES. HENCE HER FEAR AND ANGER.
IT'S HARD WORK EATING, ISN'T IT JILL?
YES.
WITH PATIENTS LIKE THIS, A BALANCE HAS TO BE FOUND BETWEEN GIVING THEM MEDICATION THAT WILL HELP WITH THEIR ANXIETY, AND OVER-SEDATING THEM.
ONCE THEY WOULD HAVE SIMPLY SEDATED DIFFICULT PATIENTS.
ZZZ!
ZZZ!

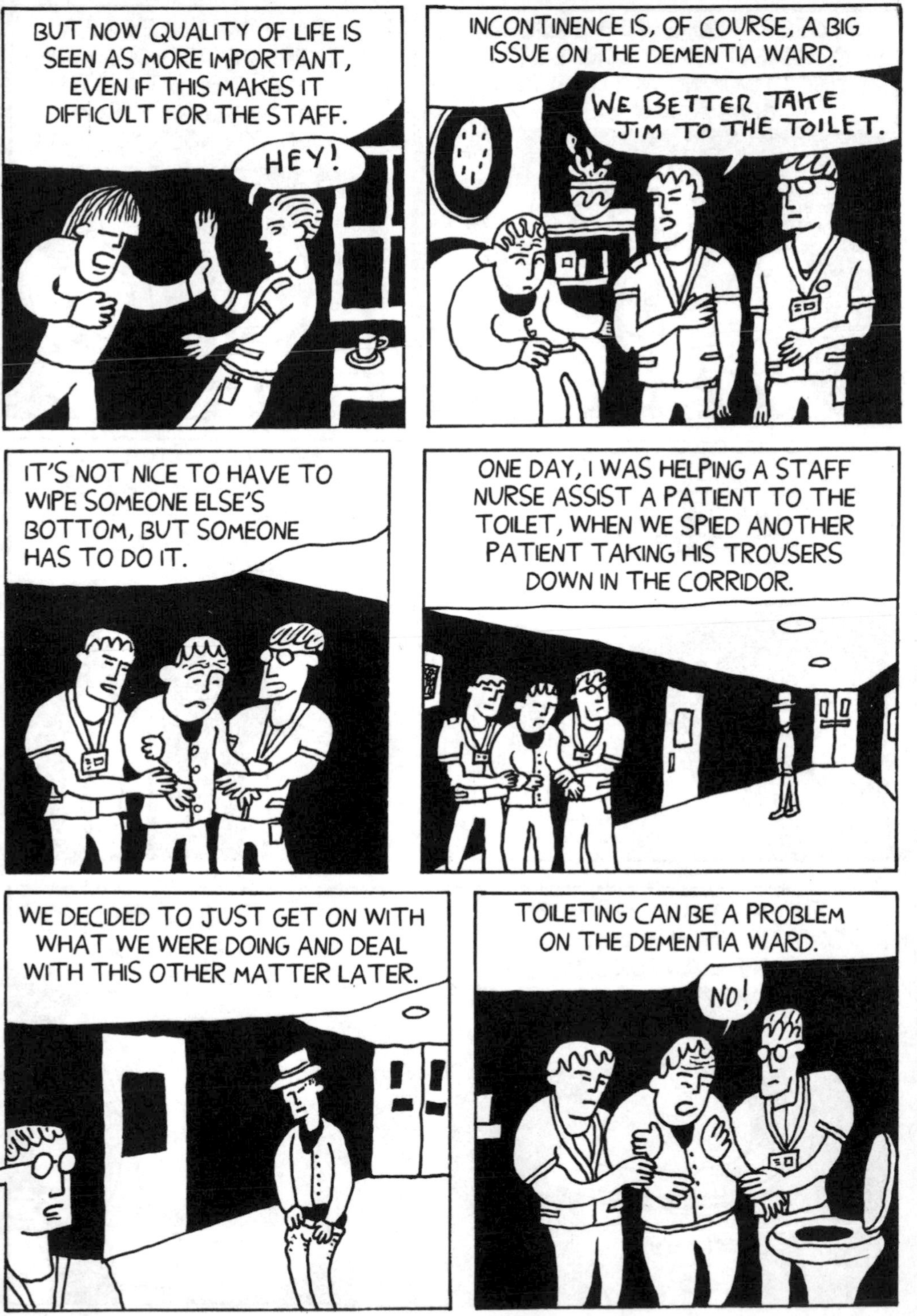
BUT NOW QUALITY OF LIFE IS SEEN AS MORE IMPORTANT, EVEN IF THIS MAKES IT DIFFICULT FOR THE STAFF.
HEY!
INCONTINENCE IS, OF COURSE, A BIG ISSUE ON THE DEMENTIA WARD.
WE BETTER TAKE JIM TO THE TOILET.
IT'S NOT NICE TO HAVE TO WIPE SOMEONE ELSE'S BOTTOM, BUT SOMEONE HAS TO DO IT.
ONE DAY, I WAS HELPING A STAFF NURSE ASSIST A PATIENT TO THE TOILET, WHEN WE SPIED ANOTHER PATIENT TAKING HIS TROUSERS DOWN IN THE CORRIDOR.
WE DECIDED TO JUST GET ON WITH WHAT WE WERE DOING AND DEAL WITH THIS OTHER MATTER LATER.
TOILETING CAN BE A PROBLEM ON THE DEMENTIA WARD.
NO!

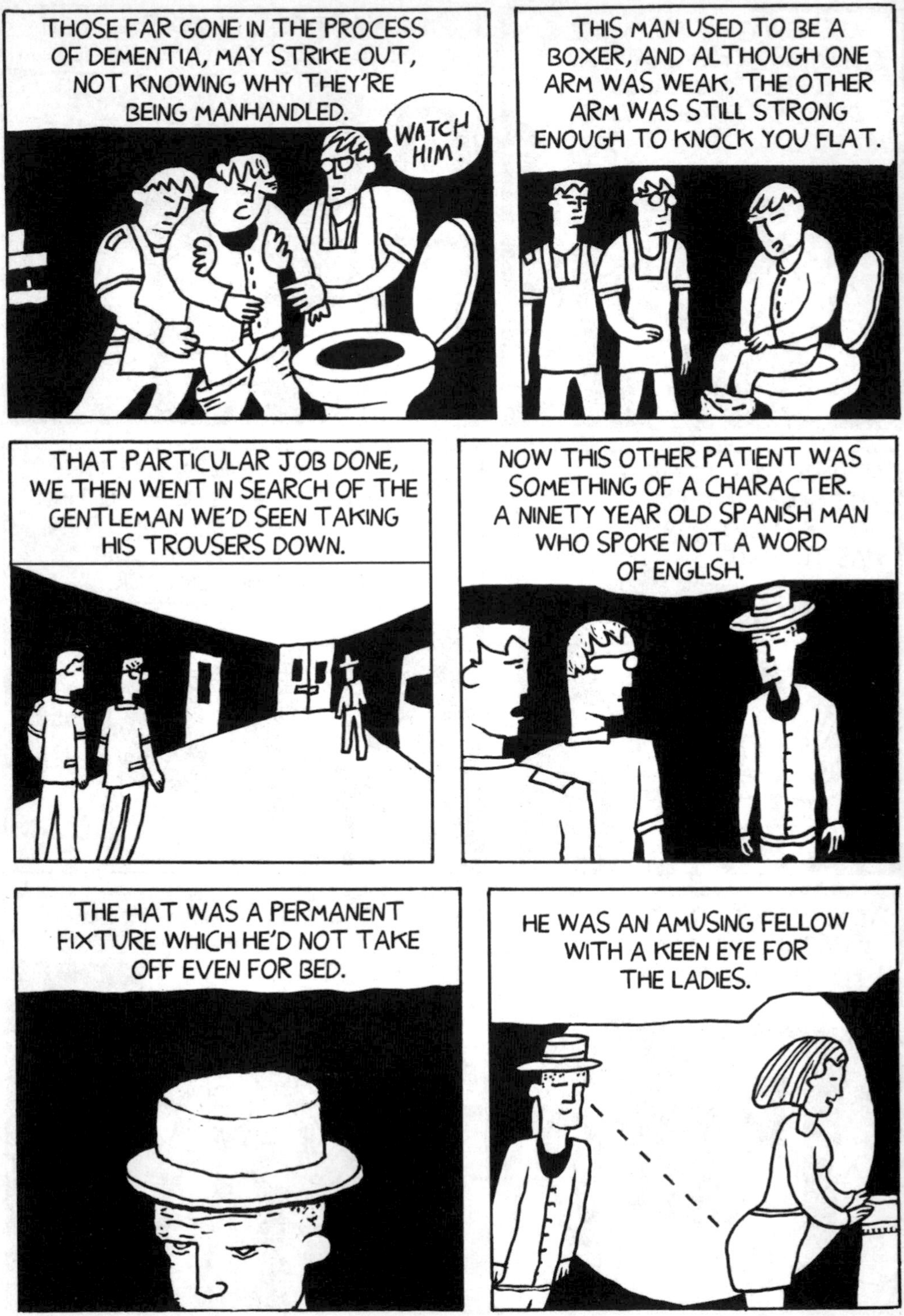
THOSE FAR GONE IN THE PROCESS OF DEMENTIA, MAY STRIKE OUT, NOT KNOWING WHY THEY'RE BEING MANHANDLED.
WATCH HIM!
THIS MAN USED TO BE A BOXER, AND ALTHOUGH ONE ARM WAS WEAK, THE OTHER ARM WAS STILL STRONG ENOUGH TO KNOCK YOU FLAT.
THAT PARTICULAR JOB DONE, WE THEN WENT IN SEARCH OF THE GENTLEMAN WE'D SEEN TAKING HIS TROUSERS DOWN.
NOW THIS OTHER PATIENT WAS SOMETHING OF A CHARACTER. A NINETY YEAR OLD SPANISH MAN WHO SPOKE NOT A WORD OF ENGLISH.
THE HAT WAS A PERMANENT FIXTURE WHICH HE'D NOT TAKE OFF EVEN FOR BED.
HE WAS AN AMUSING FELLOW WITH A KEEN EYE FOR THE LADIES.

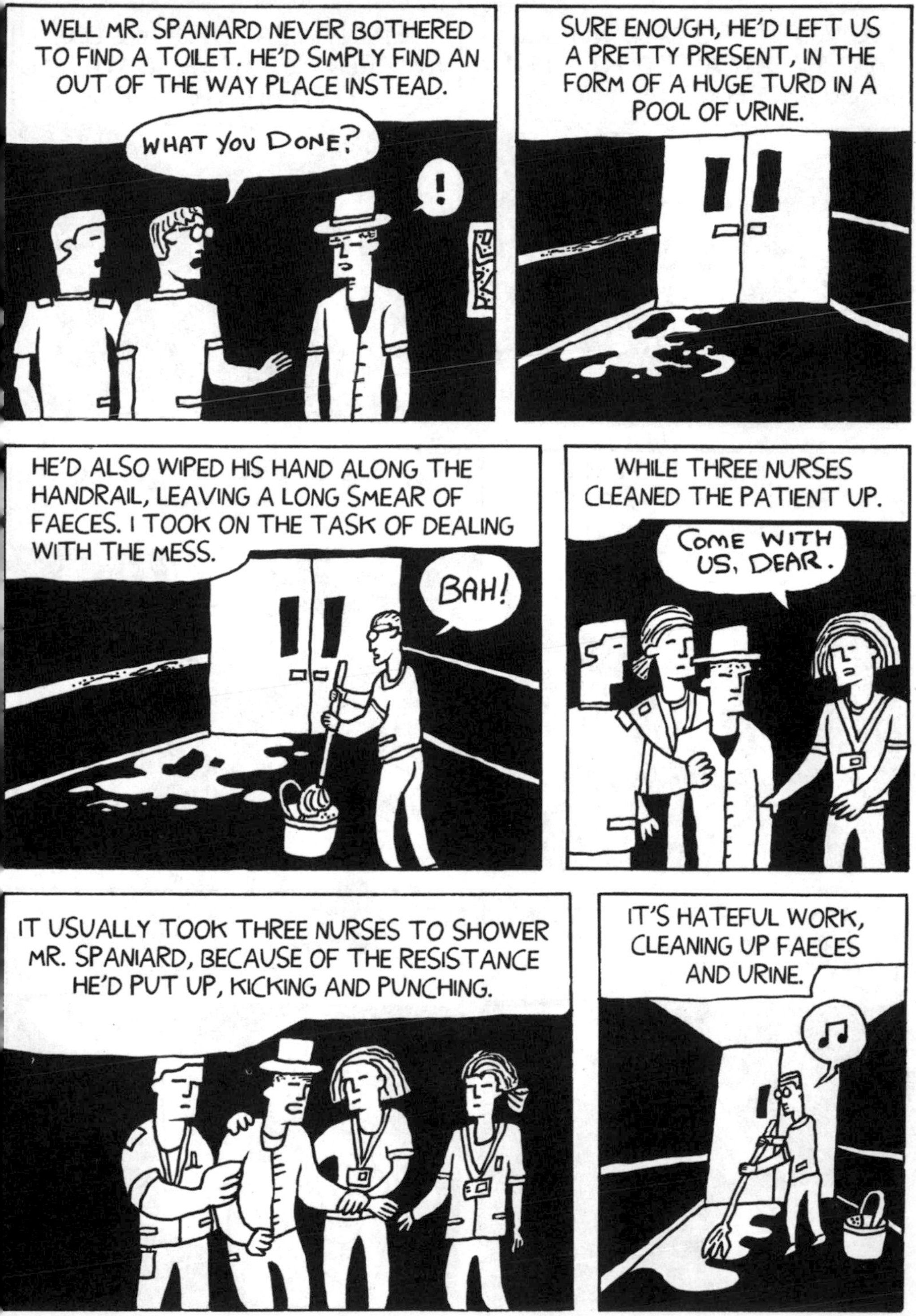
WELL MR. SPANIARD NEVER BOTHERED TO FIND A TOILET. HE'D SIMPLY FIND AN OUT OF THE WAY PLACE INSTEAD.
WHAT YOU DONE?
!
SURE ENOUGH, HE'D LEFT US A PRETTY PRESENT, IN THE FORM OF A HUGE TURD IN A POOL OF URINE.
HE'D ALSO WIPED HIS HAND ALONG THE HANDRAIL, LEAVING A LONG SMEAR OF FAECES. I TOOK ON THE TASK OF DEALING WITH THE MESS.
BAH!
WHILE THREE NURSES CLEANED THE PATIENT UP.
COME WITH US, DEAR.
IT USUALLY TOOK THREE NURSES TO SHOWER MR. SPANIARD, BECAUSE OF THE RESISTANCE HE'D PUT UP, KICKING AND PUNCHING.
IT'S HATEFUL WORK, CLEANING UP FAECES AND URINE.

HOWEVER, IT'S BASIC NURSING AND IF YOU CAN'T DO IT, THEN YOU SHOULDN'T BE A NURSE.

DEMENTIA PATIENTS ARE LIKE CHILDREN. YOU HAVE TO WATCH THEM ALL THE TIME.

ON ONE OCCASION THE SPANISH PATIENT HAD LEFT A BOWL MOVEMENT IN THE CORRIDOR.

BY THE TIME THE TURD WAS DISCOVERED

IT WAS UNFORTUNATELY IN THE HANDS OF ANOTHER PATIENT

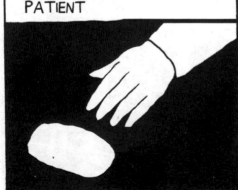

WHO WAS EATING IT, THINKING THAT IT WAS A CHOCOLATE BAR.

OH NO!

END

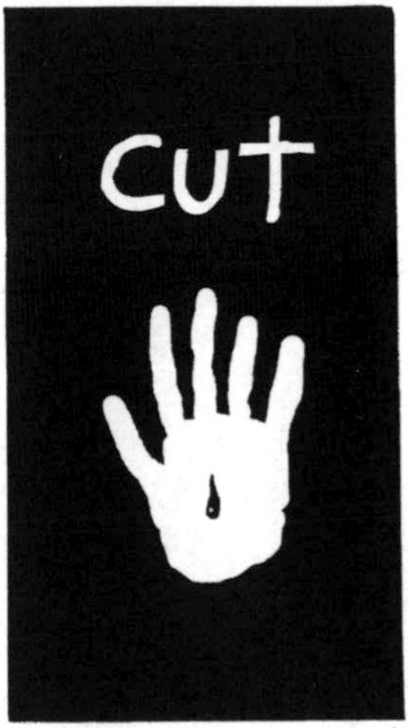
CUT

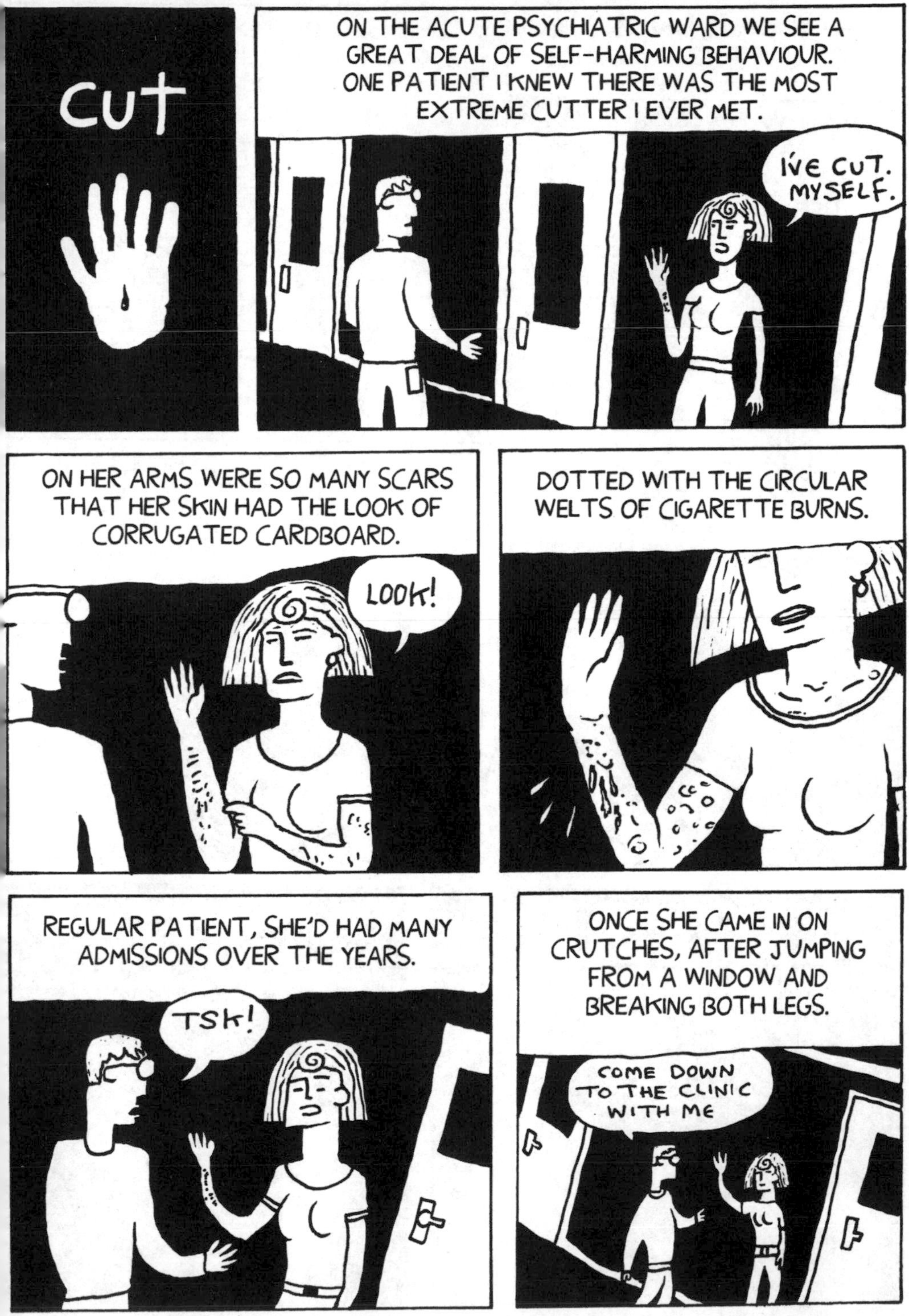
CUT
ON THE ACUTE PSYCHIATRIC WARD WE SEE A GREAT DEAL OF SELF-HARMING BEHAVIOUR. ONE PATIENT I KNEW THERE WAS THE MOST EXTREME CUTTER I EVER MET.
I'VE CUT. MYSELF.
ON HER ARMS WERE SO MANY SCARS THAT HER SKIN HAD THE LOOK OF CORRUGATED CARDBOARD.
LOOK!
DOTTED WITH THE CIRCULAR WELTS OF CIGARETTE BURNS.
REGULAR PATIENT, SHE'D HAD MANY ADMISSIONS OVER THE YEARS.
TSK!
ONCE SHE CAME IN ON CRUTCHES, AFTER JUMPING FROM A WINDOW AND BREAKING BOTH LEGS.
COME DOWN TO THE CLINIC WITH ME

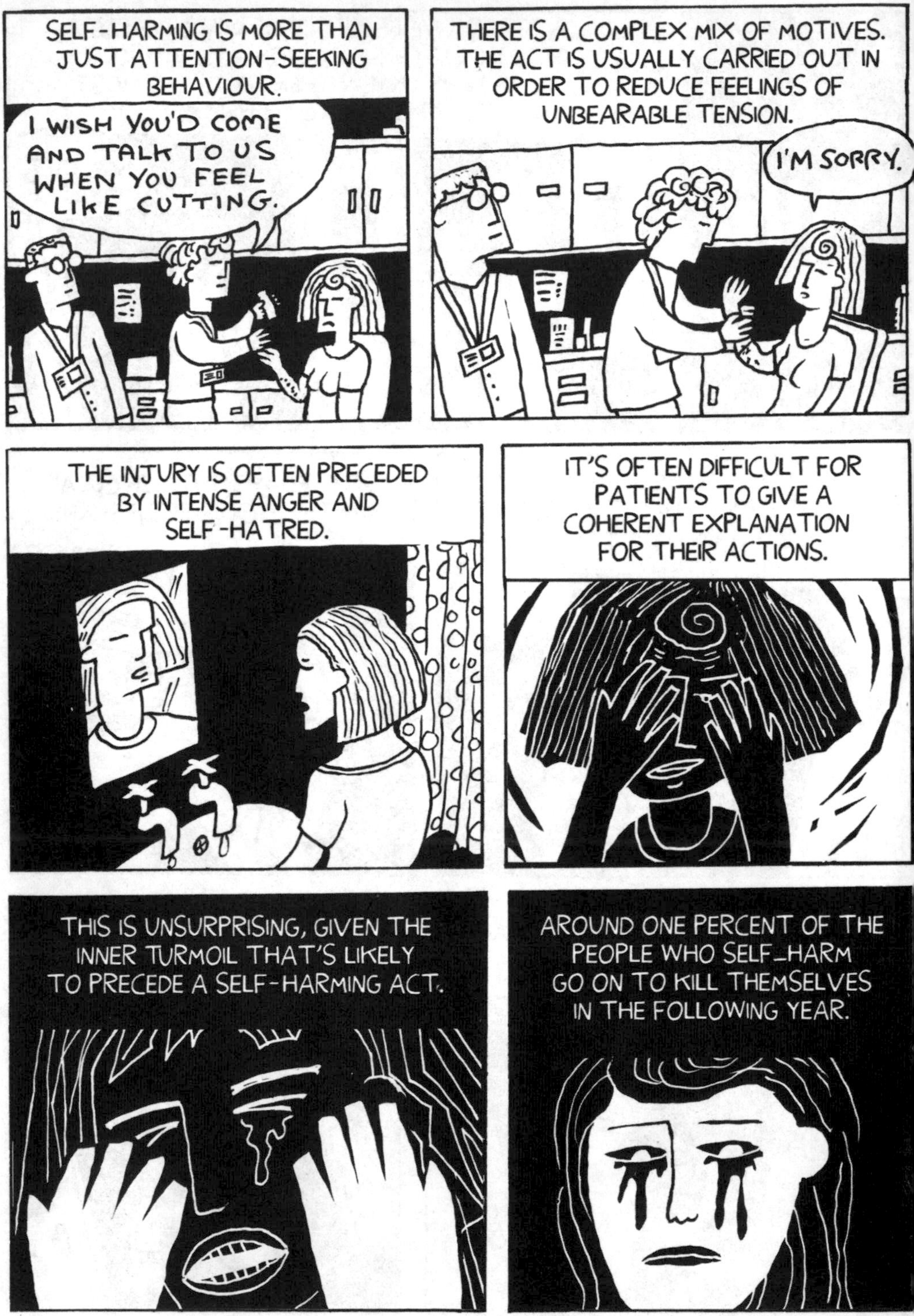
SELF-HARMING IS MORE THAN JUST ATTENTION-SEEKING BEHAVIOUR.
I WISH YOU'D COME AND TALK TO US WHEN YOU FEEL LIKE CUTTING.
THERE IS A COMPLEX MIX OF MOTIVES. THE ACT IS USUALLY CARRIED OUT IN ORDER TO REDUCE FEELINGS OF UNBEARABLE TENSION.
I'M SORRY.
THE INJURY IS OFTEN PRECEDED BY INTENSE ANGER AND SELF-HATRED.
IT'S OFTEN DIFFICULT FOR PATIENTS TO GIVE A COHERENT EXPLANATION FOR THEIR ACTIONS.
THIS IS UNSURPRISING, GIVEN THE INNER TURMOIL THAT'S LIKELY TO PRECEDE A SELF-HARMING ACT.
AROUND ONE PERCENT OF THE PEOPLE WHO SELF-HARM GO ON TO KILL THEMSELVES IN THE FOLLOWING YEAR.

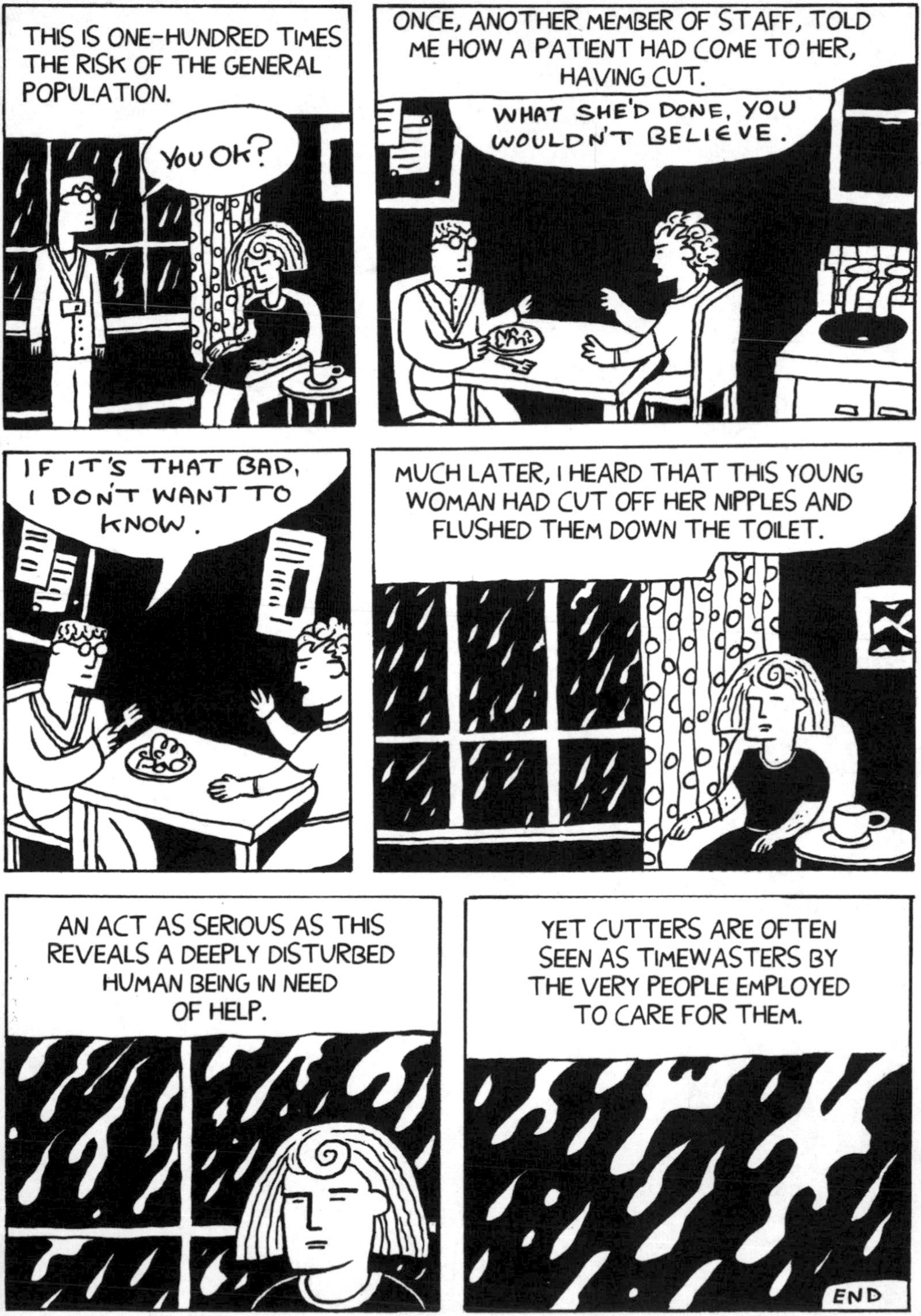

THIS IS ONE-HUNDRED TIMES THE RISK OF THE GENERAL POPULATION.
YOU OK?
ONCE, ANOTHER MEMBER OF STAFF, TOLD ME HOW A PATIENT HAD COME TO HER, HAVING CUT.
WHAT SHE'D DONE, YOU WOULDN'T BELIEVE.
IF IT'S THAT BAD, I DON'T WANT TO KNOW.
MUCH LATER, I HEARD THAT THIS YOUNG WOMAN HAD CUT OFF HER NIPPLES AND FLUSHED THEM DOWN THE TOILET.
AN ACT AS SERIOUS AS THIS REVEALS A DEEPLY DISTURBED HUMAN BEING IN NEED OF HELP.
YET CUTTERS ARE OFTEN SEEN AS TIMEWASTERS BY THE VERY PEOPLE EMPLOYED TO CARE FOR THEM.
END

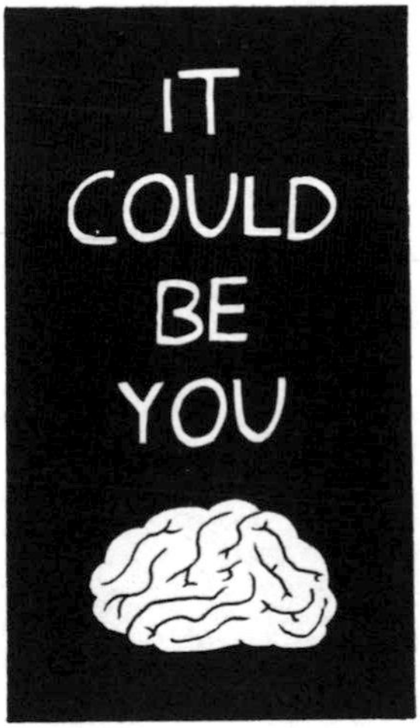
IT
COULD
BE
YOU

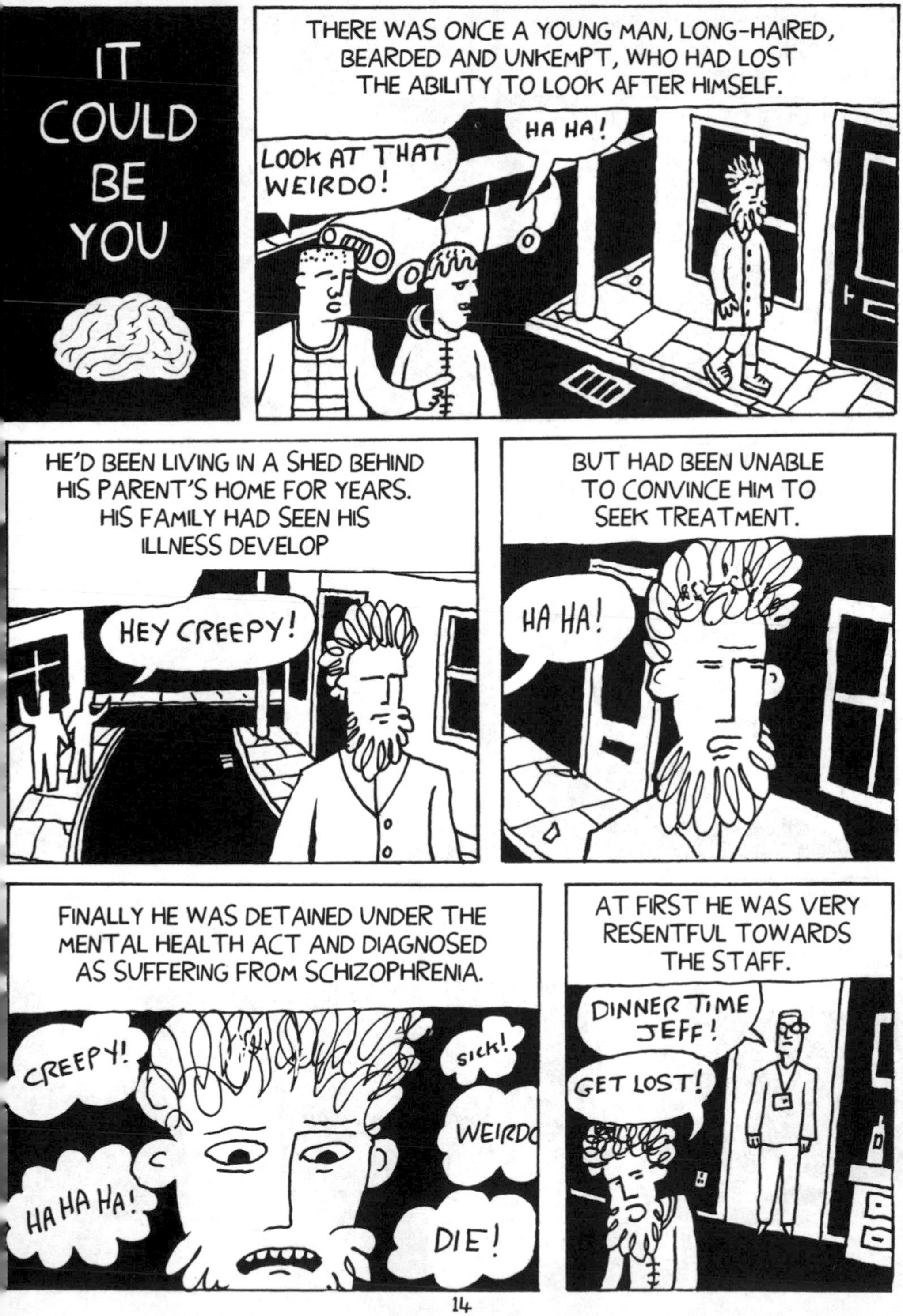
IT COULD BE YOU
THERE WAS ONCE A YOUNG MAN, LONG-HAIRED, BEARDED AND UNKEMPT, WHO HAD LOST THE ABILITY TO LOOK AFTER HIMSELF.
LOOK AT THAT WEIRDO!
HA HA!
HE'D BEEN LIVING IN A SHED BEHIND HIS PARENT'S HOME FOR YEARS. HIS FAMILY HAD SEEN HIS ILLNESS DEVELOP
HEY CREEPY!
BUT HAD BEEN UNABLE TO CONVINCE HIM TO SEEK TREATMENT.
HA HA!
FINALLY HE WAS DETAINED UNDER THE MENTAL HEALTH ACT AND DIAGNOSED AS SUFFERING FROM SCHIZOPHRENIA.
CREEPY!
SICK!
WEIRDO
HA HA HA!
DIE!
AT FIRST HE WAS VERY RESENTFUL TOWARDS THE STAFF.
DINNER TIME JEFF!
GET LOST!

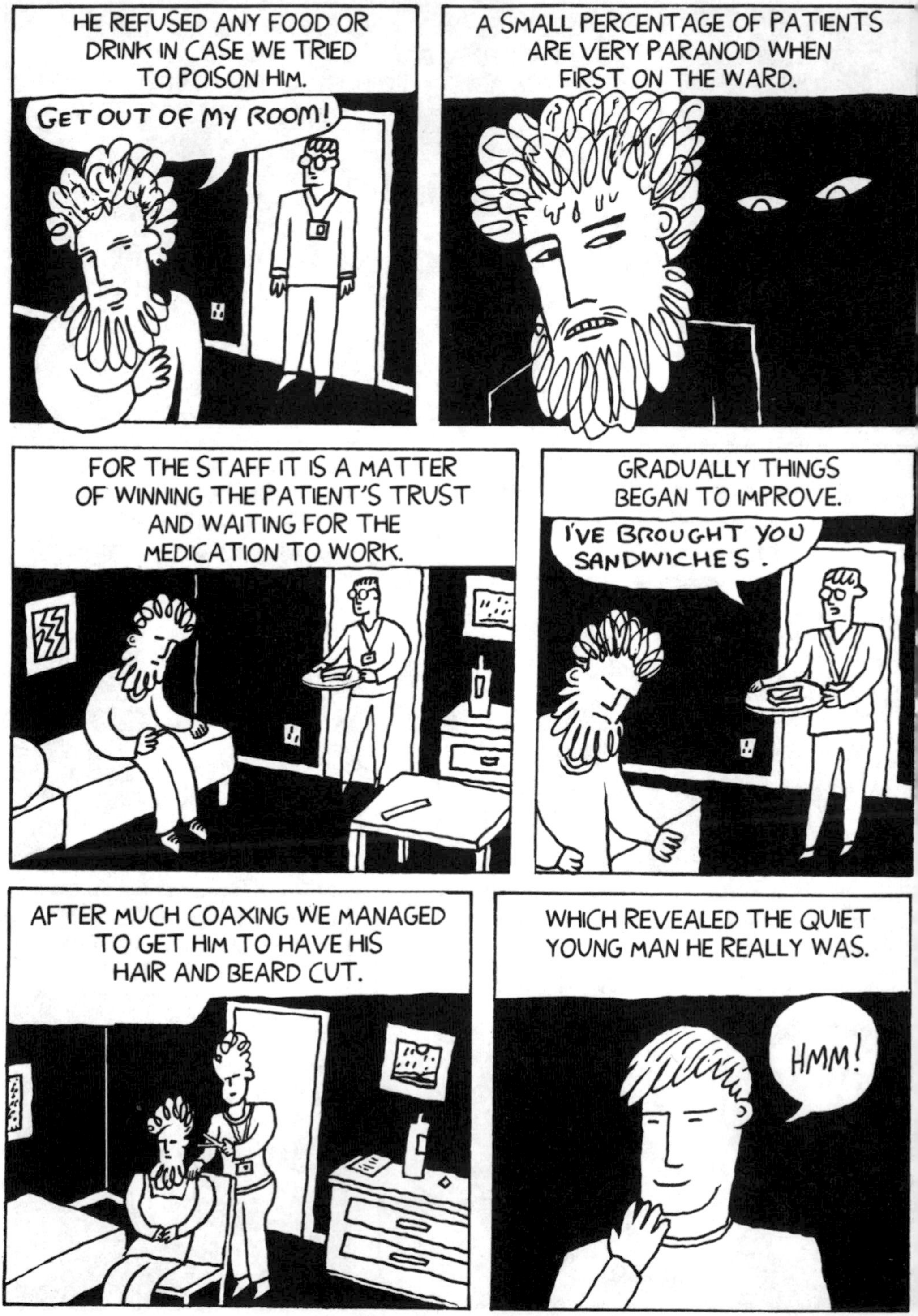
HE REFUSED ANY FOOD OR DRINK IN CASE WE TRIED TO POISON HIM.
GET OUT OF MY ROOM!
A SMALL PERCENTAGE OF PATIENTS ARE VERY PARANOID WHEN FIRST ON THE WARD.
FOR THE STAFF IT IS A MATTER OF WINNING THE PATIENT'S TRUST AND WAITING FOR THE MEDICATION TO WORK.
GRADUALLY THINGS BEGAN TO IMPROVE.
I'VE BROUGHT YOU SANDWICHES.
AFTER MUCH COAXING WE MANAGED TO GET HIM TO HAVE HIS HAIR AND BEARD CUT.
WHICH REVEALED THE QUIET YOUNG MAN HE REALLY WAS.
HMM!

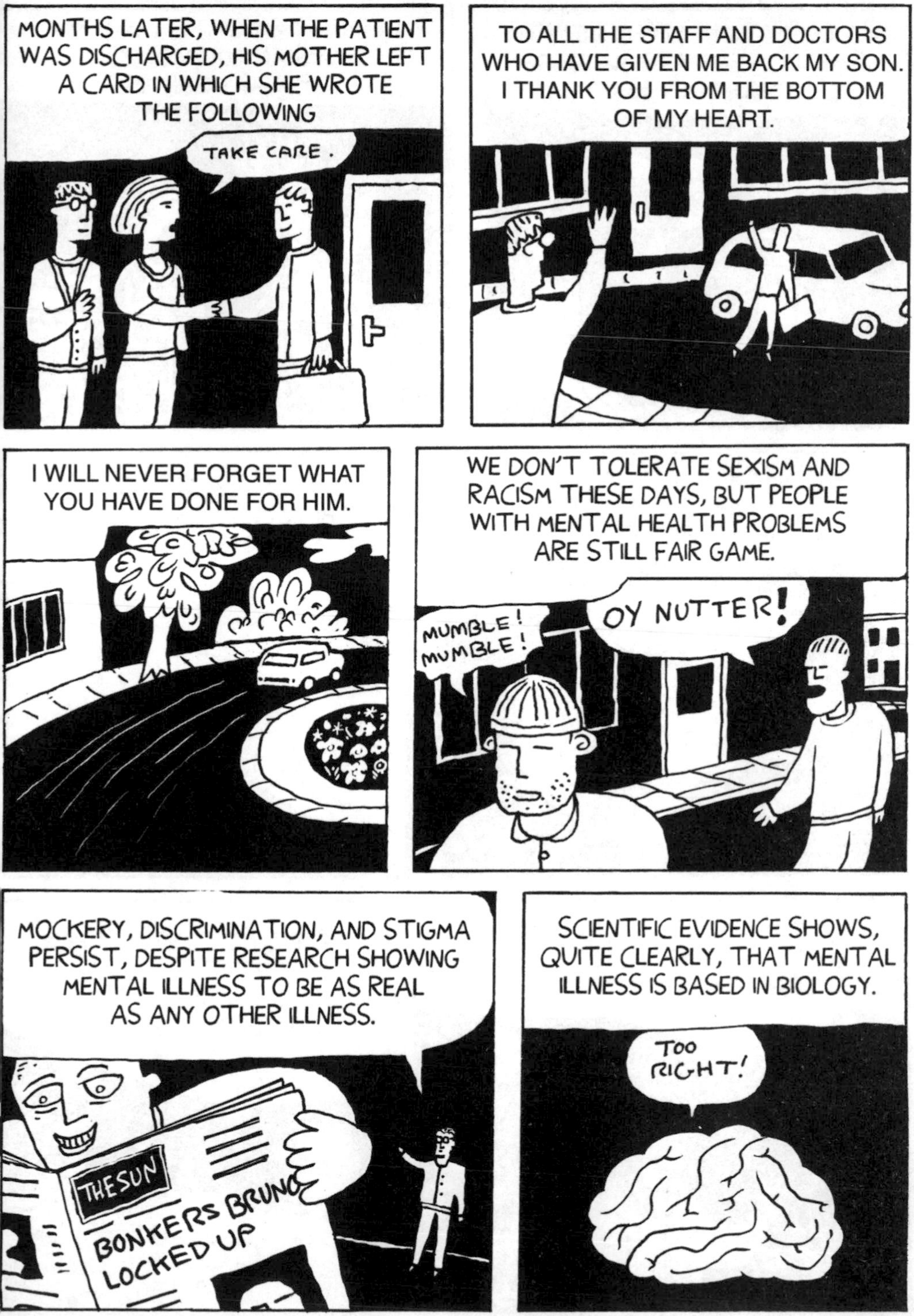
MONTHS LATER, WHEN THE PATIENT WAS DISCHARGED, HIS MOTHER LEFT A CARD IN WHICH SHE WROTE THE FOLLOWING
TAKE CARE.
TO ALL THE STAFF AND DOCTORS WHO HAVE GIVEN ME BACK MY SON. I THANK YOU FROM THE BOTTOM OF MY HEART.
I WILL NEVER FORGET WHAT YOU HAVE DONE FOR HIM.
WE DON'T TOLERATE SEXISM AND RACISM THESE DAYS, BUT PEOPLE WITH MENTAL HEALTH PROBLEMS ARE STILL FAIR GAME.
MUMBLE! MUMBLE!
OY NUTTER!
MOCKERY, DISCRIMINATION, AND STIGMA PERSIST, DESPITE RESEARCH SHOWING MENTAL ILLNESS TO BE AS REAL AS ANY OTHER ILLNESS.
THE SUN
BONKERS BRUNO LOCKED UP
SCIENTIFIC EVIDENCE SHOWS, QUITE CLEARLY, THAT MENTAL ILLNESS IS BASED IN BIOLOGY.
TOO RIGHT!

HALLUCINATIONS IN PEOPLE WITH SCHIZOPHRENIA ARE ALLAYED BY MEDICINES.

LITHIUM TAMES THE TERRIFYING UPS AND DOWNS OF BIPOLAR DISORDER.

BRAIN SCANS SHOW ABNORMAL BIOCHEMISTRY IN PEOPLE WHO ARE DEPRESSED.

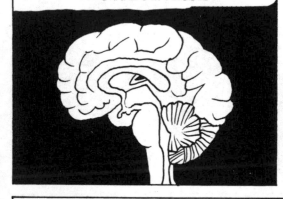

DEPRESSION IS MORE THAN JUST THE BLUES. IT'S A SERIOUS DISORDER WHICH CAN KILL.

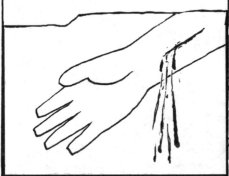

A MENTAL ILLNESS IS A BRAIN DISEASE. JUST AS A STROKE OR A BRAIN TUMOUR IS A BRAIN DISEASE.

THERE IS NO JUSTIFICATION FOR SEPARATING OUT MENTAL ILLNESSES FROM OTHER BRAIN DISORDERS.

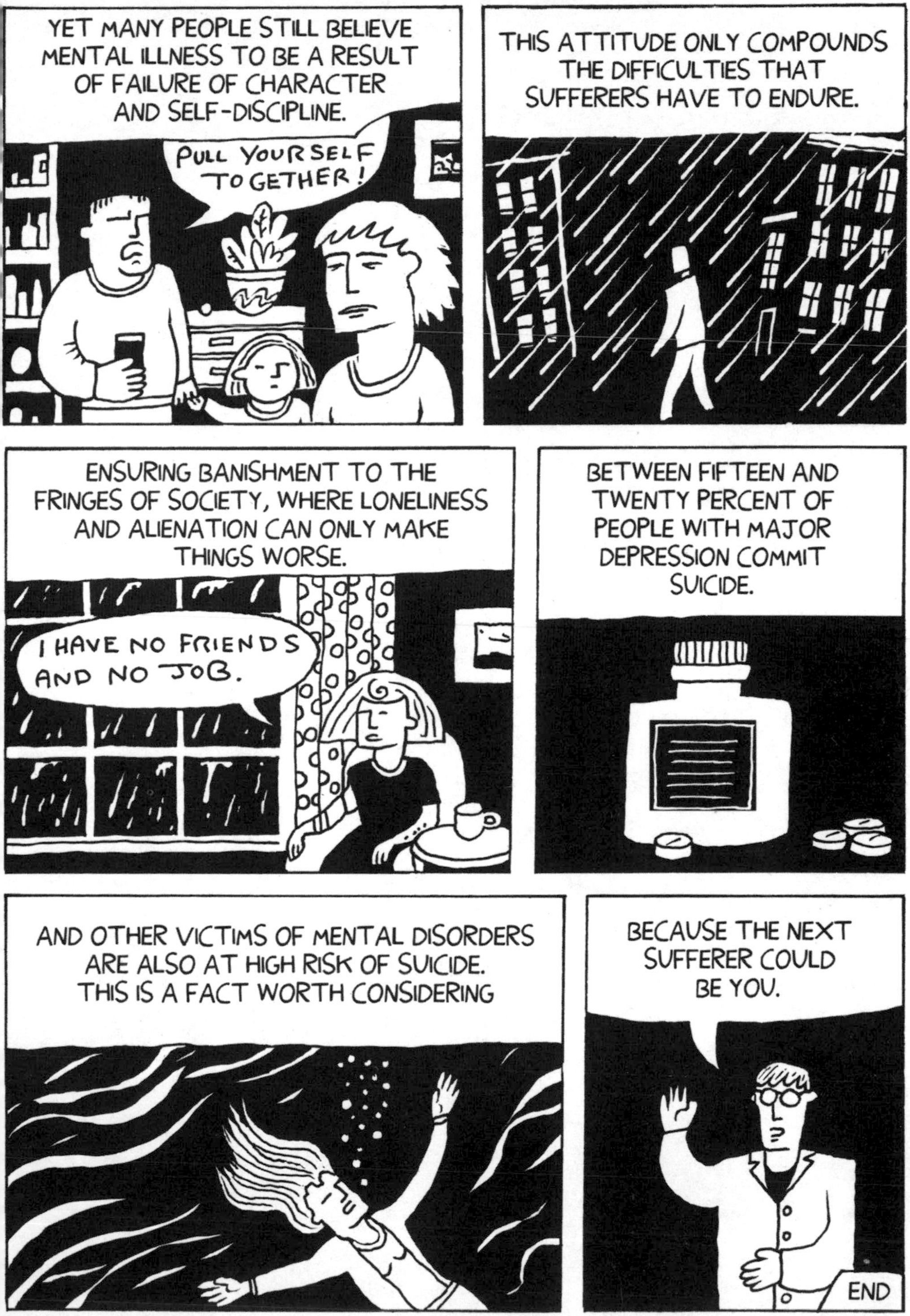
YET MANY PEOPLE STILL BELIEVE MENTAL ILLNESS TO BE A RESULT OF FAILURE OF CHARACTER AND SELF-DISCIPLINE.
PULL YOURSELF TOGETHER!
THIS ATTITUDE ONLY COMPOUNDS THE DIFFICULTIES THAT SUFFERERS HAVE TO ENDURE.
ENSURING BANISHMENT TO THE FRINGES OF SOCIETY, WHERE LONELINESS AND ALIENATION CAN ONLY MAKE THINGS WORSE.
I HAVE NO FRIENDS AND NO JOB.
BETWEEN FIFTEEN AND TWENTY PERCENT OF PEOPLE WITH MAJOR DEPRESSION COMMIT SUICIDE.
AND OTHER VICTIMS OF MENTAL DISORDERS ARE ALSO AT HIGH RISK OF SUICIDE. THIS IS A FACT WORTH CONSIDERING
BECAUSE THE NEXT SUFFERER COULD BE YOU.
END

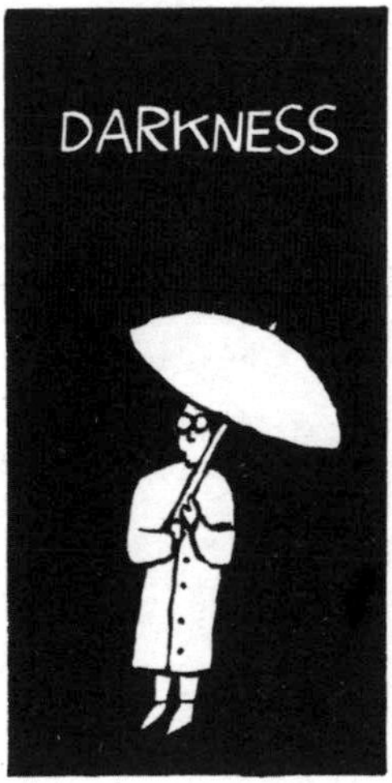
DARKNESS

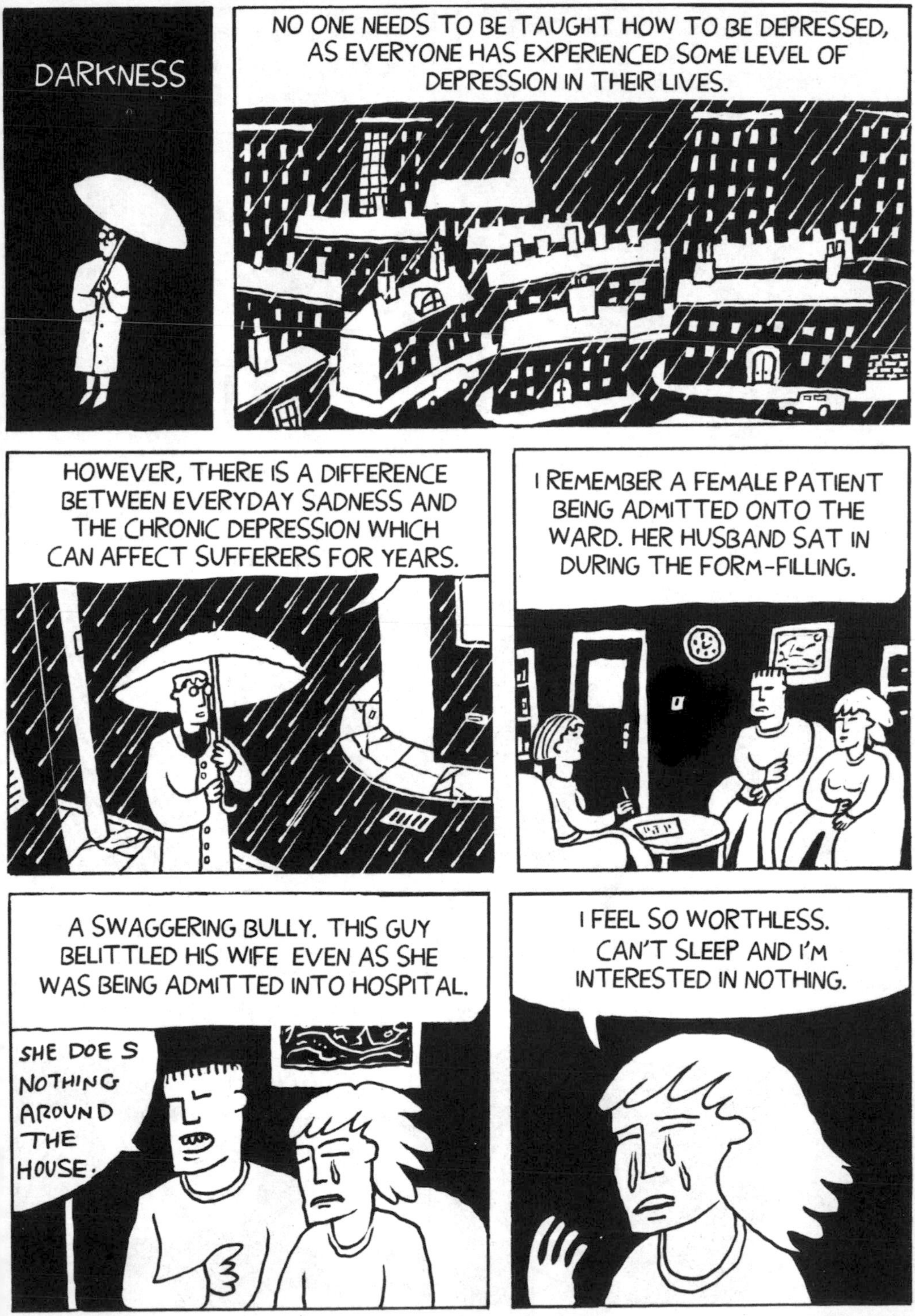
DARKNESS
NO ONE NEEDS TO BE TAUGHT HOW TO BE DEPRESSED, AS EVERYONE HAS EXPERIENCED SOME LEVEL OF DEPRESSION IN THEIR LIVES.
HOWEVER, THERE IS A DIFFERENCE BETWEEN EVERYDAY SADNESS AND THE CHRONIC DEPRESSION WHICH CAN AFFECT SUFFERERS FOR YEARS.
I REMEMBER A FEMALE PATIENT BEING ADMITTED ONTO THE WARD. HER HUSBAND SAT IN DURING THE FORM-FILLING.
A SWAGGERING BULLY. THIS GUY BELITTLED HIS WIFE EVEN AS SHE WAS BEING ADMITTED INTO HOSPITAL.
SHE DOE S NOTHING AROUND THE HOUSE.
I FEEL SO WORTHLESS. CAN'T SLEEP AND I'M INTERESTED IN NOTHING.

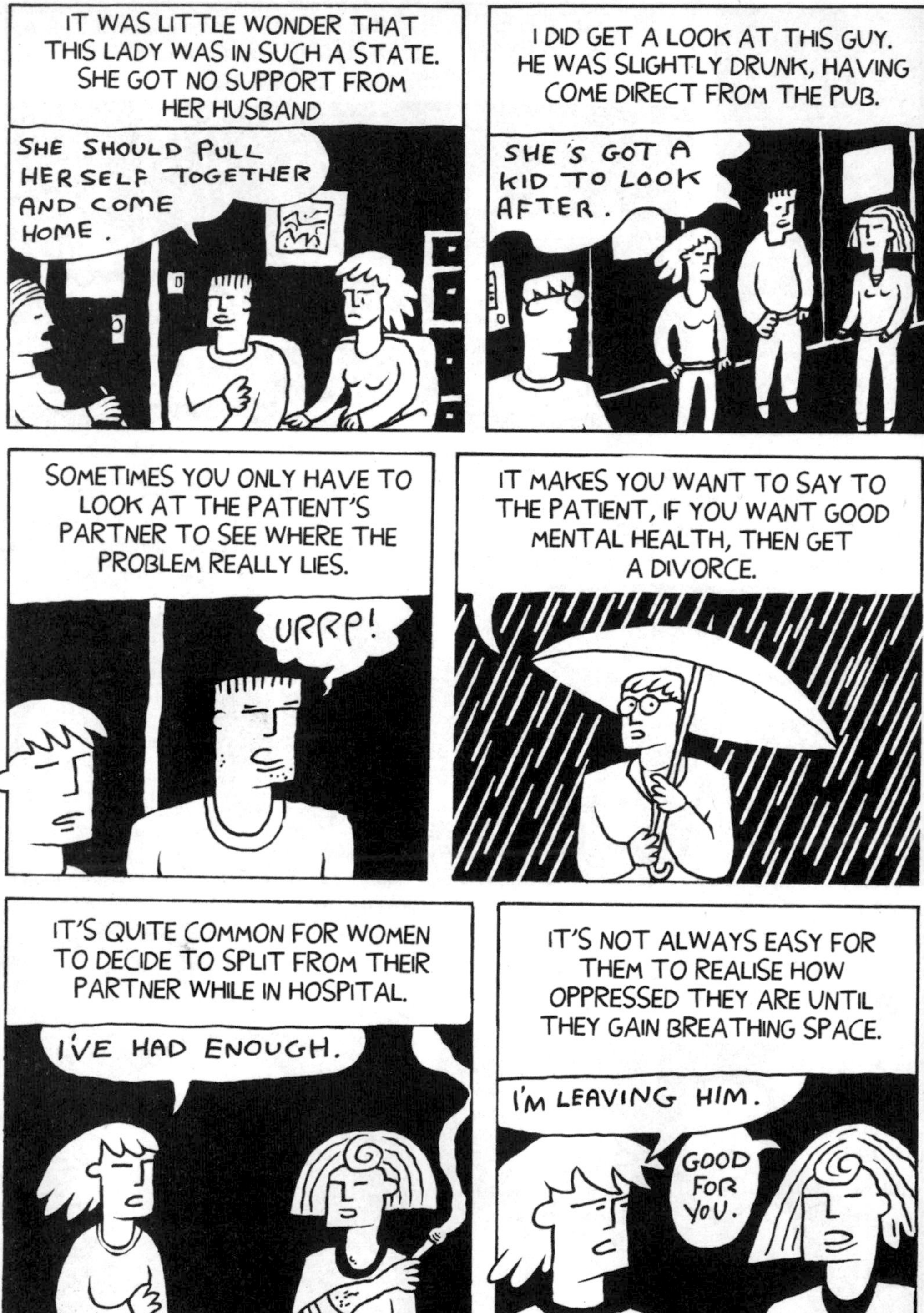
IT WAS LITTLE WONDER THAT THIS LADY WAS IN SUCH A STATE. SHE GOT NO SUPPORT FROM HER HUSBAND
SHE SHOULD PULL HERSELF TOGETHER AND COME HOME.
I DID GET A LOOK AT THIS GUY. HE WAS SLIGHTLY DRUNK, HAVING COME DIRECT FROM THE PUB.
SHE'S GOT A KID TO LOOK AFTER.
SOMETIMES YOU ONLY HAVE TO LOOK AT THE PATIENT'S PARTNER TO SEE WHERE THE PROBLEM REALLY LIES.
URRP!
IT MAKES YOU WANT TO SAY TO THE PATIENT, IF YOU WANT GOOD MENTAL HEALTH, THEN GET A DIVORCE.
IT'S QUITE COMMON FOR WOMEN TO DECIDE TO SPLIT FROM THEIR PARTNER WHILE IN HOSPITAL.
I'VE HAD ENOUGH.
IT'S NOT ALWAYS EASY FOR THEM TO REALISE HOW OPPRESSED THEY ARE UNTIL THEY GAIN BREATHING SPACE.
I'M LEAVING HIM.
GOOD FOR YOU.

DEPRESSION ISN'T A BLUE MOOD YOU CAN JUST SNAP OUT OF. IT'S A SERIOUS BIOLOGICAL ILLNESS
FOR YEARS I'VE HAD NO LIFE OF MY OWN.
WHICH AFFECTS BEHAVIOUR, THOUGHTS AND FEELINGS.
I KNOW EXACTLY WHAT YOU MEAN, DEAR.
IN THE BRAIN THERE ARE NATURALLY OCCURRING SUBSTANCES CALLED NEUROTRANSMITTERS.
WILL THIS RAIN EVER STOP?
THESE ARE THE CHEMICAL MESSENGERS WHICH CARRY ELECTRICAL SIGNALS FROM ONE NERVE CELL TO ANOTHER.
ACROSS SPACES CALLED SYNAPSES.
NEUROTRANSMITTER
NERVE CELL BODY
AXON
SYNAPSE
THE NEUROTRANSMITTERS THAT PLAY A SIGNIFICANT ROLE IN MAINTAINING OUR MOOD ARE SEROTONIN AND NOREPINEPHRINE.
NERVE CELL BODY

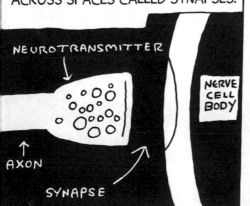

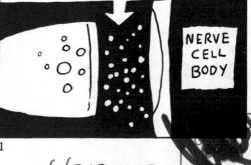

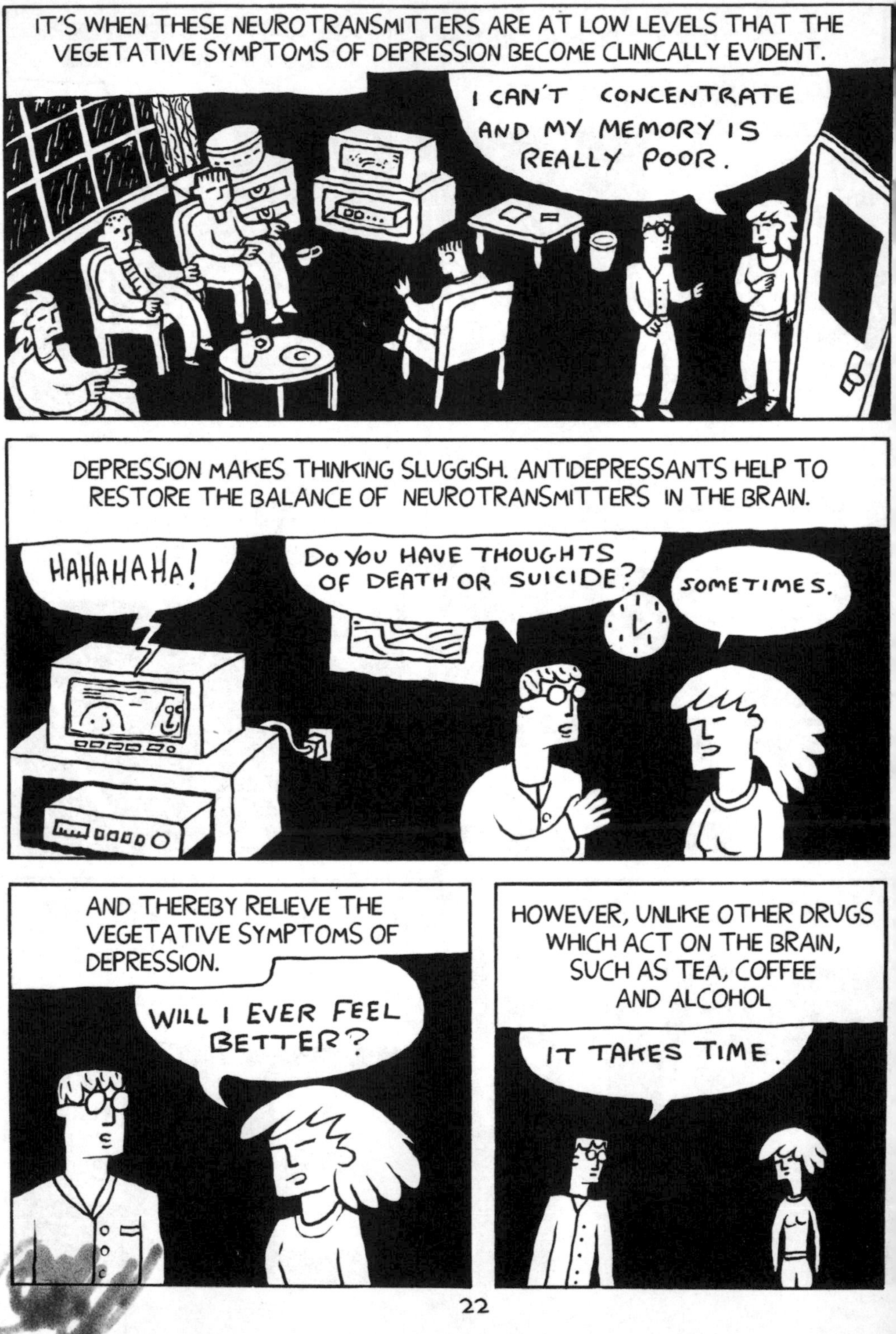
IT'S WHEN THESE NEUROTRANSMITTERS ARE AT LOW LEVELS THAT THE VEGETATIVE SYMPTOMS OF DEPRESSION BECOME CLINICALLY EVIDENT.
I CAN'T CONCENTRATE AND MY MEMORY IS REALLY POOR.
DEPRESSION MAKES THINKING SLUGGISH. ANTIDEPRESSANTS HELP TO RESTORE THE BALANCE OF NEUROTRANSMITTERS IN THE BRAIN.
HAHAHAHA!
DO YOU HAVE THOUGHTS OF DEATH OR SUICIDE?
SOMETIMES.
AND THEREBY RELIEVE THE VEGETATIVE SYMPTOMS OF DEPRESSION.
WILL I EVER FEEL BETTER?
HOWEVER, UNLIKE OTHER DRUGS WHICH ACT ON THE BRAIN, SUCH AS TEA, COFFEE AND ALCOHOL
IT TAKES TIME.

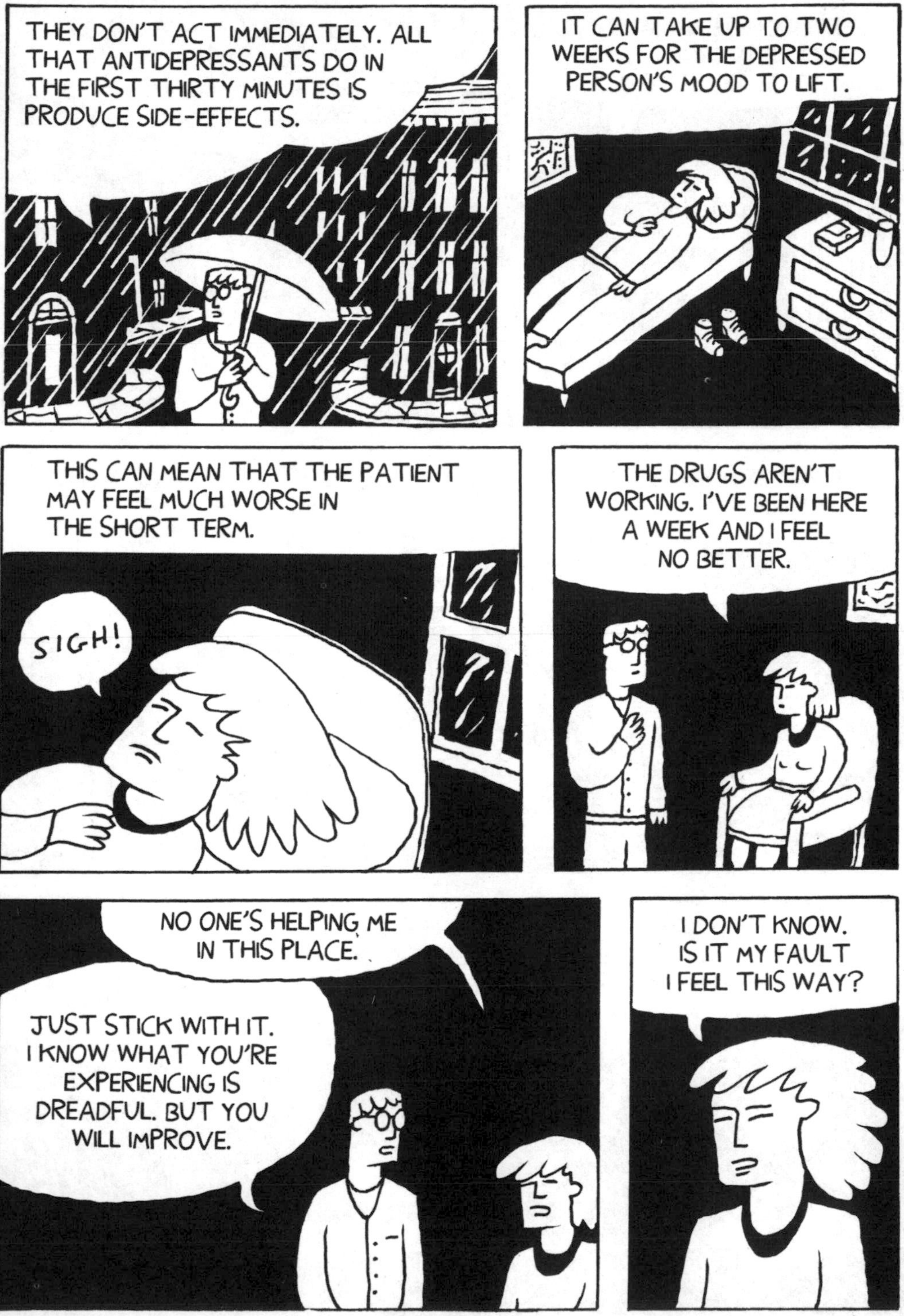

THEY DON'T ACT IMMEDIATELY. ALL THAT ANTIDEPRESSANTS DO IN THE FIRST THIRTY MINUTES IS PRODUCE SIDE-EFFECTS.
IT CAN TAKE UP TO TWO WEEKS FOR THE DEPRESSED PERSON'S MOOD TO LIFT.
THIS CAN MEAN THAT THE PATIENT MAY FEEL MUCH WORSE IN THE SHORT TERM.
SIGH!
THE DRUGS AREN'T WORKING. I'VE BEEN HERE A WEEK AND I FEEL NO BETTER.
NO ONE'S HELPING ME IN THIS PLACE.
JUST STICK WITH IT. I KNOW WHAT YOU'RE EXPERIENCING IS DREADFUL. BUT YOU WILL IMPROVE.
I DON'T KNOW. IS IT MY FAULT I FEEL THIS WAY?

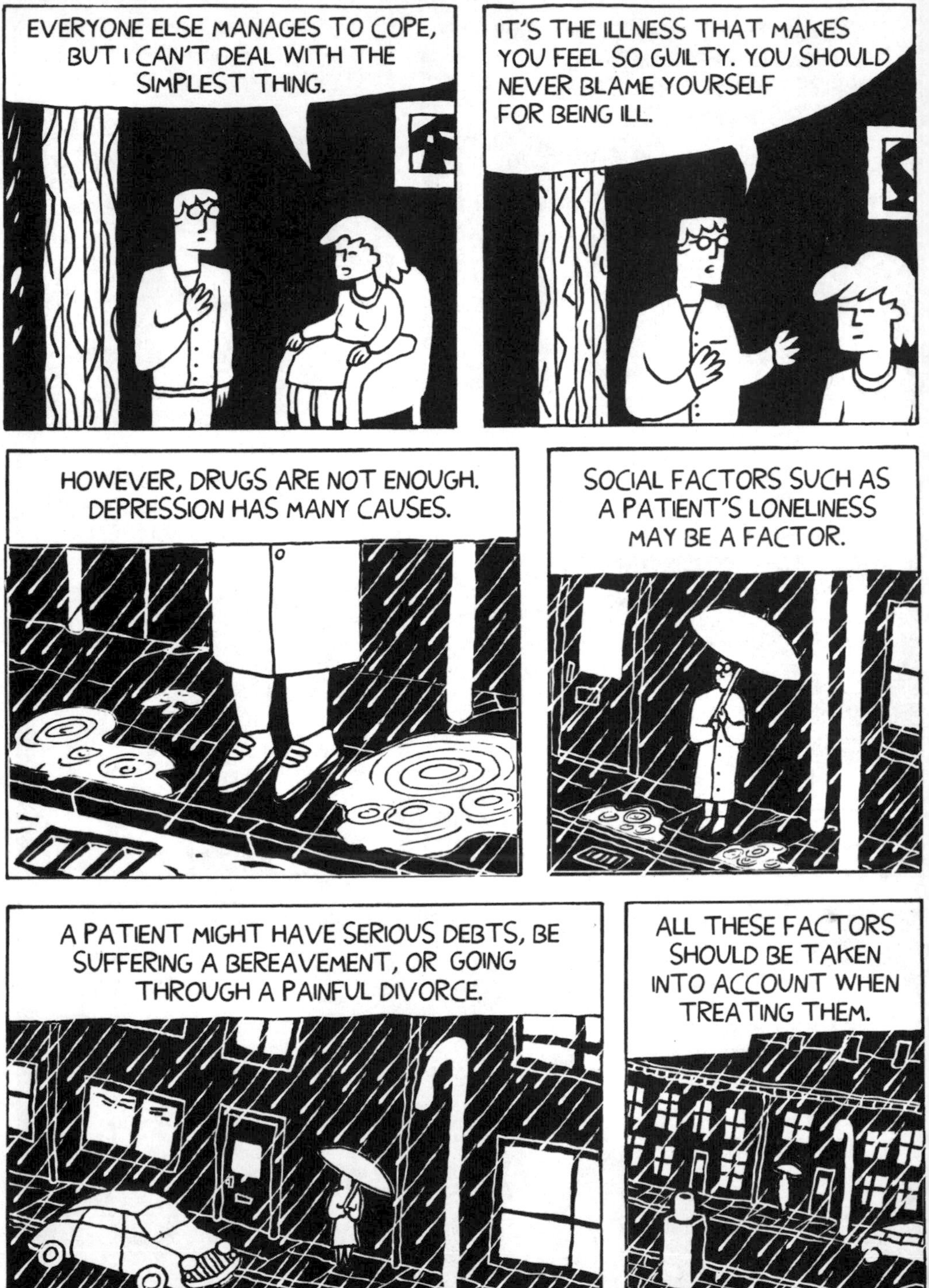
EVERYONE ELSE MANAGES TO COPE, BUT I CAN'T DEAL WITH THE SIMPLEST THING.
IT'S THE ILLNESS THAT MAKES YOU FEEL SO GUILTY. YOU SHOULD NEVER BLAME YOURSELF FOR BEING ILL.
HOWEVER, DRUGS ARE NOT ENOUGH. DEPRESSION HAS MANY CAUSES.
SOCIAL FACTORS SUCH AS A PATIENT'S LONELINESS MAY BE A FACTOR.
A PATIENT MIGHT HAVE SERIOUS DEBTS, BE SUFFERING A BEREAVEMENT, OR GOING THROUGH A PAINFUL DIVORCE.
ALL THESE FACTORS SHOULD BE TAKEN INTO ACCOUNT WHEN TREATING THEM.

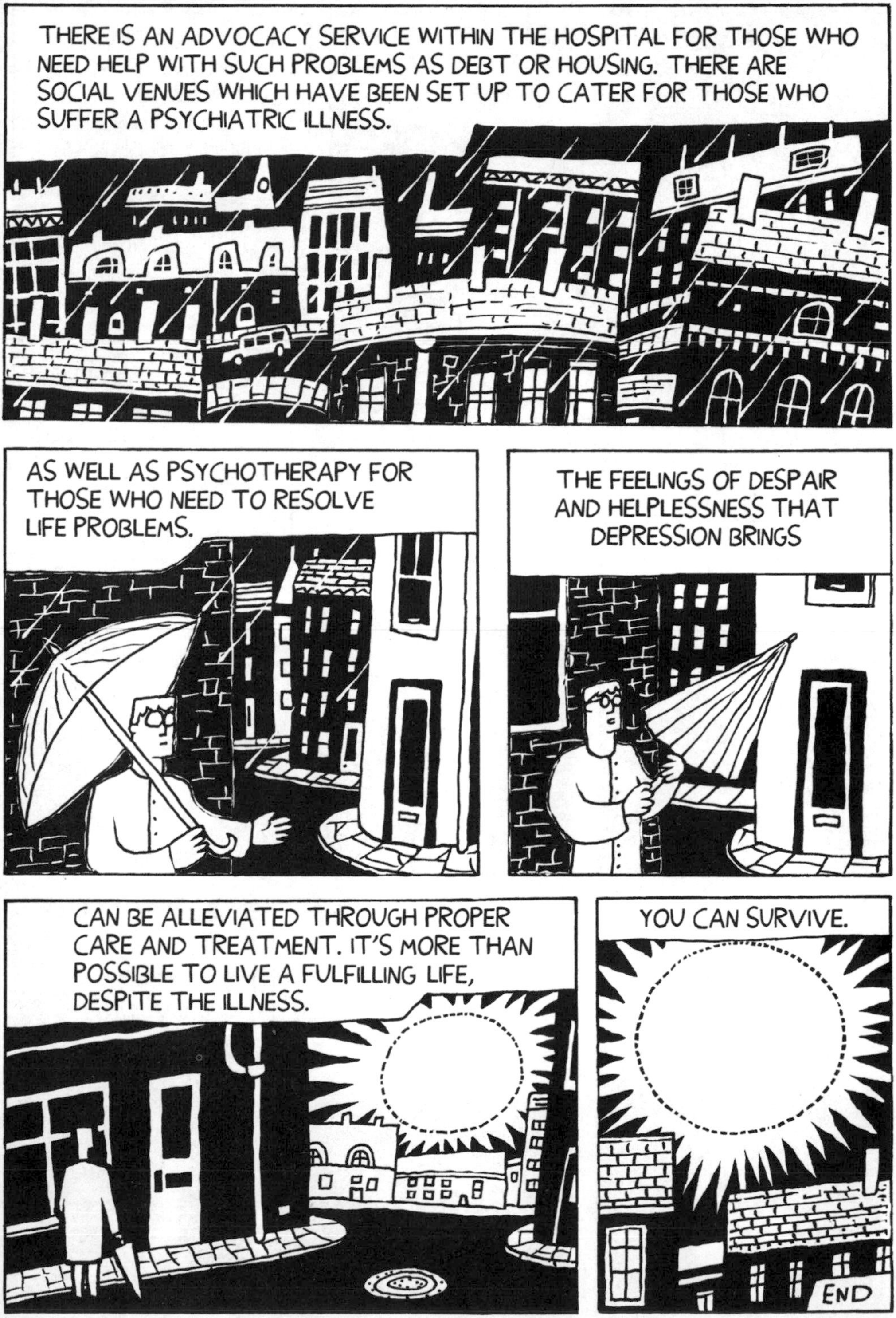
THERE IS AN ADVOCACY SERVICE WITHIN THE HOSPITAL FOR THOSE WHO NEED HELP WITH SUCH PROBLEMS AS DEBT OR HOUSING. THERE ARE SOCIAL VENUES WHICH HAVE BEEN SET UP TO CATER FOR THOSE WHO SUFFER A PSYCHIATRIC ILLNESS.
AS WELL AS PSYCHOTHERAPY FOR THOSE WHO NEED TO RESOLVE LIFE PROBLEMS.
THE FEELINGS OF DESPAIR AND HELPLESSNESS THAT DEPRESSION BRINGS
CAN BE ALLEVIATED THROUGH PROPER CARE AND TREATMENT. IT'S MORE THAN POSSIBLE TO LIVE A FULFILLING LIFE, DESPITE THE ILLNESS.
YOU CAN SURVIVE.
END

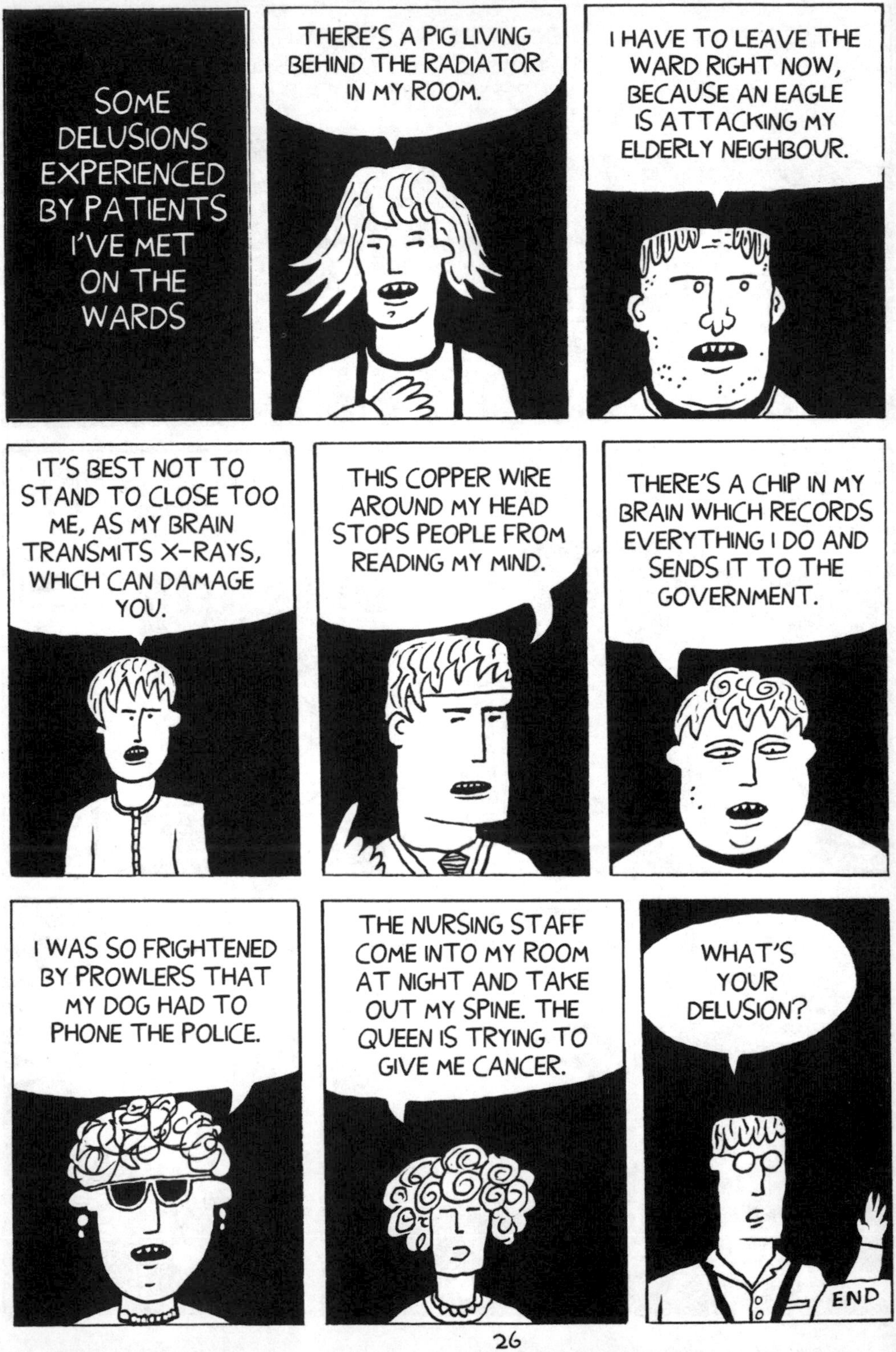
SOME DELUSIONS EXPERIENCED BY PATIENTS I'VE MET ON THE WARDS
THERE'S A PIG LIVING BEHIND THE RADIATOR IN MY ROOM.
I HAVE TO LEAVE THE WARD RIGHT NOW, BECAUSE AN EAGLE IS ATTACKING MY ELDERLY NEIGHBOUR.
IT'S BEST NOT TO STAND TO CLOSE TOO ME, AS MY BRAIN TRANSMITS X-RAYS, WHICH CAN DAMAGE YOU.
THIS COPPER WIRE AROUND MY HEAD STOPS PEOPLE FROM READING MY MIND.
THERE'S A CHIP IN MY BRAIN WHICH RECORDS EVERYTHING I DO AND SENDS IT TO THE GOVERNMENT.
I WAS SO FRIGHTENED BY PROWLERS THAT MY DOG HAD TO PHONE THE POLICE.
THE NURSING STAFF COME INTO MY ROOM AT NIGHT AND TAKE OUT MY SPINE. THE QUEEN IS TRYING TO GIVE ME CANCER.
WHAT'S YOUR DELUSION?
END

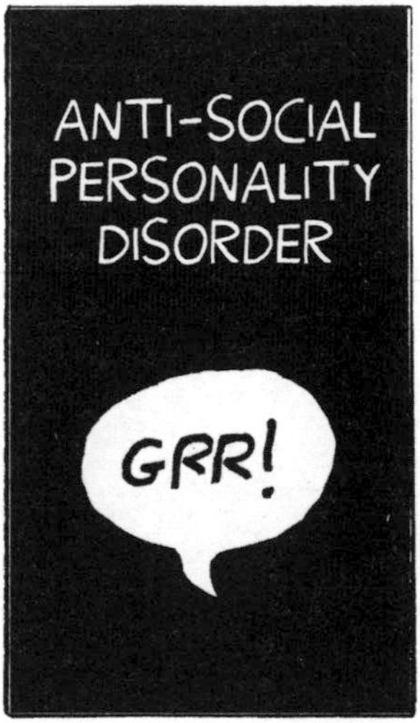
ANTI-SOCIAL PERSONALITY DISORDER
GRR!

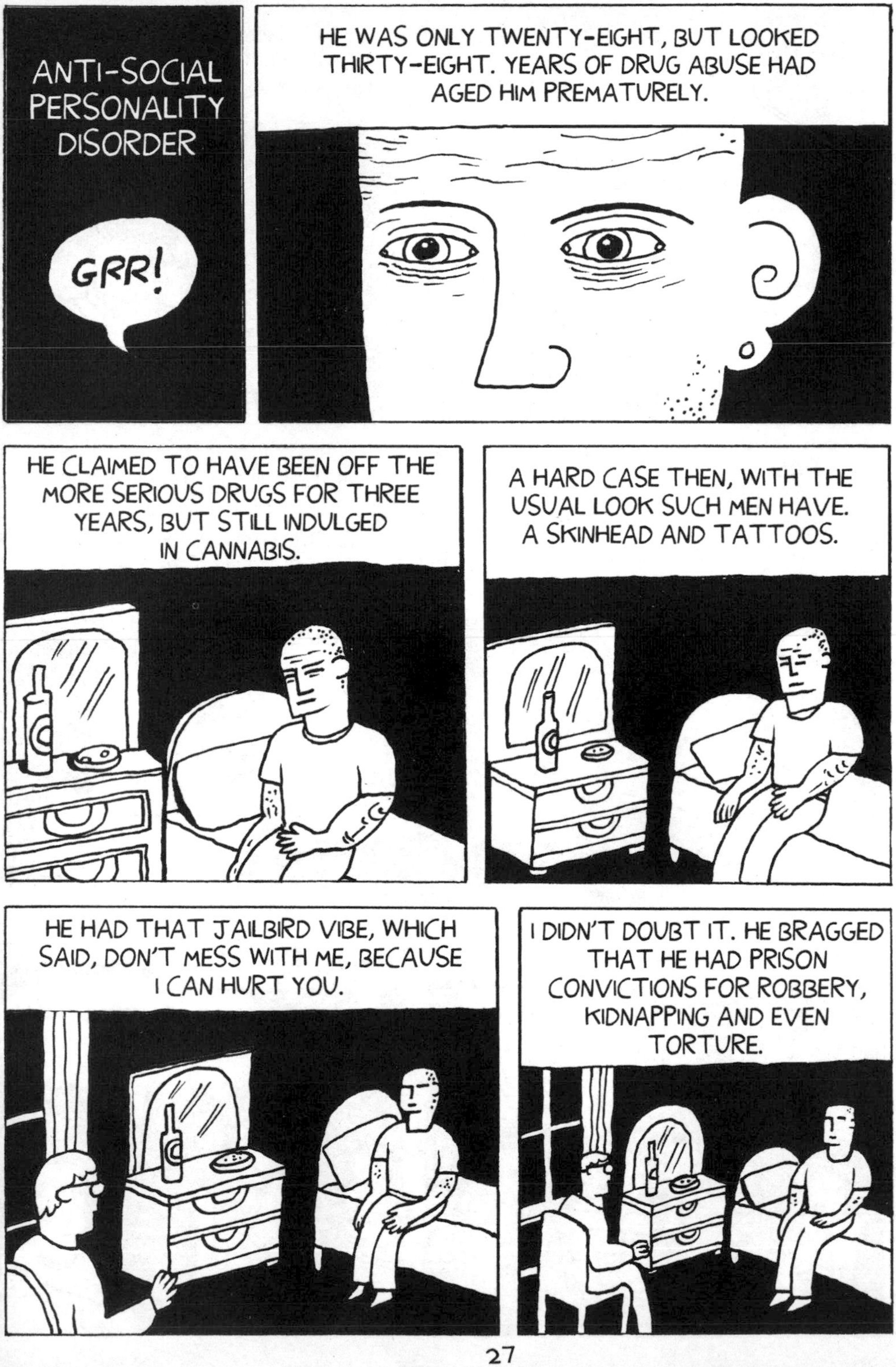
ANTI-SOCIAL PERSONALITY DISORDER
GRR!
HE WAS ONLY TWENTY-EIGHT, BUT LOOKED THIRTY-EIGHT. YEARS OF DRUG ABUSE HAD AGED HIM PREMATURELY.
HE CLAIMED TO HAVE BEEN OFF THE MORE SERIOUS DRUGS FOR THREE YEARS, BUT STILL INDULGED IN CANNABIS.
A HARD CASE THEN, WITH THE USUAL LOOK SUCH MEN HAVE. A SKINHEAD AND TATTOOS.
HE HAD THAT JAILBIRD VIBE, WHICH SAID, DON'T MESS WITH ME, BECAUSE I CAN HURT YOU.
I DIDN'T DOUBT IT. HE BRAGGED THAT HE HAD PRISON CONVICTIONS FOR ROBBERY, KIDNAPPING AND EVEN TORTURE.

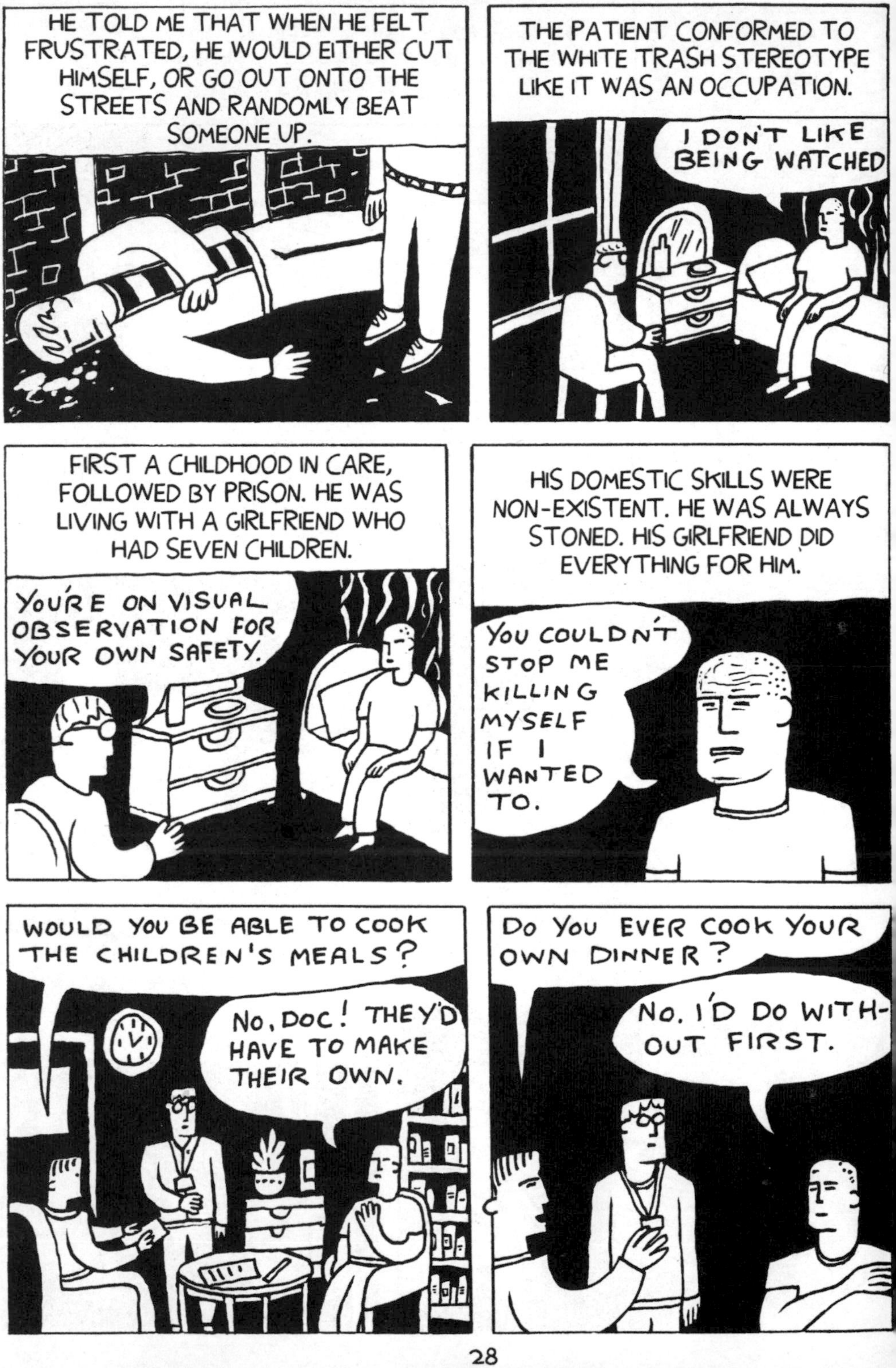
HE TOLD ME THAT WHEN HE FELT FRUSTRATED, HE WOULD EITHER CUT HIMSELF, OR GO OUT ONTO THE STREETS AND RANDOMLY BEAT SOMEONE UP.
THE PATIENT CONFORMED TO THE WHITE TRASH STEREOTYPE LIKE IT WAS AN OCCUPATION.
I DON'T LIKE BEING WATCHED
FIRST A CHILDHOOD IN CARE, FOLLOWED BY PRISON. HE WAS LIVING WITH A GIRLFRIEND WHO HAD SEVEN CHILDREN.
YOU'RE ON VISUAL OBSERVATION FOR YOUR OWN SAFETY.
HIS DOMESTIC SKILLS WERE NON-EXISTENT. HE WAS ALWAYS STONED. HIS GIRLFRIEND DID EVERYTHING FOR HIM.
YOU COULDN'T STOP ME KILLING MYSELF IF I WANTED TO.
WOULD YOU BE ABLE TO COOK THE CHILDREN'S MEALS?
NO, DOC! THEY'D HAVE TO MAKE THEIR OWN.
DO YOU EVER COOK YOUR OWN DINNER?
NO. I'D DO WITH-OUT FIRST.

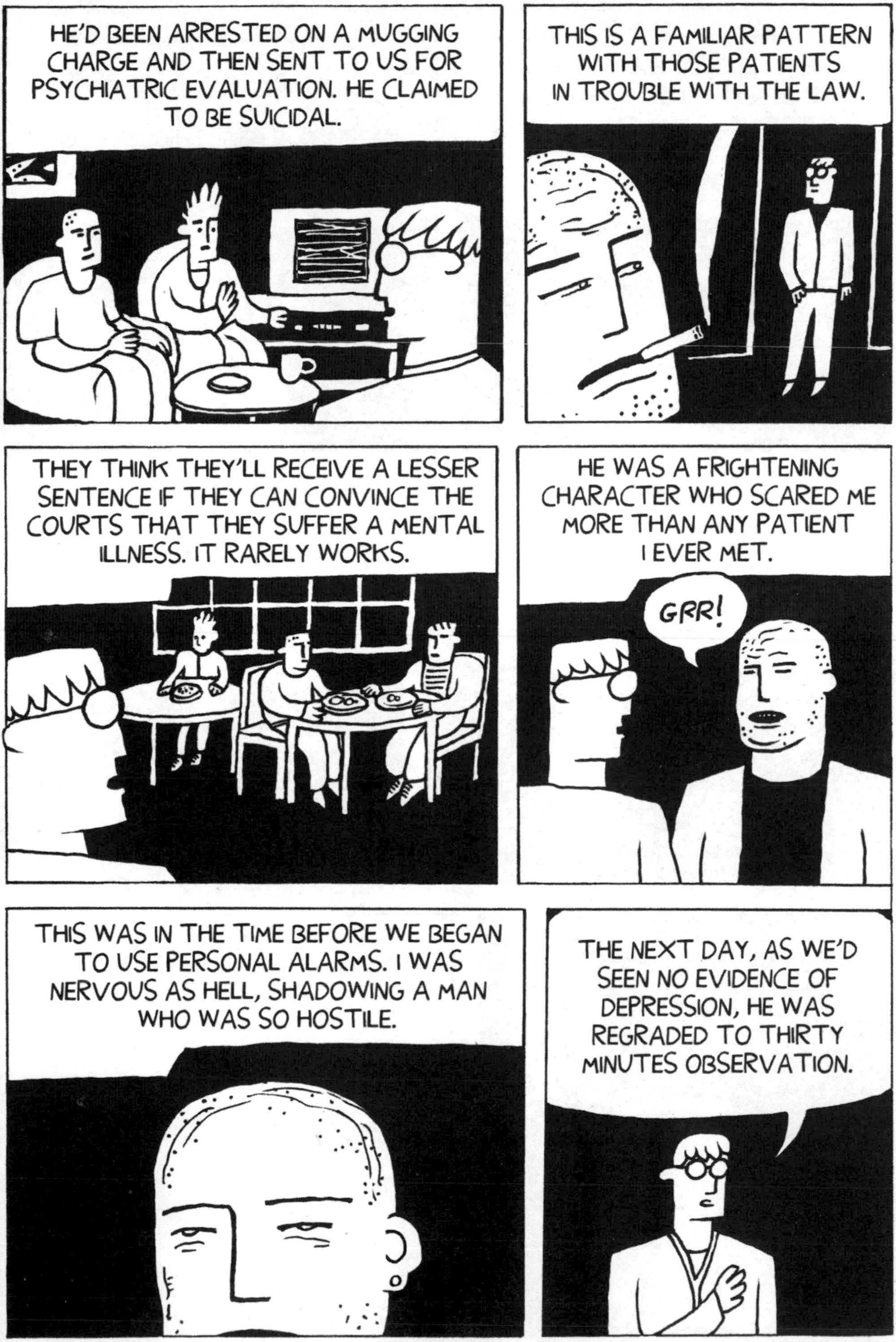
HE'D BEEN ARRESTED ON A MUGGING CHARGE AND THEN SENT TO US FOR PSYCHIATRIC EVALUATION. HE CLAIMED TO BE SUICIDAL.
THIS IS A FAMILIAR PATTERN WITH THOSE PATIENTS IN TROUBLE WITH THE LAW.
THEY THINK THEY'LL RECEIVE A LESSER SENTENCE IF THEY CAN CONVINCE THE COURTS THAT THEY SUFFER A MENTAL ILLNESS. IT RARELY WORKS.
HE WAS A FRIGHTENING CHARACTER WHO SCARED ME MORE THAN ANY PATIENT I EVER MET.
GRR!
THIS WAS IN THE TIME BEFORE WE BEGAN TO USE PERSONAL ALARMS. I WAS NERVOUS AS HELL, SHADOWING A MAN WHO WAS SO HOSTILE.
THE NEXT DAY, AS WE'D SEEN NO EVIDENCE OF DEPRESSION, HE WAS REGRADED TO THIRTY MINUTES OBSERVATION.

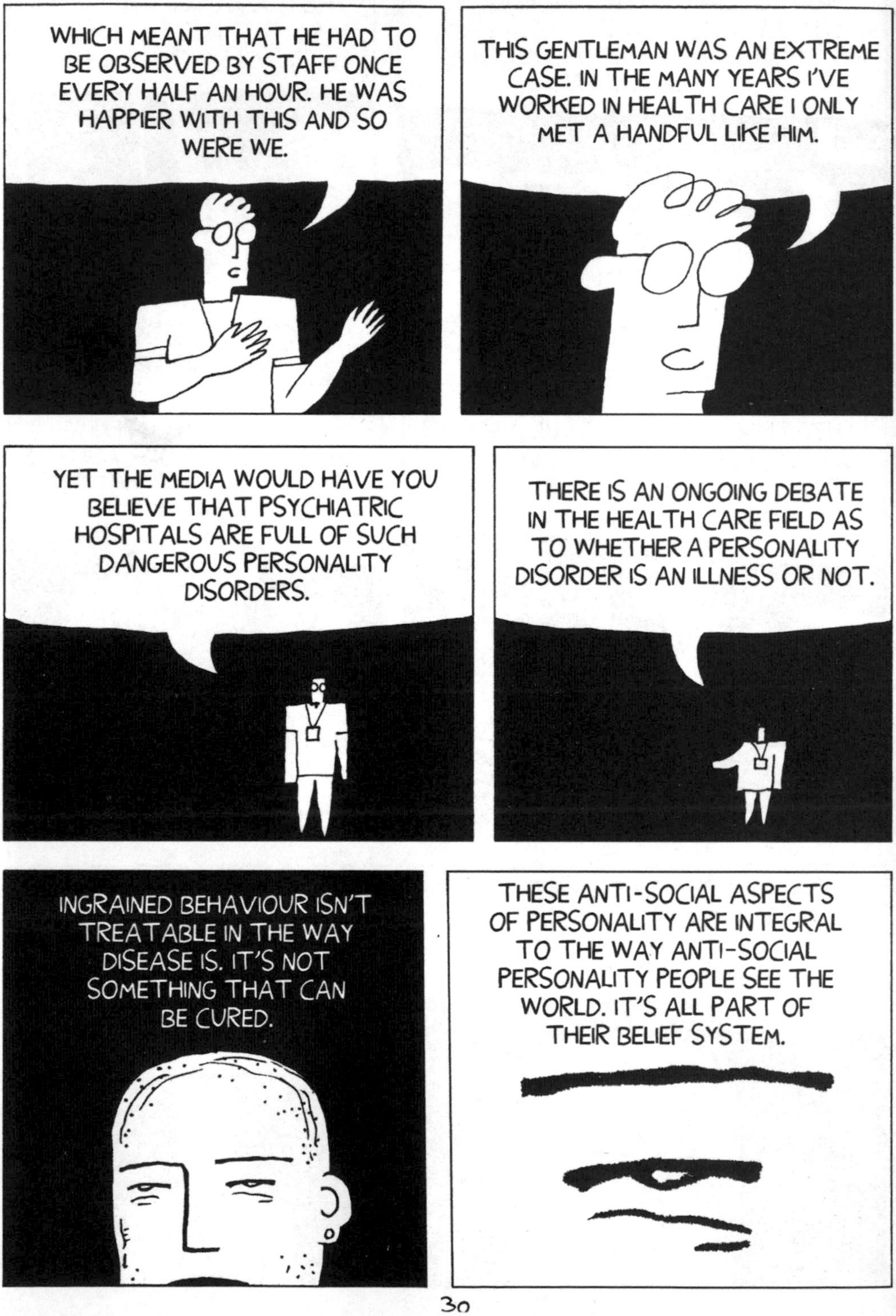
WHICH MEANT THAT HE HAD TO BE OBSERVED BY STAFF ONCE EVERY HALF AN HOUR. HE WAS HAPPIER WITH THIS AND SO WERE WE.
THIS GENTLEMAN WAS AN EXTREME CASE. IN THE MANY YEARS I'VE WORKED IN HEALTH CARE I ONLY MET A HANDFUL LIKE HIM.
YET THE MEDIA WOULD HAVE YOU BELIEVE THAT PSYCHIATRIC HOSPITALS ARE FULL OF SUCH DANGEROUS PERSONALITY DISORDERS.
THERE IS AN ONGOING DEBATE IN THE HEALTH CARE FIELD AS TO WHETHER A PERSONALITY DISORDER IS AN ILLNESS OR NOT.
INGRAINED BEHAVIOUR ISN'T TREATABLE IN THE WAY DISEASE IS. IT'S NOT SOMETHING THAT CAN BE CURED.
THESE ANTI-SOCIAL ASPECTS OF PERSONALITY ARE INTEGRAL TO THE WAY ANTI-SOCIAL PERSONALITY PEOPLE SEE THE WORLD. IT'S ALL PART OF THEIR BELIEF SYSTEM.

A BELIEF SYSTEM WHICH MAKES THEM OBLIVIOUS TO SOCIAL NORMS.

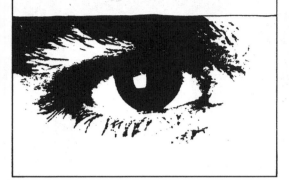

THERE'S A CALLOUS UNCONCERN FOR OTHERS.

AN INABILITY TO MAINTAIN RELATIONSHIPS, EVEN THOUGH THEY HAVE NO DIFFICULTY ESTABLISHING THEM.

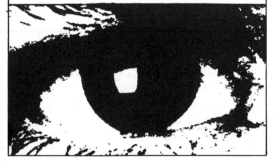

THEY HAVE A VERY LOW TOLERANCE FOR FRUSTRATION, AND ARE BOTH QUICK TO ANGER AND PRONE TO VIOLENCE.

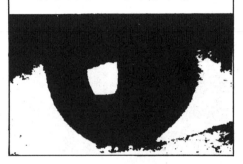

THEY LACK GUILT. DON'T LEARN FROM EXPERIENCE AND ARE IMPERVIOUS TO PUNISHMENT.

THEY REFUSE TO ACCEPT RESPONSIBILITY FOR THEIR ACTIONS AND TEND TO BLAME OTHERS FOR THEIR BEHAVIOUR.

I DON'T KNOW WHAT HAPPENED TO THIS PATIENT. I WENT ON HOLIDAY AND WHEN I RETURNED HE WAS GONE.

I PRESUMED THAT HAVING BEEN ASSESSED HE'D BEEN TAKEN BACK INTO CUSTODY.

NOT ALL PEOPLE WITH THIS TYPE OF PERSONALITY DISORDER ARE CRIMINALS.

WE LIVE IN A SOCIETY WHERE MANY OF THESE PSYCHOPATHIC TRAITS ARE CONSIDERED QUITE REASONABLE.

SELFISHNESS, LACK OF EMPATHY, SUPERFICIALITY, AND MANIPULATIVENESS

ARE TRAITS THAT ARE HIGHLY VALUED IN THE WORLDS OF BUSINESS, POLITICS, THE LAW, AND ACADEMIA.

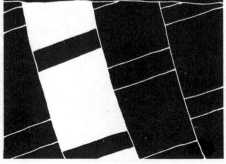

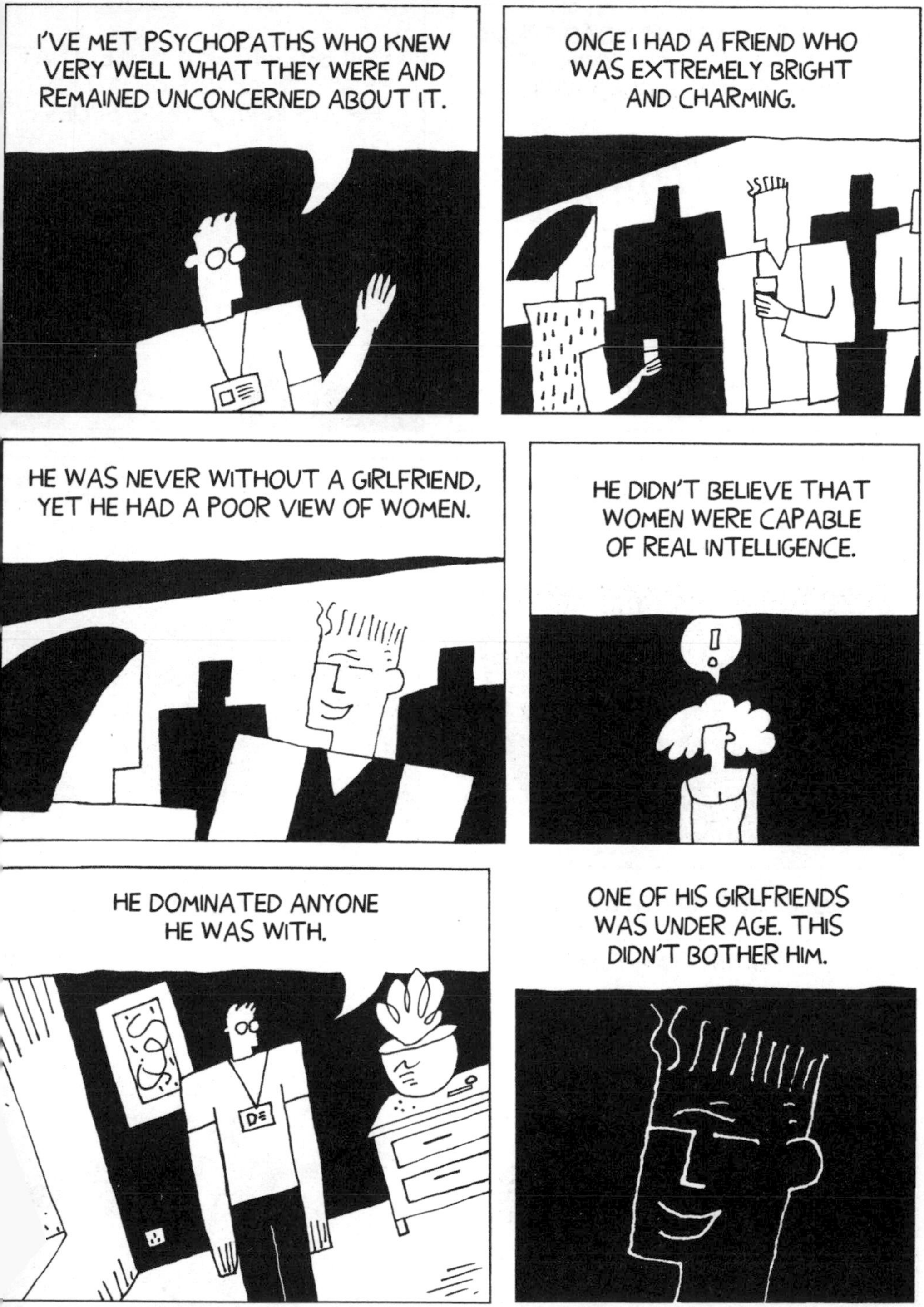
I'VE MET PSYCHOPATHS WHO KNEW VERY WELL WHAT THEY WERE AND REMAINED UNCONCERNED ABOUT IT.
ONCE I HAD A FRIEND WHO WAS EXTREMELY BRIGHT AND CHARMING.
HE WAS NEVER WITHOUT A GIRLFRIEND, YET HE HAD A POOR VIEW OF WOMEN.
HE DIDN'T BELIEVE THAT WOMEN WERE CAPABLE OF REAL INTELLIGENCE.
!
HE DOMINATED ANYONE HE WAS WITH.
ONE OF HIS GIRLFRIENDS WAS UNDER AGE. THIS DIDN'T BOTHER HIM.

AFTER A PARTICULARLY BAD BREAK UP WITH A GIRL, HE TOOK TO CARRYING A KNIFE AROUND WITH HIM.

I REALISED, AFTER A WHILE, THAT HE WAS INCAPABLE OF PUTTING HIMSELF IN ANOTHER'S SHOES.

HE LACKED IMAGINATION. HE WOULD JOKE ABOUT GASSING THE WORKING CLASSES.

HE COULDN'T THINK WHY ANYONE WOULD WORK IN HEALTH CARE OR SOCIAL SERVICES.

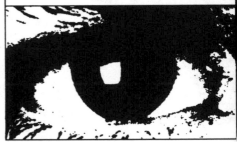

ASSUMING THAT IT WAS ONLY BECAUSE THEY COULDN'T DO ANYTHING ELSE.

YEARS LATER, I HEARD THAT HE'D BECOME A LAWYER.

END

PEOPLE
WITH
MENTAL
ILLNESS
ENRICH
OUR
LIVES

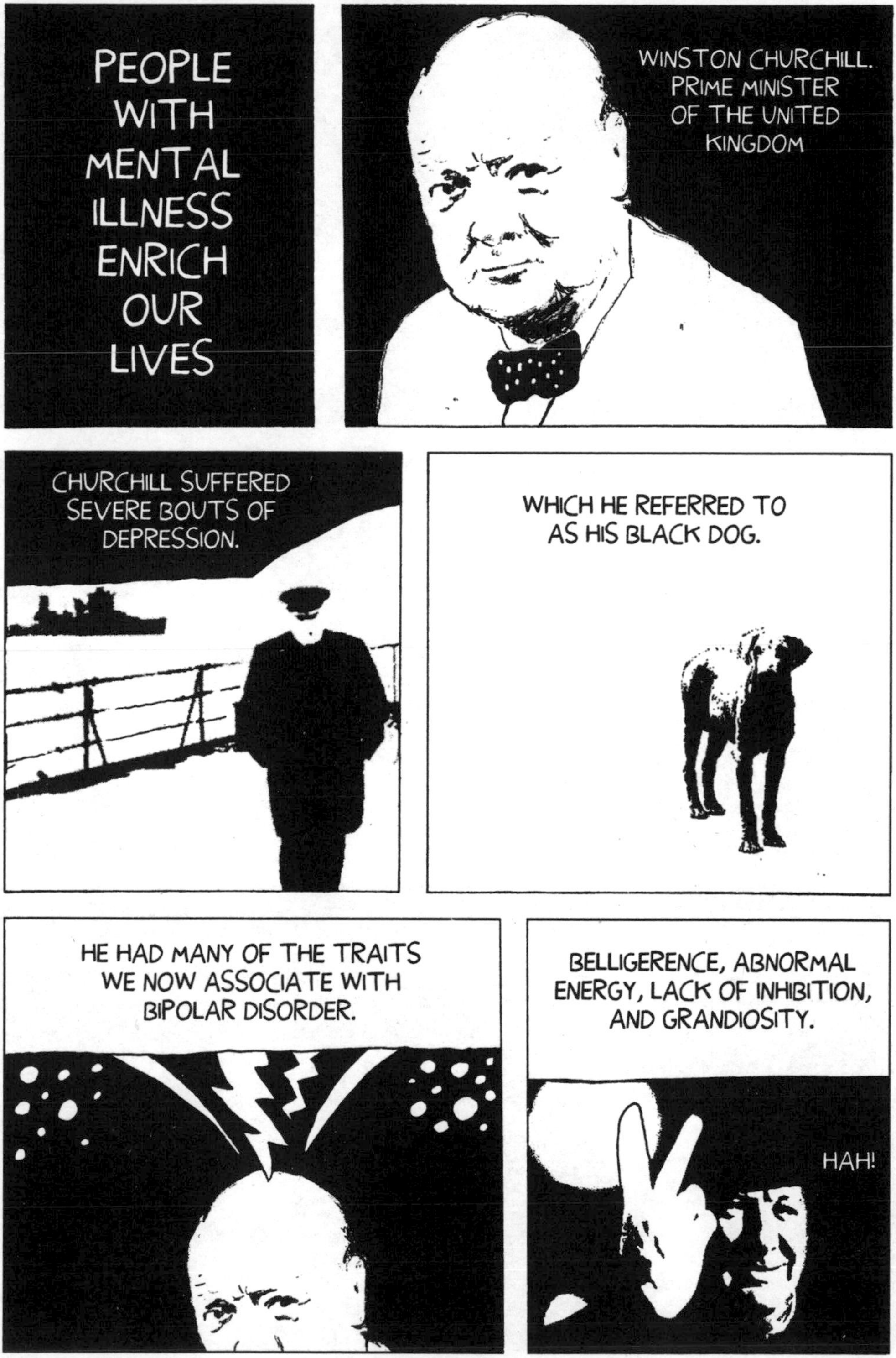
PEOPLE WITH MENTAL ILLNESS ENRICH OUR LIVES
WINSTON CHURCHILL. PRIME MINISTER OF THE UNITED KINGDOM
CHURCHILL SUFFERED SEVERE BOUTS OF DEPRESSION.
WHICH HE REFERRED TO AS HIS BLACK DOG.
HE HAD MANY OF THE TRAITS WE NOW ASSOCIATE WITH BIPOLAR DISORDER.
BELLIGERENCE, ABNORMAL ENERGY, LACK OF INHIBITION, AND GRANDIOSITY.
HAH!

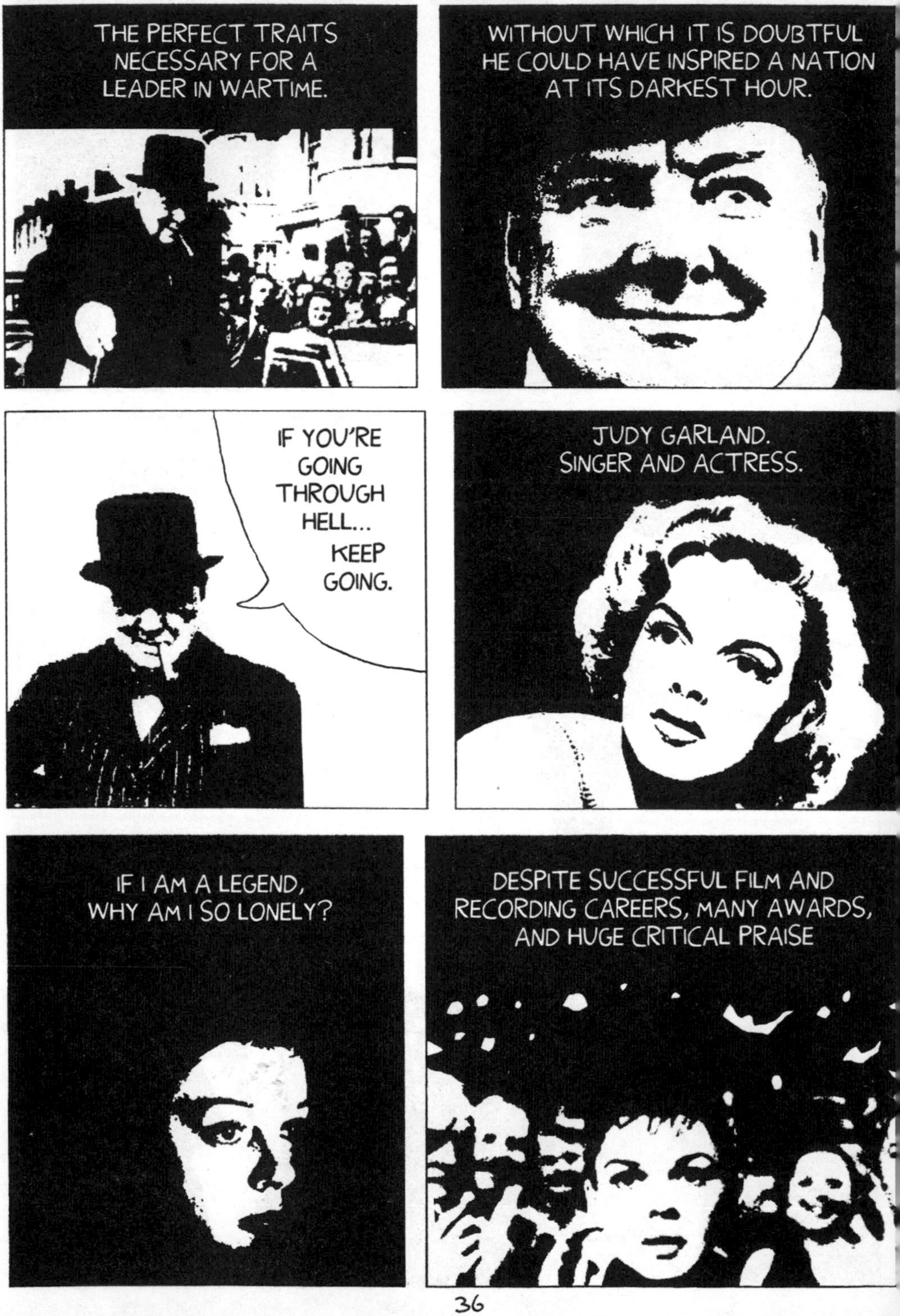
THE PERFECT TRAITS NECESSARY FOR A LEADER IN WARTIME.
WITHOUT WHICH IT IS DOUBTFUL HE COULD HAVE INSPIRED A NATION AT ITS DARKEST HOUR.
IF YOU'RE GOING THROUGH HELL... KEEP GOING.
JUDY GARLAND. SINGER AND ACTRESS.
IF I AM A LEGEND, WHY AM I SO LONELY?
DESPITE SUCCESSFUL FILM AND RECORDING CAREERS, MANY AWARDS, AND HUGE CRITICAL PRAISE

GARLAND SUFFERED THROUGHOUT HER LIFE FROM LACERATING SELF-DOUBT.

SHE REQUIRED CONSTANT REASSURANCE THAT SHE WAS TALENTED AND ATTRACTIVE.

AS A TEENAGE STAR SHE WAS PLIED WITH DRUGS IN ORDER TO KEEP HER WEIGHT DOWN.

A SITUATION THAT BROUGHT ABOUT A LIFE-LONG STRUGGLE WITH ADDICTION.

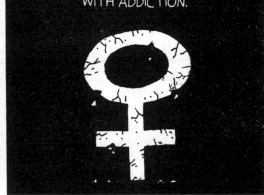

WHICH ENDED WITH HER DEATH FROM AN ACCIDENTAL OVERDOSE.

YET OUT OF THE CHAOS OF HER LIFE, GARLAND LEFT A LASTING LEGACY.

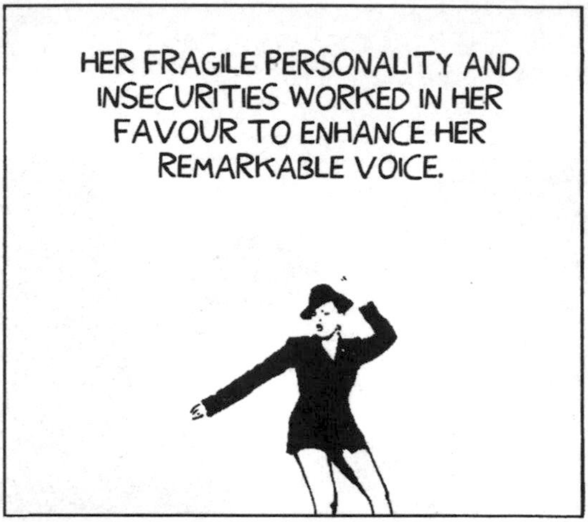
HER FRAGILE PERSONALITY AND INSECURITIES WORKED IN HER FAVOUR TO ENHANCE HER REMARKABLE VOICE.

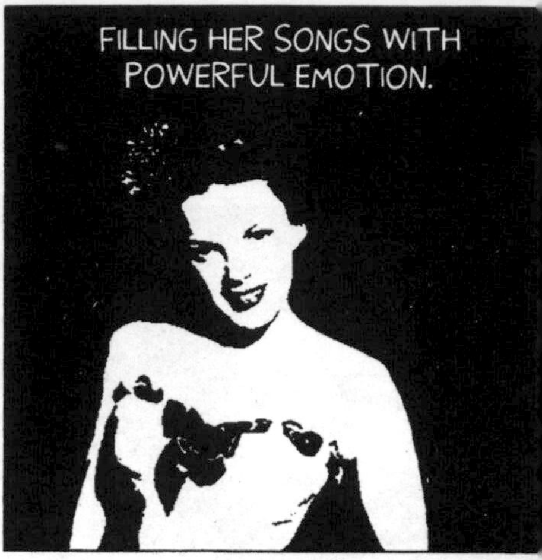
FILLING HER SONGS WITH POWERFUL EMOTION.

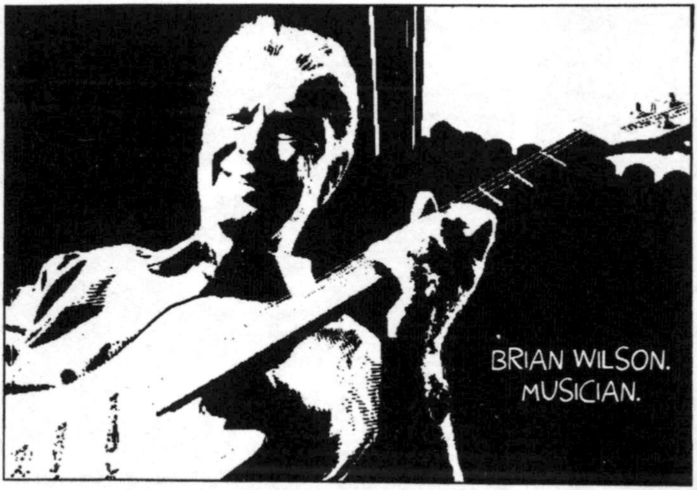
BRIAN WILSON.
MUSICIAN.

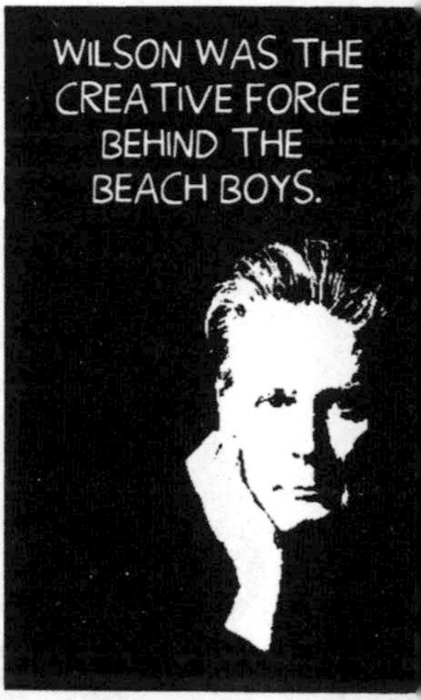
WILSON WAS THE CREATIVE FORCE BEHIND THE BEACH BOYS.

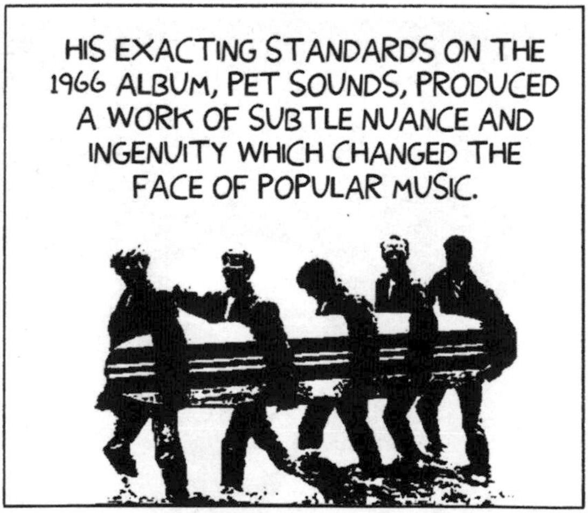
HIS EXACTING STANDARDS ON THE 1966 ALBUM, PET SOUNDS, PRODUCED A WORK OF SUBTLE NUANCE AND INGENUITY WHICH CHANGED THE FACE OF POPULAR MUSIC.

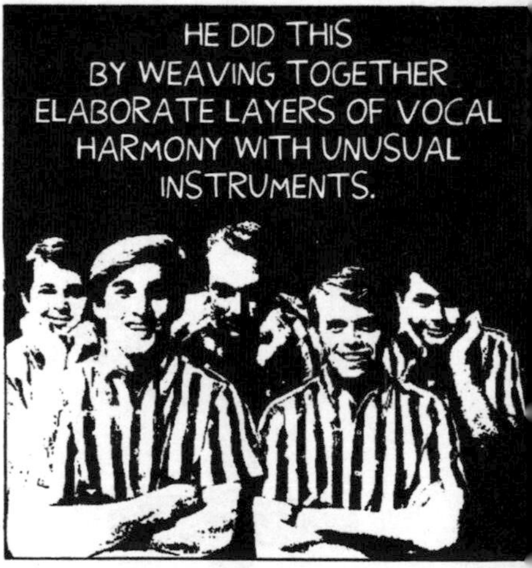
HE DID THIS BY WEAVING TOGETHER ELABORATE LAYERS OF VOCAL HARMONY WITH UNUSUAL INSTRUMENTS.

IN HIS MID-TWENTIES, WILSON, BEGAN TO EXPERIENCE AUDITORY HALLUCINATIONS.

HEY!

DEROGATORY VOICES, TAUNTING HIM.

YOU'RE GOING TO DIE SOON!

THESE VOICES NEVER LEFT WILSON, MAKING IT IMPOSSIBLE FOR HIM TO GO ON STAGE FOR MANY YEARS.

THIS, COMBINED WITH HIS OBSESSIVE PERFECTIONISM, AND THE GROWING TENSIONS WITHIN THE BAND

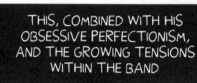

BROUGHT ABOUT AN END TO WILSON'S LEADERSHIP OF THE BEACH BOYS.

WILSON THEN SANK INTO A MORASS OF DRUG-TAKING AND OVER-EATING.

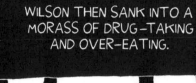

REPORTEDLY SPENDING WEEKS OR MONTHS IN BED.

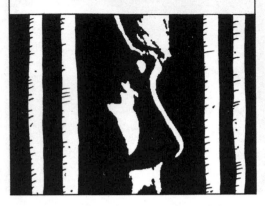

A PRISONER OF HIS TORMENTED MIND.

WILSON'S RETURN TO FUNCTIONAL LIFE TOOK DECADES.

I USED TO GO FOR LONG PERIODS WITHOUT DOING ANYTHING, BUT NOW I PLAY EVERY DAY.

FINISHING THE ALBUM SMILE WAS MY BIGGEST ACCOMPLISHMENT ... EVER.

WILSON CONTINUES TO BOTH RECORD AND PERFORM. ONE OF THE FEW TRUE GENIUSES OF POPULAR MUSIC.

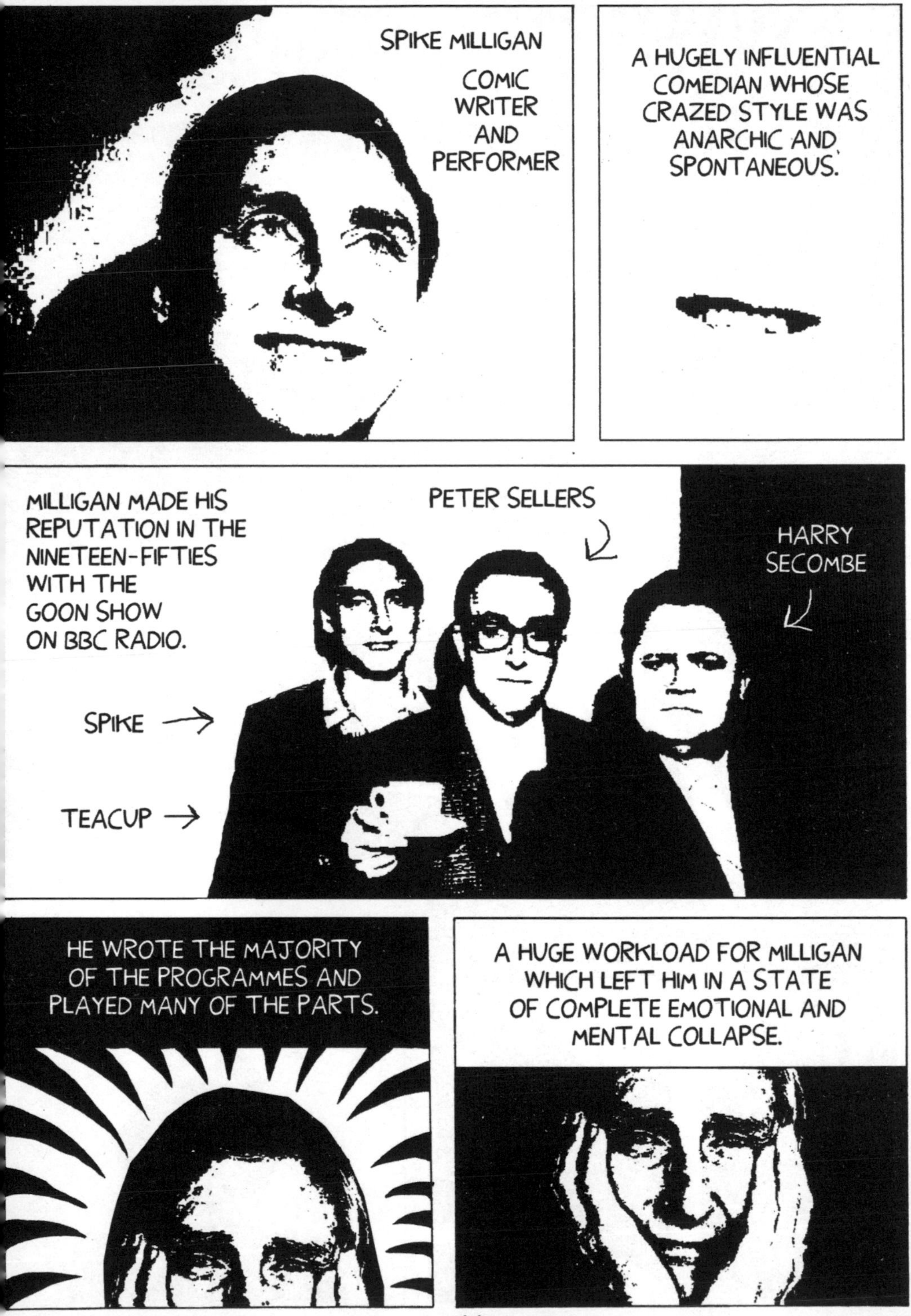
SPIKE MILLIGAN
COMIC WRITER AND PERFORMER
A HUGELY INFLUENTIAL COMEDIAN WHOSE CRAZED STYLE WAS ANARCHIC AND SPONTANEOUS.
MILLIGAN MADE HIS REPUTATION IN THE NINETEEN-FIFTIES WITH THE GOON SHOW ON BBC RADIO.
PETER SELLERS
HARRY SECOMBE
SPIKE →
TEACUP →
HE WROTE THE MAJORITY OF THE PROGRAMMES AND PLAYED MANY OF THE PARTS.
A HUGE WORKLOAD FOR MILLIGAN WHICH LEFT HIM IN A STATE OF COMPLETE EMOTIONAL AND MENTAL COLLAPSE.

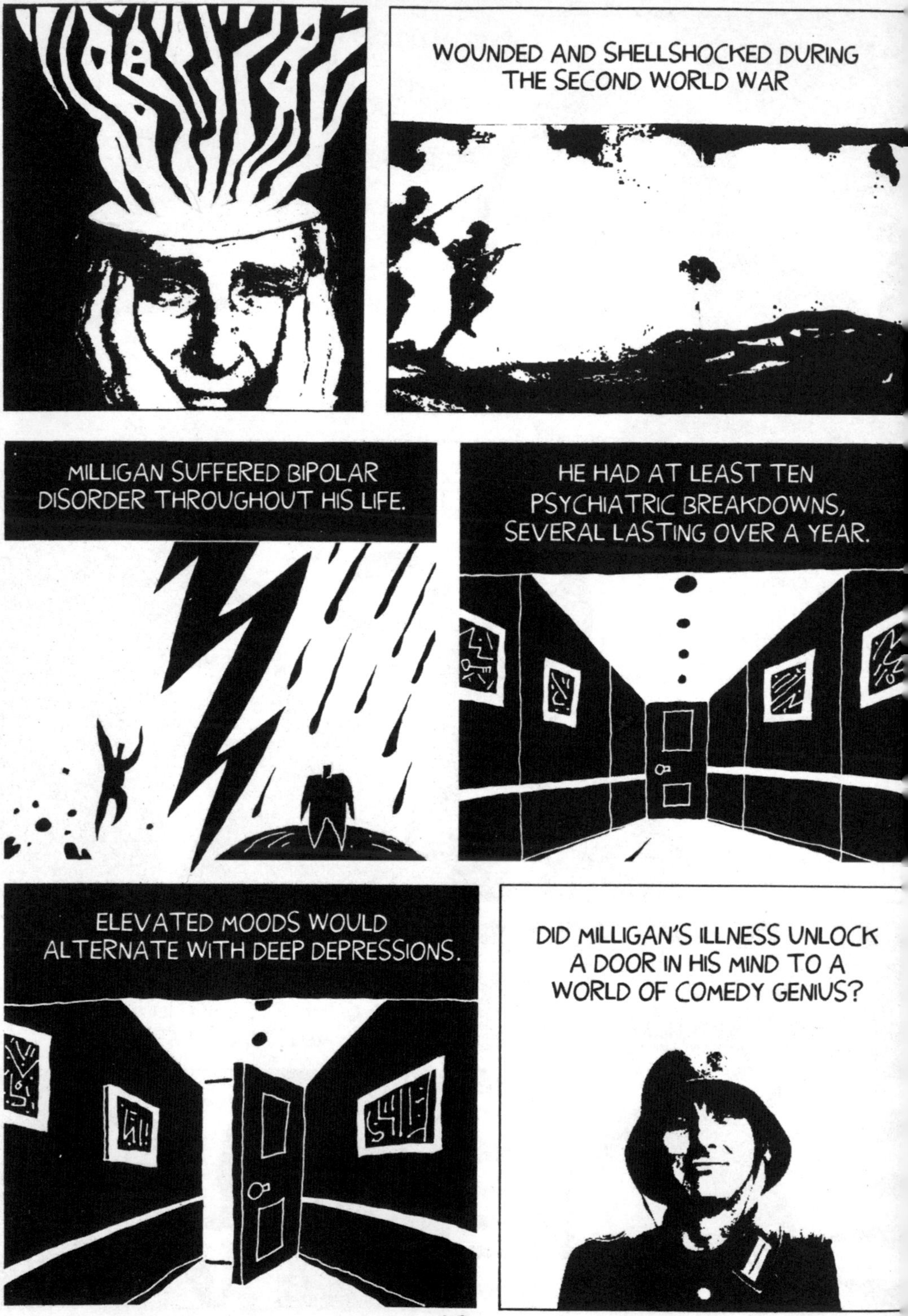
WOUNDED AND SHELLSHOCKED DURING THE SECOND WORLD WAR
MILLIGAN SUFFERED BIPOLAR DISORDER THROUGHOUT HIS LIFE.
HE HAD AT LEAST TEN PSYCHIATRIC BREAKDOWNS, SEVERAL LASTING OVER A YEAR.
ELEVATED MOODS WOULD ALTERNATE WITH DEEP DEPRESSIONS.
DID MILLIGAN'S ILLNESS UNLOCK A DOOR IN HIS MIND TO A WORLD OF COMEDY GENIUS?

AN ELEVATED MOOD WILL BRING WITH IT AN EXPLOSION OF ENERGY AND FREE-FLOWING IDEAS.

HAH!

BUT THE INGENUITY AND ABILITY TO THINK CREATIVELY HAS TO BE THERE IN THE FIRST PLACE.

MENTAL ILLNESS WILL TEND TO HINDER THE CREATIVE PROCESS, AS MUCH AS HELP IT.

IT IS DESPITE MILLIGAN'S ILLNESS THAT HE WAS A SUCCESSFUL AUTHOR, PLAYWRIGHT, POET, AND ACTOR. NOT BECAUSE OF IT.

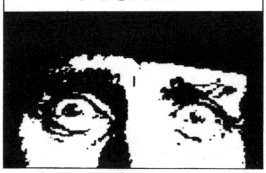

A TROUBLED, GIFTED MAN WITH A UNIQUE WORLD VIEW.

DO YOU FIND YOURSELF LOOKING BACK AT YOUR CHILDHOOD?

NO, IT HURTS MY NECK.

43

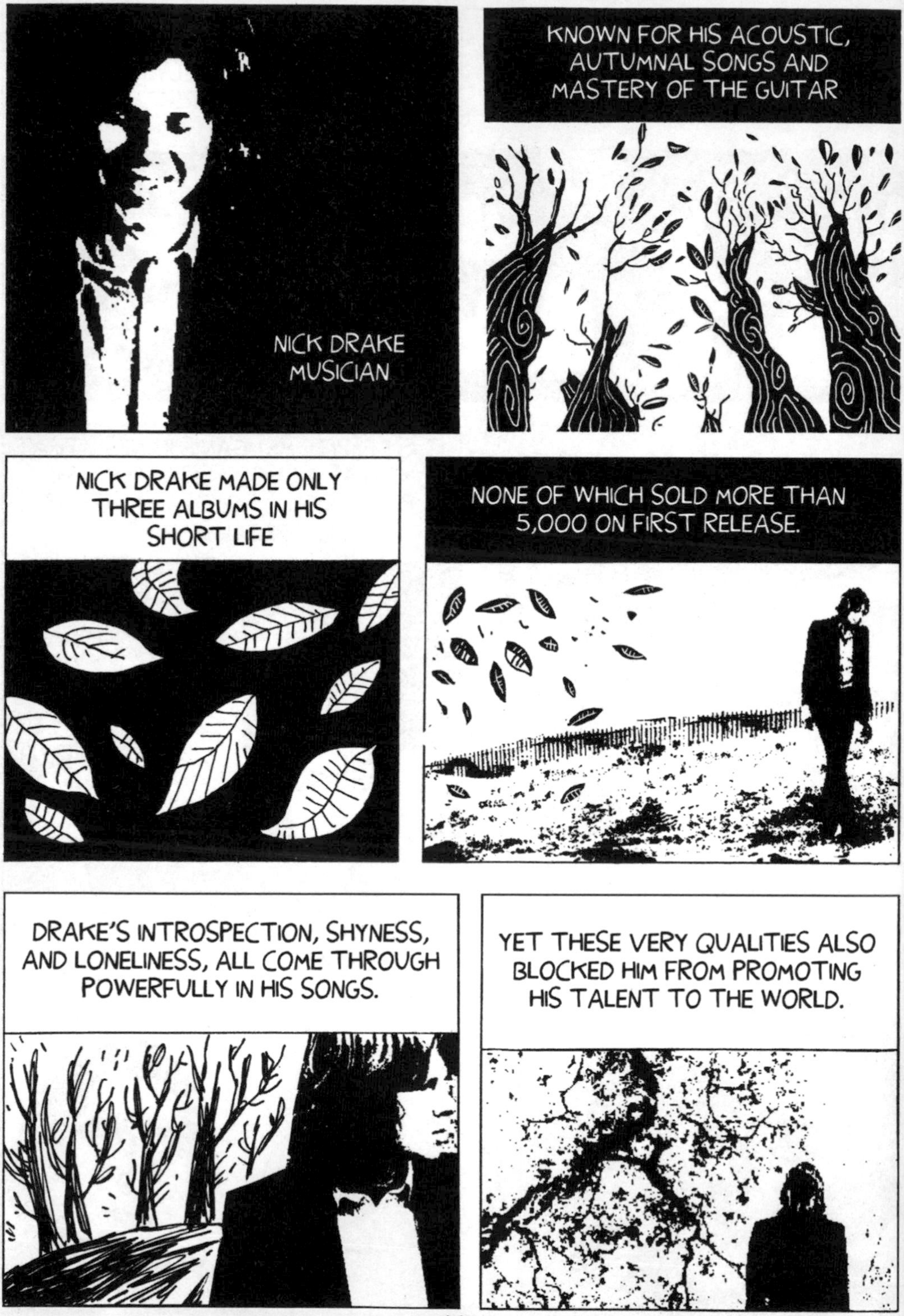
NICK DRAKE
MUSICIAN
KNOWN FOR HIS ACOUSTIC, AUTUMNAL SONGS AND MASTERY OF THE GUITAR
NICK DRAKE MADE ONLY THREE ALBUMS IN HIS SHORT LIFE
NONE OF WHICH SOLD MORE THAN 5,000 ON FIRST RELEASE.
DRAKE'S INTROSPECTION, SHYNESS, AND LONELINESS, ALL COME THROUGH POWERFULLY IN HIS SONGS.
YET THESE VERY QUALITIES ALSO BLOCKED HIM FROM PROMOTING HIS TALENT TO THE WORLD.

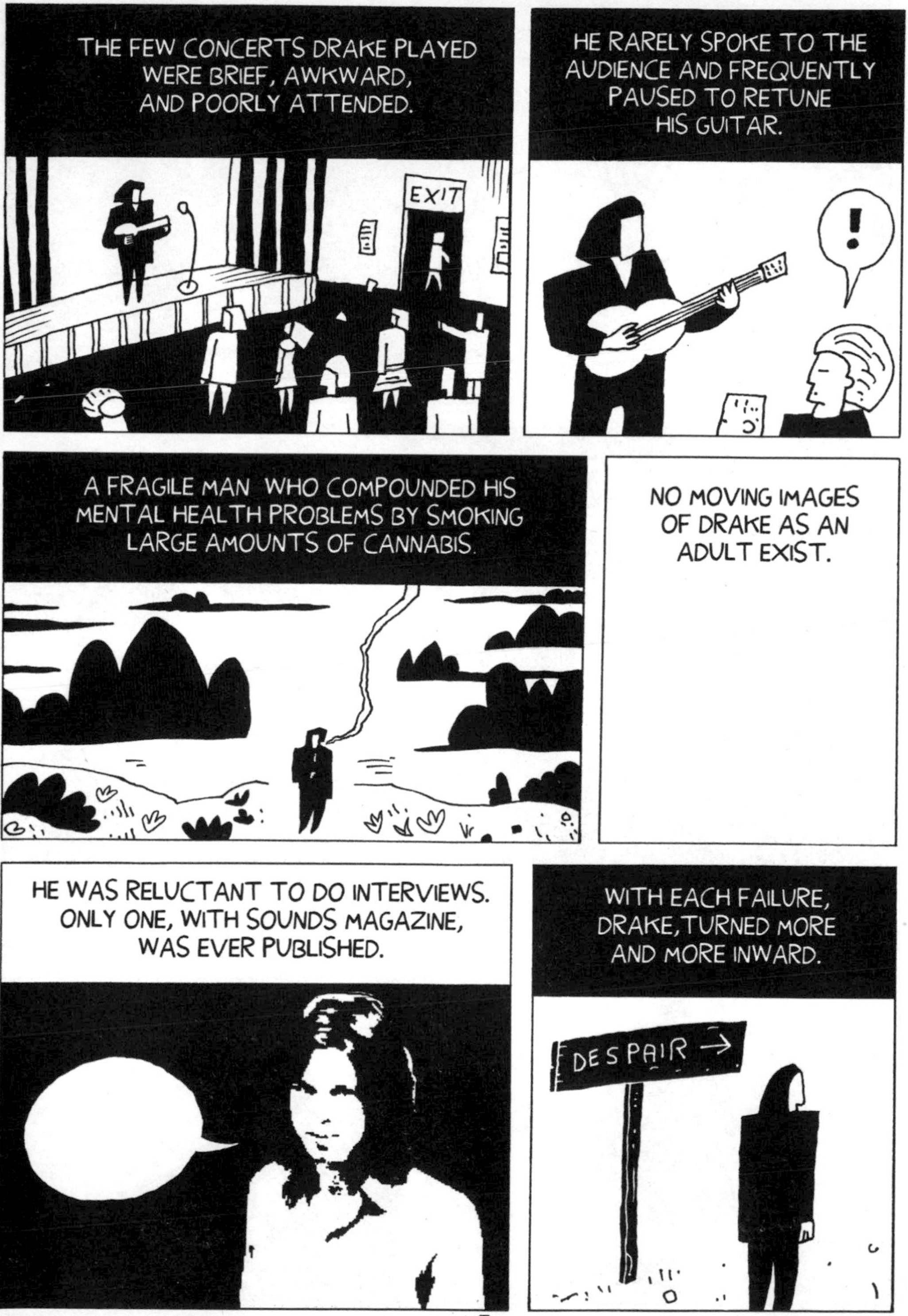
THE FEW CONCERTS DRAKE PLAYED WERE BRIEF, AWKWARD, AND POORLY ATTENDED.
EXIT
HE RARELY SPOKE TO THE AUDIENCE AND FREQUENTLY PAUSED TO RETUNE HIS GUITAR.
!
A FRAGILE MAN WHO COMPOUNDED HIS MENTAL HEALTH PROBLEMS BY SMOKING LARGE AMOUNTS OF CANNABIS.
NO MOVING IMAGES OF DRAKE AS AN ADULT EXIST.
HE WAS RELUCTANT TO DO INTERVIEWS. ONLY ONE, WITH SOUNDS MAGAZINE, WAS EVER PUBLISHED.
WITH EACH FAILURE, DRAKE, TURNED MORE AND MORE INWARD.
DESPAIR →

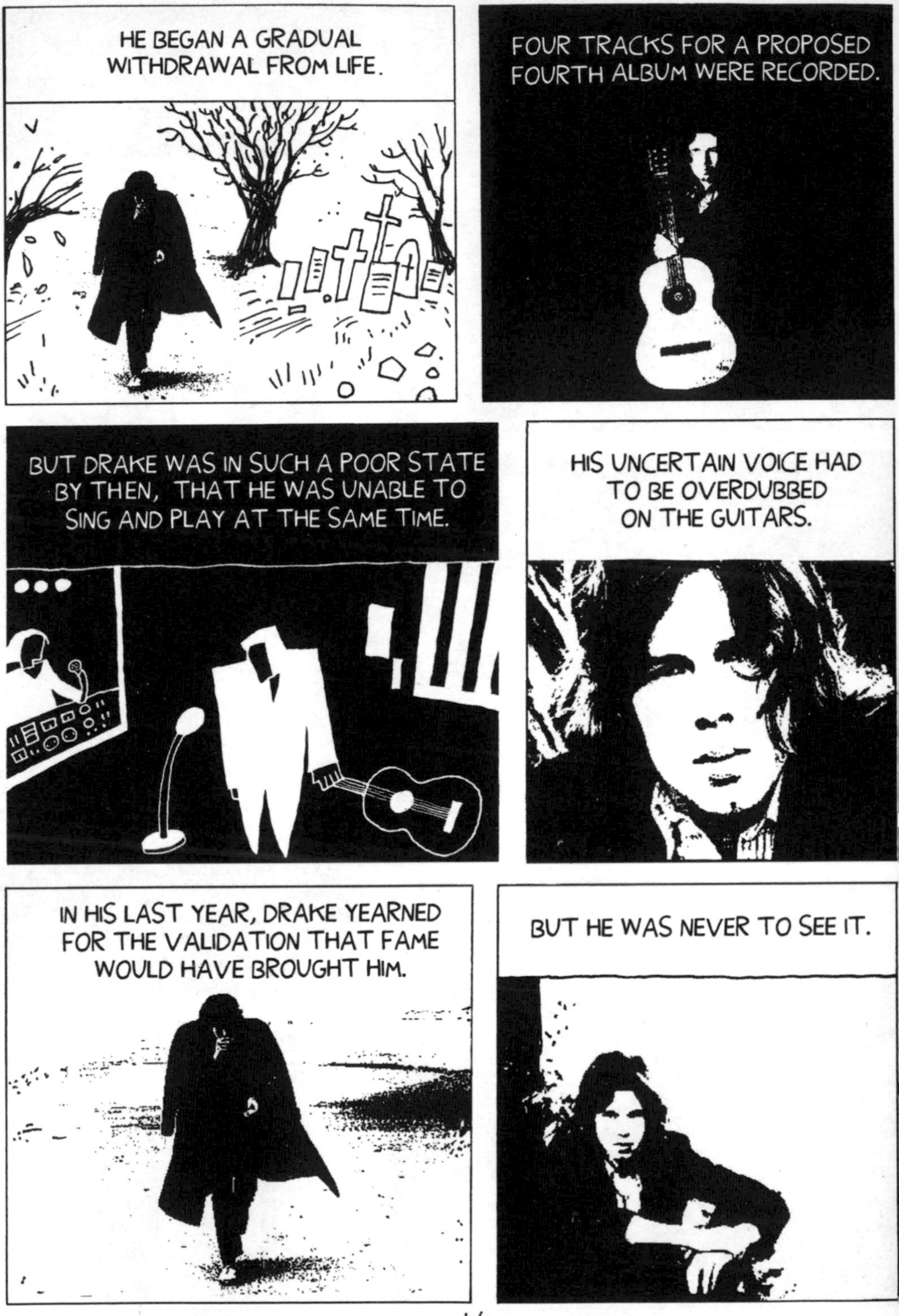
HE BEGAN A GRADUAL WITHDRAWAL FROM LIFE.
FOUR TRACKS FOR A PROPOSED FOURTH ALBUM WERE RECORDED.
BUT DRAKE WAS IN SUCH A POOR STATE BY THEN, THAT HE WAS UNABLE TO SING AND PLAY AT THE SAME TIME.
HIS UNCERTAIN VOICE HAD TO BE OVERDUBBED ON THE GUITARS.
IN HIS LAST YEAR, DRAKE YEARNED FOR THE VALIDATION THAT FAME WOULD HAVE BROUGHT HIM.
BUT HE WAS NEVER TO SEE IT.

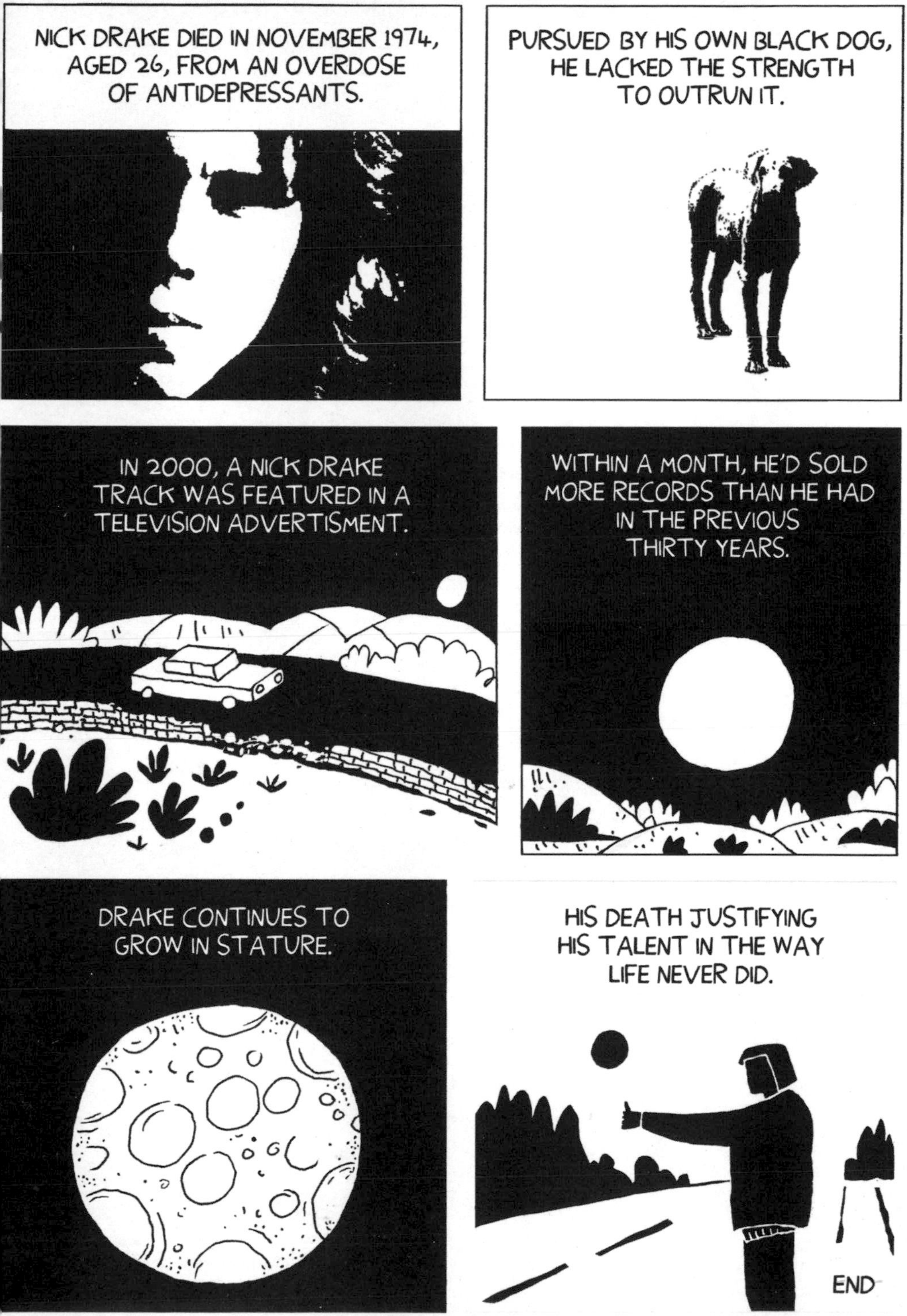
NICK DRAKE DIED IN NOVEMBER 1974, AGED 26, FROM AN OVERDOSE OF ANTIDEPRESSANTS.
PURSUED BY HIS OWN BLACK DOG, HE LACKED THE STRENGTH TO OUTRUN IT.
IN 2000, A NICK DRAKE TRACK WAS FEATURED IN A TELEVISION ADVERTISMENT.
WITHIN A MONTH, HE'D SOLD MORE RECORDS THAN HE HAD IN THE PREVIOUS THIRTY YEARS.
DRAKE CONTINUES TO GROW IN STATURE.
HIS DEATH JUSTIFYING HIS TALENT IN THE WAY LIFE NEVER DID.
END

BLOOD

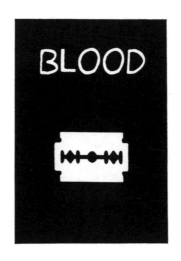

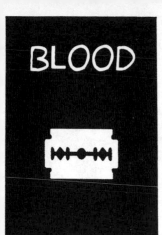

BLOOD

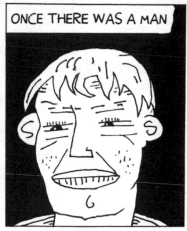

ONCE THERE WAS A MAN

AND A HAMMER.

THE MAN TOOK THE HAMMER AND REPEATEDLY HIT HIMSELF IN THE FACE.

BREAKING HIS NOSE

AND LEAVING PERMANENT SMALL DEPRESSIONS IN HIS FOREHEAD.

WHAT INNER TORMENT WOULD DRIVE A MAN TO DO SUCH A THING?

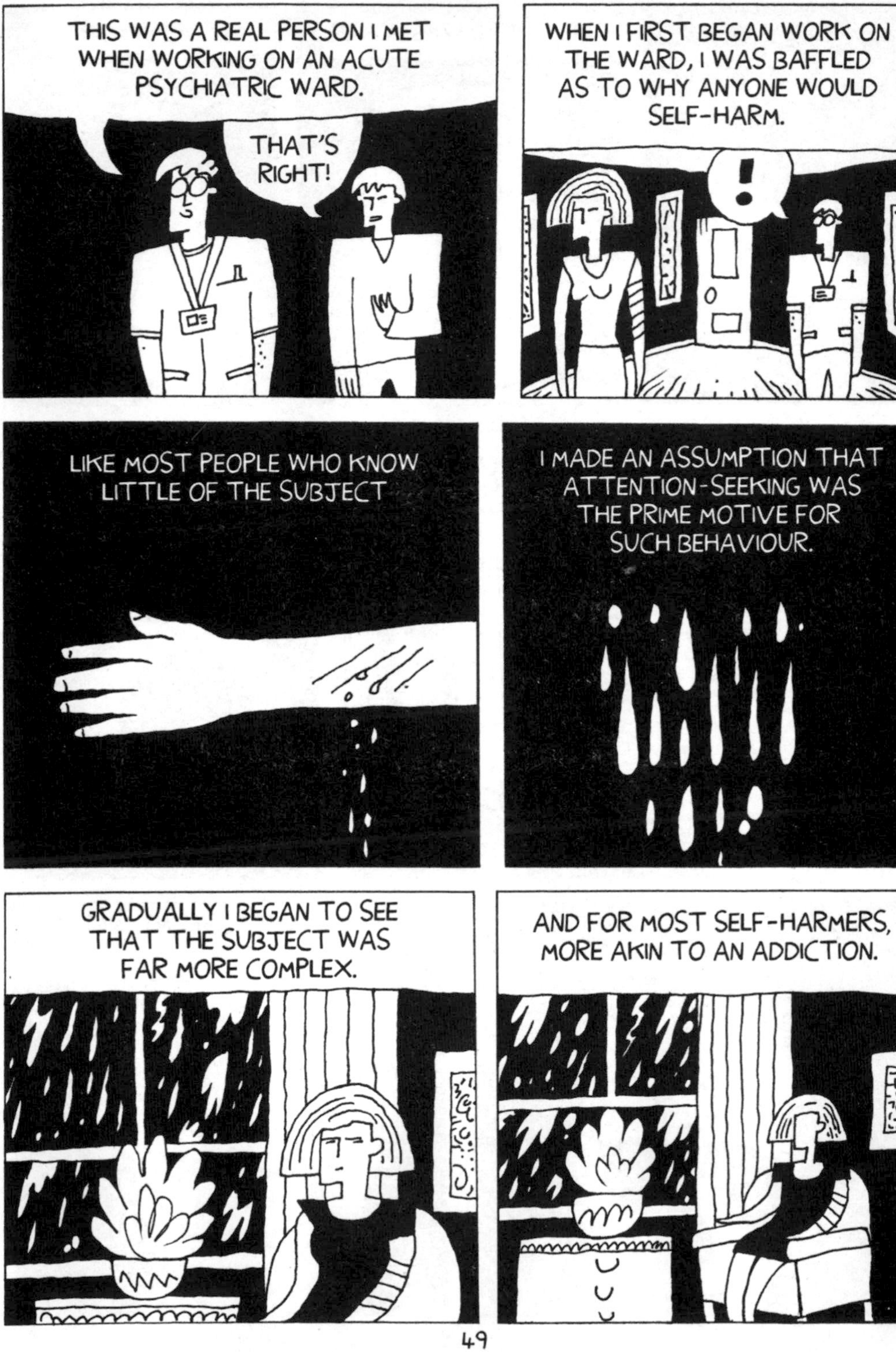
THIS WAS A REAL PERSON I MET WHEN WORKING ON AN ACUTE PSYCHIATRIC WARD.
THAT'S RIGHT!
WHEN I FIRST BEGAN WORK ON THE WARD, I WAS BAFFLED AS TO WHY ANYONE WOULD SELF-HARM.
!
LIKE MOST PEOPLE WHO KNOW LITTLE OF THE SUBJECT
I MADE AN ASSUMPTION THAT ATTENTION-SEEKING WAS THE PRIME MOTIVE FOR SUCH BEHAVIOUR.
GRADUALLY I BEGAN TO SEE THAT THE SUBJECT WAS FAR MORE COMPLEX.
AND FOR MOST SELF-HARMERS, MORE AKIN TO AN ADDICTION.

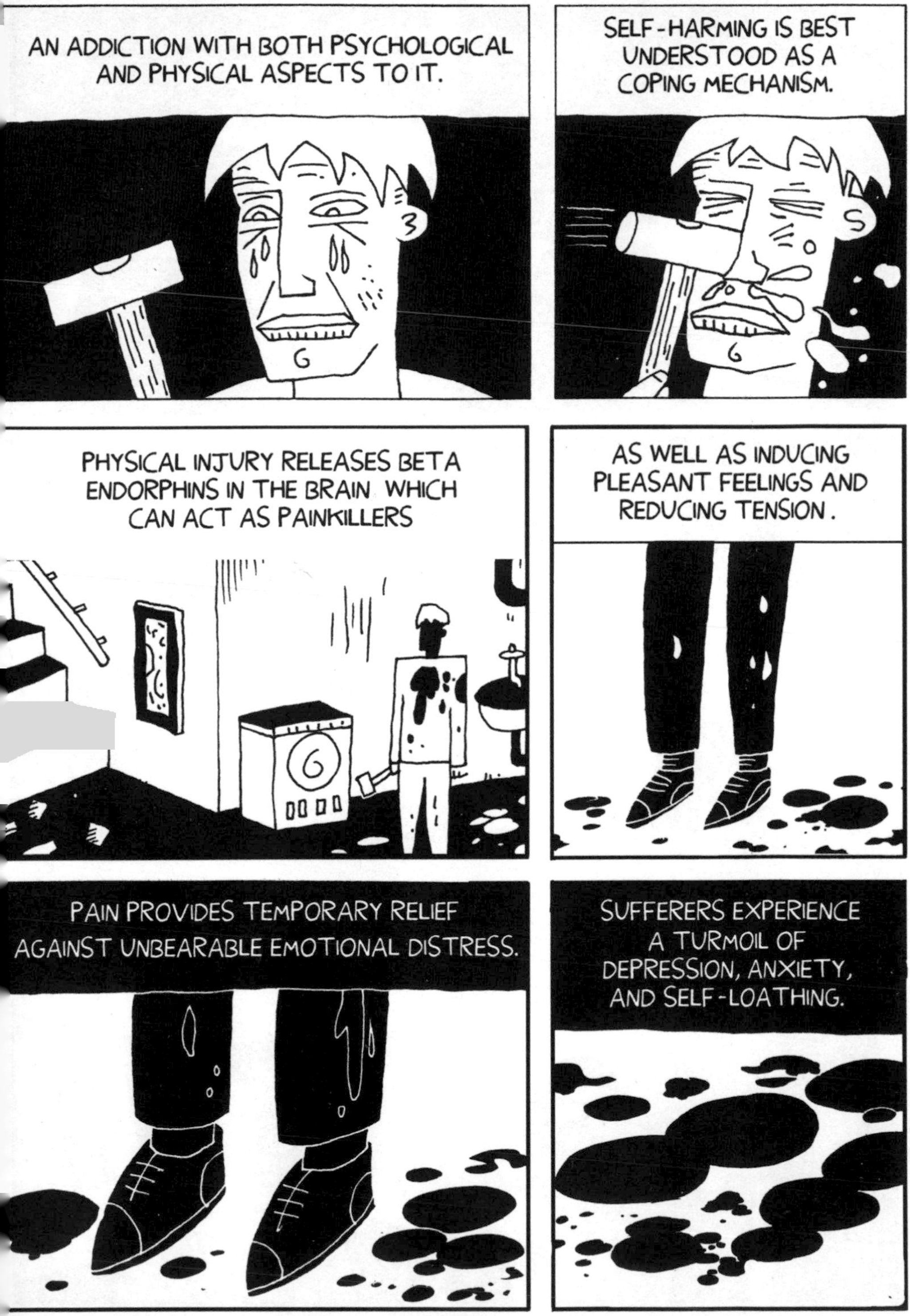
AN ADDICTION WITH BOTH PSYCHOLOGICAL AND PHYSICAL ASPECTS TO IT.
SELF-HARMING IS BEST UNDERSTOOD AS A COPING MECHANISM.
PHYSICAL INJURY RELEASES BETA ENDORPHINS IN THE BRAIN WHICH CAN ACT AS PAINKILLERS
AS WELL AS INDUCING PLEASANT FEELINGS AND REDUCING TENSION.
PAIN PROVIDES TEMPORARY RELIEF AGAINST UNBEARABLE EMOTIONAL DISTRESS.
SUFFERERS EXPERIENCE A TURMOIL OF DEPRESSION, ANXIETY, AND SELF-LOATHING.

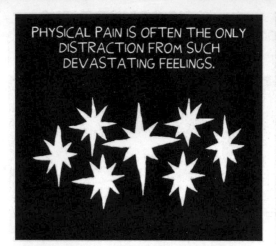

PHYSICAL PAIN IS OFTEN THE ONLY DISTRACTION FROM SUCH DEVASTATING FEELINGS.

SELF-HARMING GIVES THE SUFFERER AN ESCAPE FROM SUCH TORMENT AND OFFERS CONTROL.

ESCAPE FROM AN INNER BLACKNESS THAT FRIENDS AND FAMILY ARE USUALLY UNAWARE OF.

WHY DO YOU DO IT? IS IT FOR ATTENTION?

I SAW PATIENTS ON THE WARDS WHO WERE HAPPY TO DISPLAY THEIR SCARS.

MAKING A STATEMENT ABOUT THEMSELVES AS MARTYRS OR VICTIMS, PERHAPS?

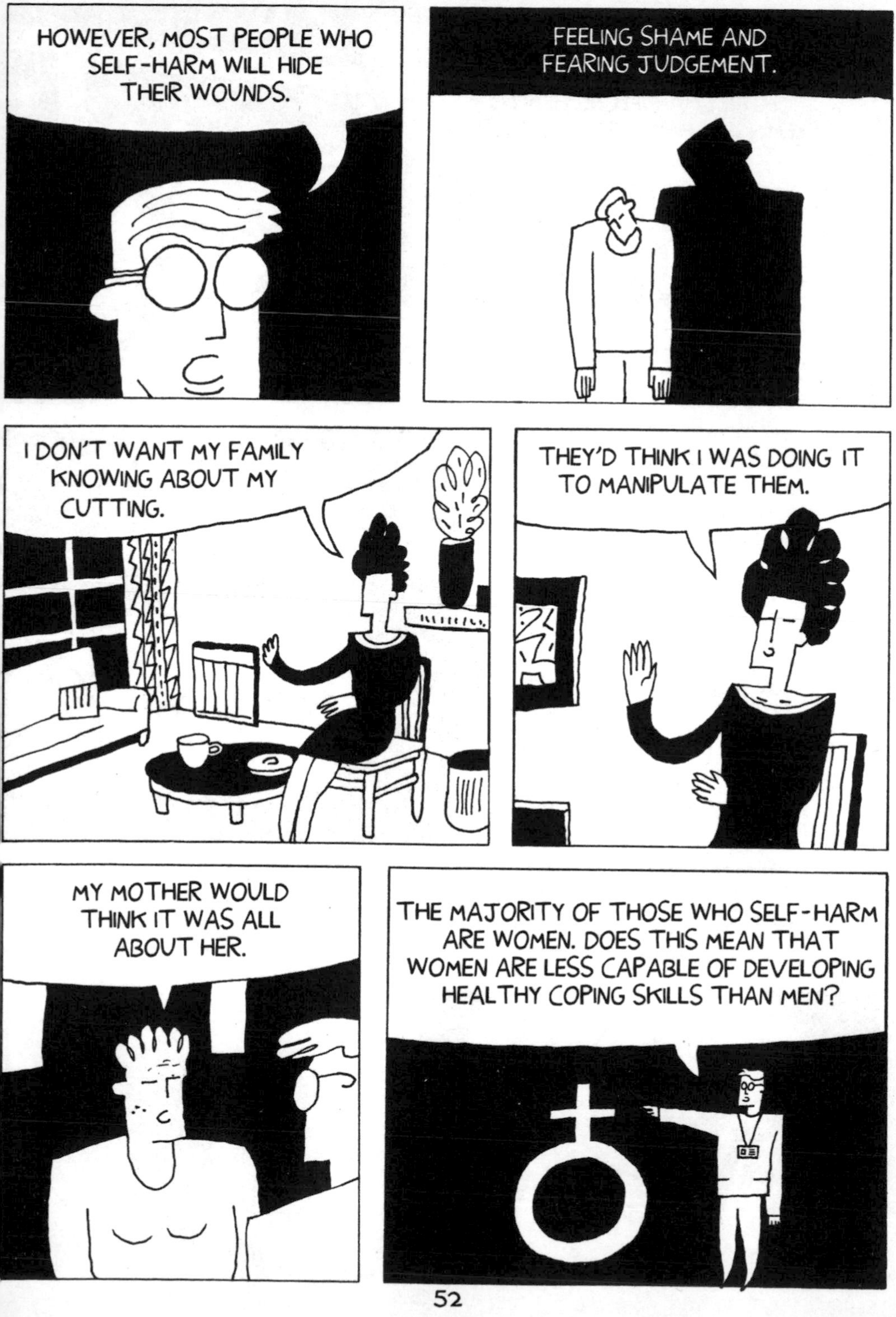
HOWEVER, MOST PEOPLE WHO SELF-HARM WILL HIDE THEIR WOUNDS.
FEELING SHAME AND FEARING JUDGEMENT.
I DON'T WANT MY FAMILY KNOWING ABOUT MY CUTTING.
THEY'D THINK I WAS DOING IT TO MANIPULATE THEM.
MY MOTHER WOULD THINK IT WAS ALL ABOUT HER.
THE MAJORITY OF THOSE WHO SELF-HARM ARE WOMEN. DOES THIS MEAN THAT WOMEN ARE LESS CAPABLE OF DEVELOPING HEALTHY COPING SKILLS THAN MEN?

IT SEEMS NOT. MEN FIND IT EASIER TO EXTERNALISE EMOTIONAL PAIN, OFTEN CHANNELLING IT INTO SEEMINGLY UNRELATED VIOLENCE.

AND THOSE MEN WHO DO SELF-HARM TEND TO BE MORE EXTREME IN THEIR METHODS.

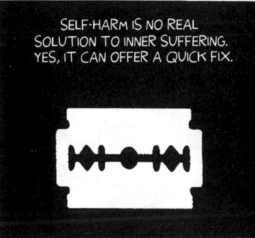

SELF-HARM IS NO REAL SOLUTION TO INNER SUFFERING. YES, IT CAN OFFER A QUICK FIX.

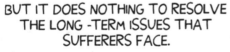

BUT IT DOES NOTHING TO RESOLVE THE LONG-TERM ISSUES THAT SUFFERERS FACE.

OF LOW SELF-ESTEEM, DESPAIR, AND CHRONIC ANXIETY.

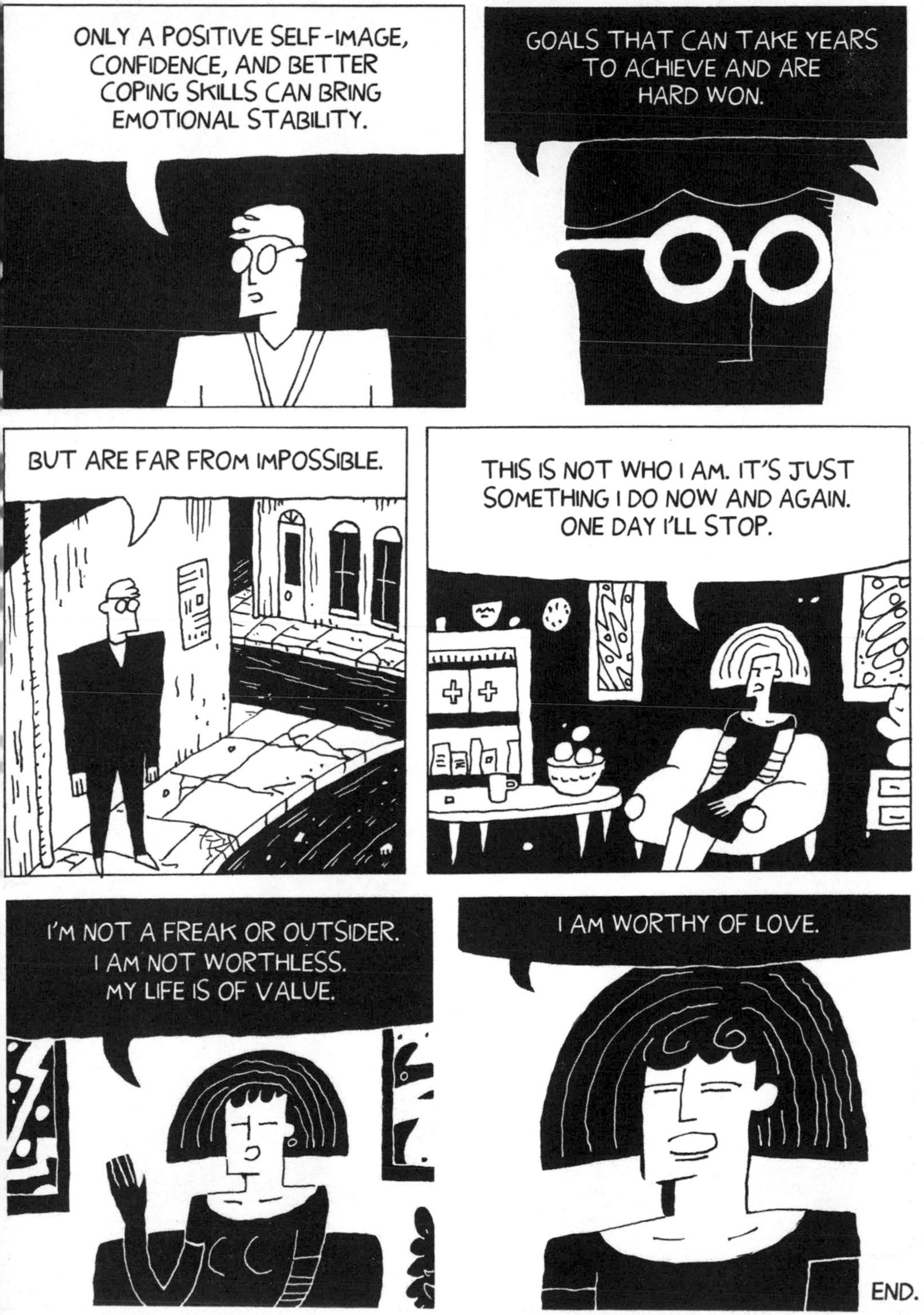
ONLY A POSITIVE SELF-IMAGE, CONFIDENCE, AND BETTER COPING SKILLS CAN BRING EMOTIONAL STABILITY.
GOALS THAT CAN TAKE YEARS TO ACHIEVE AND ARE HARD WON.
BUT ARE FAR FROM IMPOSSIBLE.
THIS IS NOT WHO I AM. IT'S JUST SOMETHING I DO NOW AND AGAIN. ONE DAY I'LL STOP.
I'M NOT A FREAK OR OUTSIDER. I AM NOT WORTHLESS. MY LIFE IS OF VALUE.
I AM WORTHY OF LOVE.
END.

BIPOLAR
DISORDER

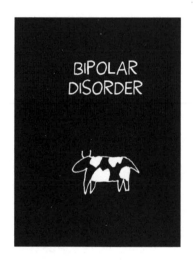

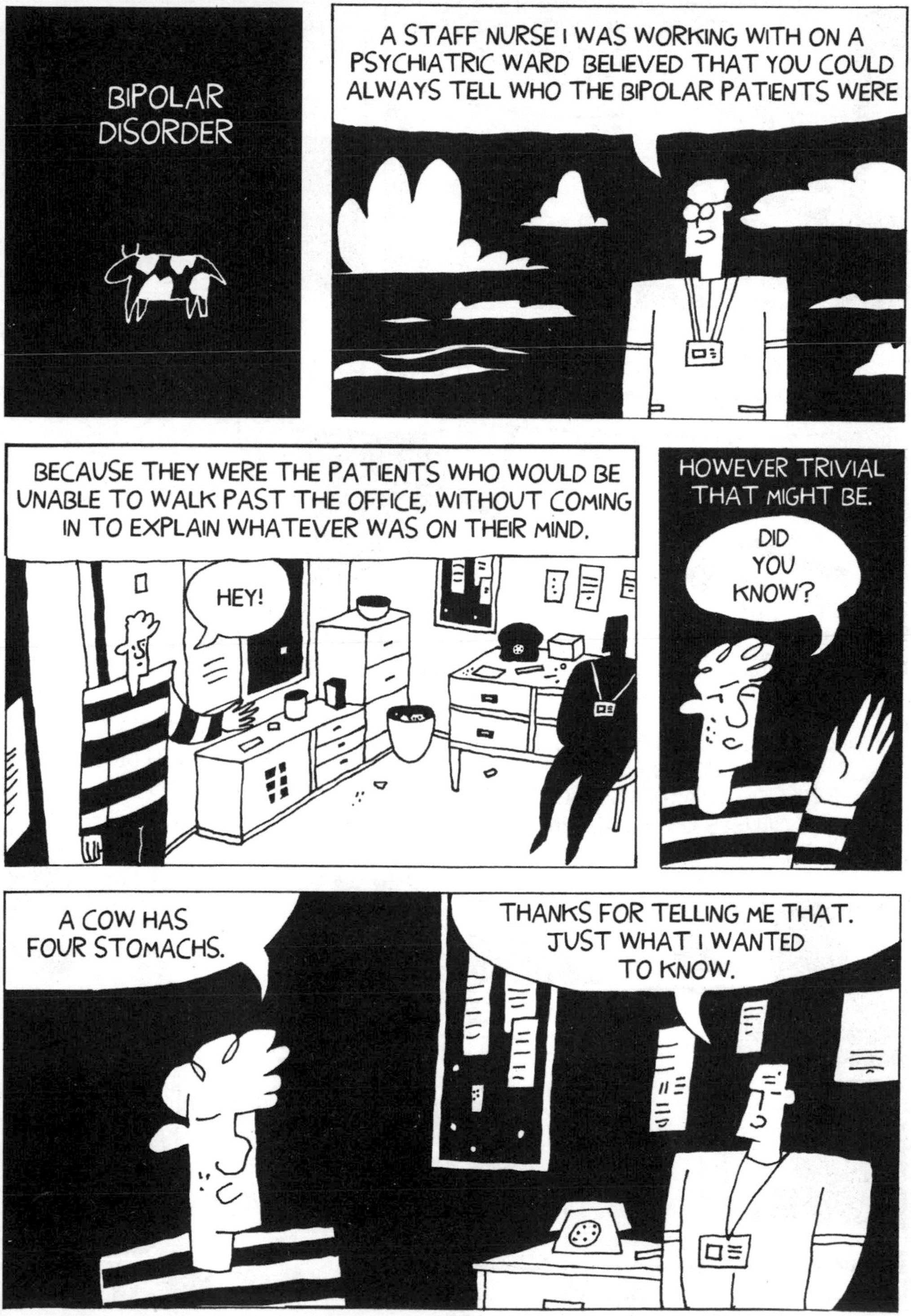
BIPOLAR DISORDER
A STAFF NURSE I WAS WORKING WITH ON A PSYCHIATRIC WARD BELIEVED THAT YOU COULD ALWAYS TELL WHO THE BIPOLAR PATIENTS WERE
BECAUSE THEY WERE THE PATIENTS WHO WOULD BE UNABLE TO WALK PAST THE OFFICE, WITHOUT COMING IN TO EXPLAIN WHATEVER WAS ON THEIR MIND.
HEY!
HOWEVER TRIVIAL THAT MIGHT BE.
DID YOU KNOW?
A COW HAS FOUR STOMACHS.
THANKS FOR TELLING ME THAT. JUST WHAT I WANTED TO KNOW.

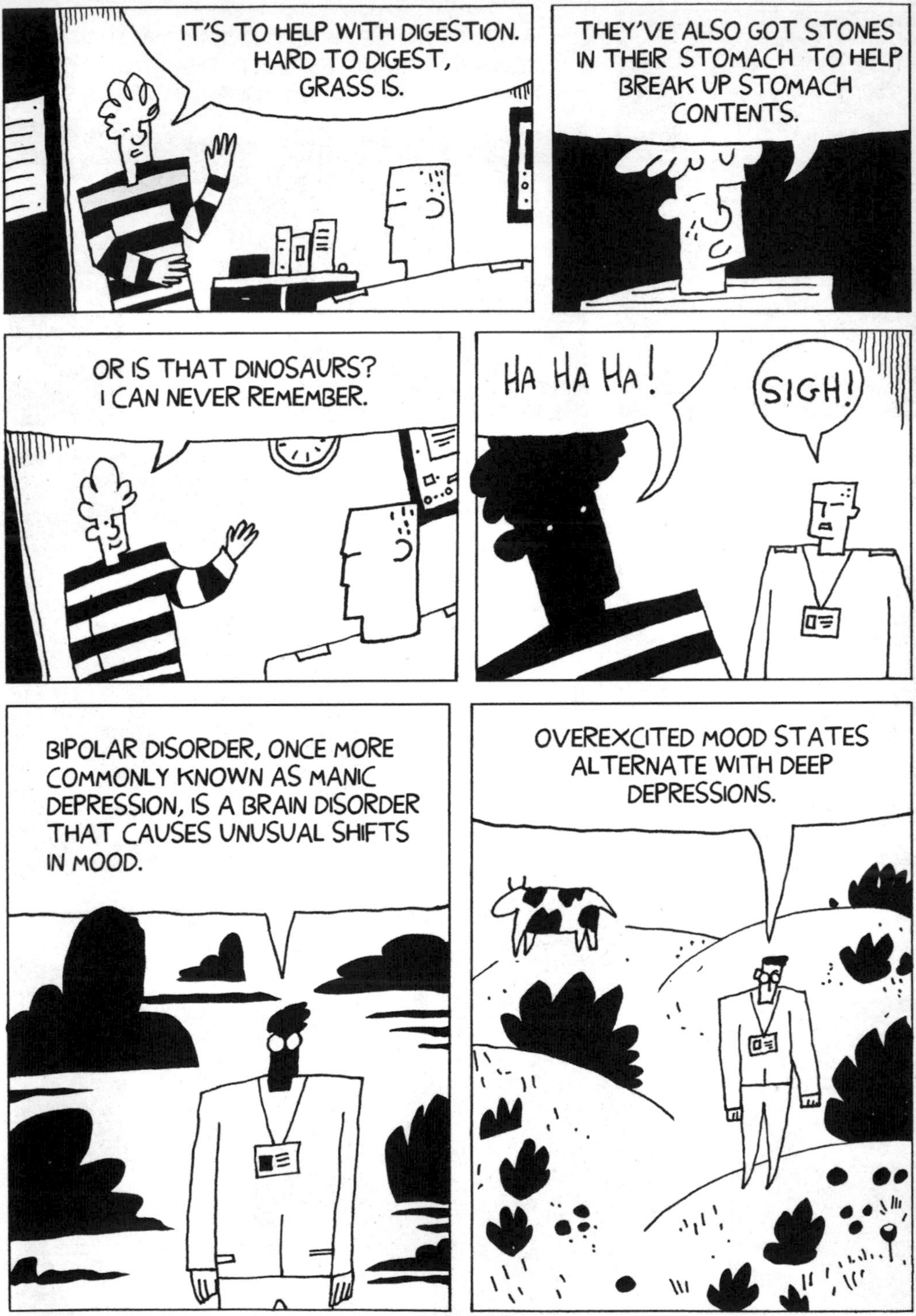
IT'S TO HELP WITH DIGESTION. HARD TO DIGEST, GRASS IS.
THEY'VE ALSO GOT STONES IN THEIR STOMACH TO HELP BREAK UP STOMACH CONTENTS.
OR IS THAT DINOSAURS? I CAN NEVER REMEMBER.
HA HA HA!
SIGH!
BIPOLAR DISORDER, ONCE MORE COMMONLY KNOWN AS MANIC DEPRESSION, IS A BRAIN DISORDER THAT CAUSES UNUSUAL SHIFTS IN MOOD.
OVEREXCITED MOOD STATES ALTERNATE WITH DEEP DEPRESSIONS.

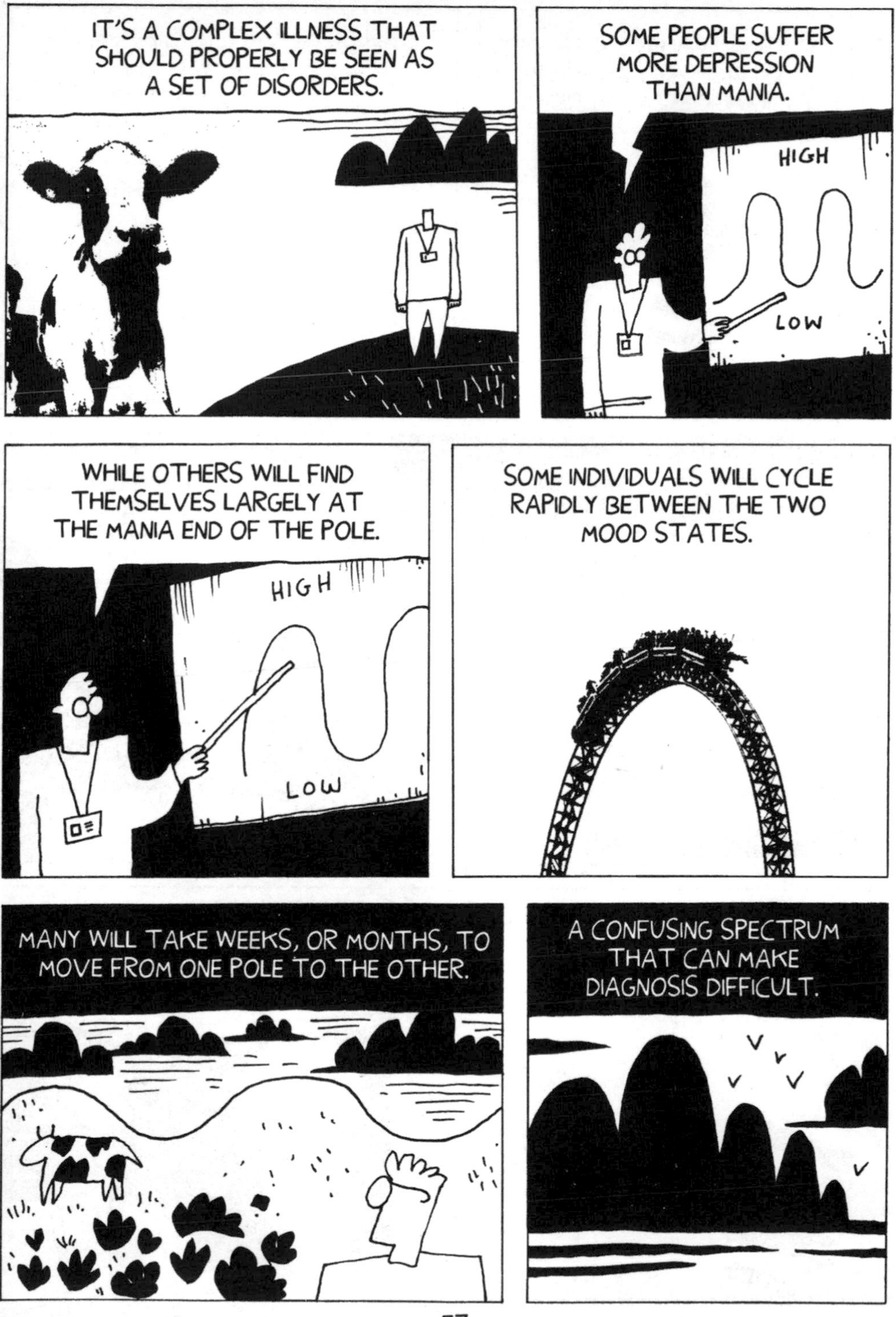
IT'S A COMPLEX ILLNESS THAT SHOULD PROPERLY BE SEEN AS A SET OF DISORDERS.
SOME PEOPLE SUFFER MORE DEPRESSION THAN MANIA.
HIGH
LOW
WHILE OTHERS WILL FIND THEMSELVES LARGELY AT THE MANIA END OF THE POLE.
HIGH
LOW
SOME INDIVIDUALS WILL CYCLE RAPIDLY BETWEEN THE TWO MOOD STATES.
MANY WILL TAKE WEEKS, OR MONTHS, TO MOVE FROM ONE POLE TO THE OTHER.
A CONFUSING SPECTRUM THAT CAN MAKE DIAGNOSIS DIFFICULT.

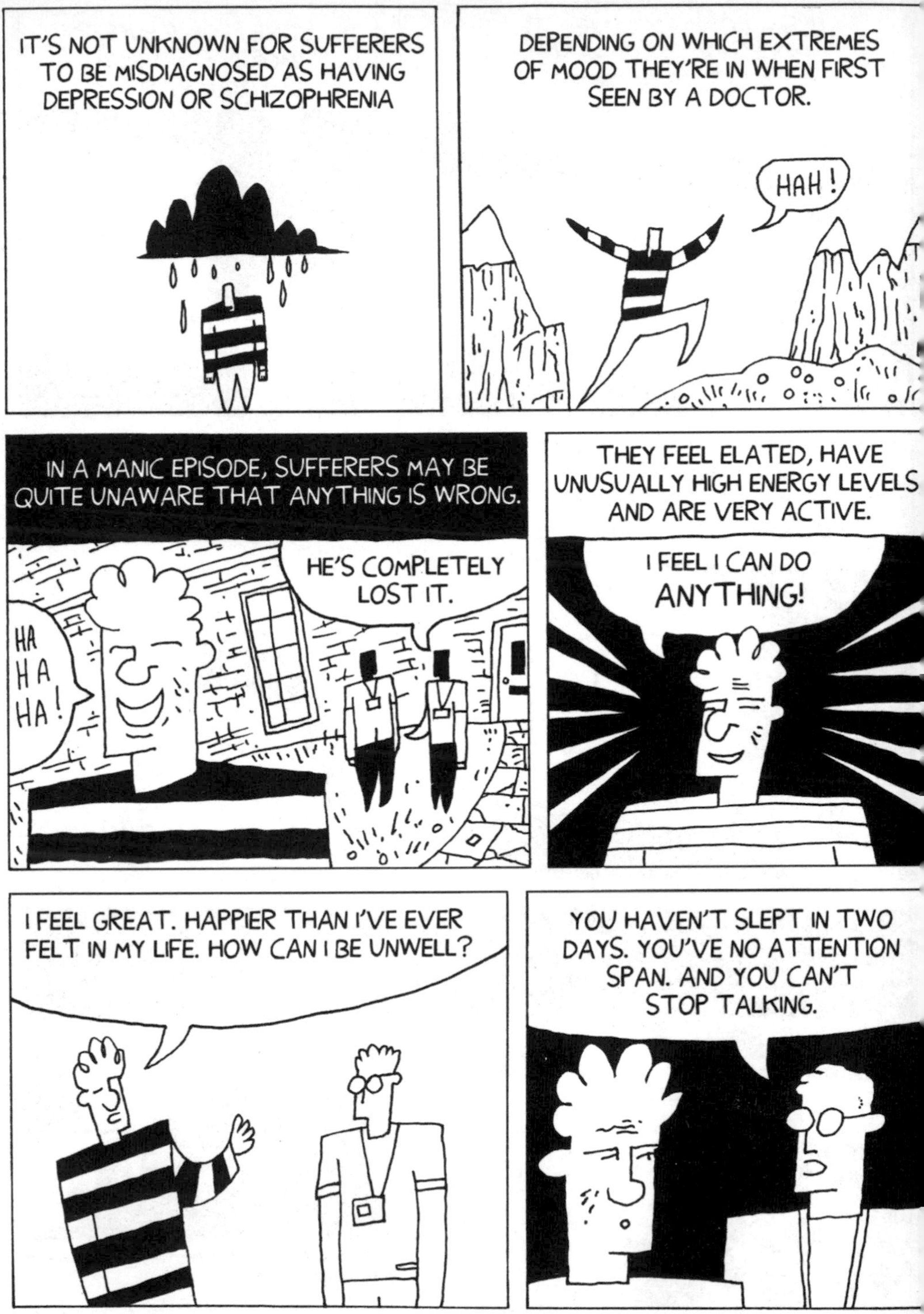
IT'S NOT UNKNOWN FOR SUFFERERS TO BE MISDIAGNOSED AS HAVING DEPRESSION OR SCHIZOPHRENIA
DEPENDING ON WHICH EXTREMES OF MOOD THEY'RE IN WHEN FIRST SEEN BY A DOCTOR.
HAH!
IN A MANIC EPISODE, SUFFERERS MAY BE QUITE UNAWARE THAT ANYTHING IS WRONG.
HA HA HA!
HE'S COMPLETELY LOST IT.
THEY FEEL ELATED, HAVE UNUSUALLY HIGH ENERGY LEVELS AND ARE VERY ACTIVE.
I FEEL I CAN DO ANYTHING!
I FEEL GREAT. HAPPIER THAN I'VE EVER FELT IN MY LIFE. HOW CAN I BE UNWELL?
YOU HAVEN'T SLEPT IN TWO DAYS. YOU'VE NO ATTENTION SPAN. AND YOU CAN'T STOP TALKING.

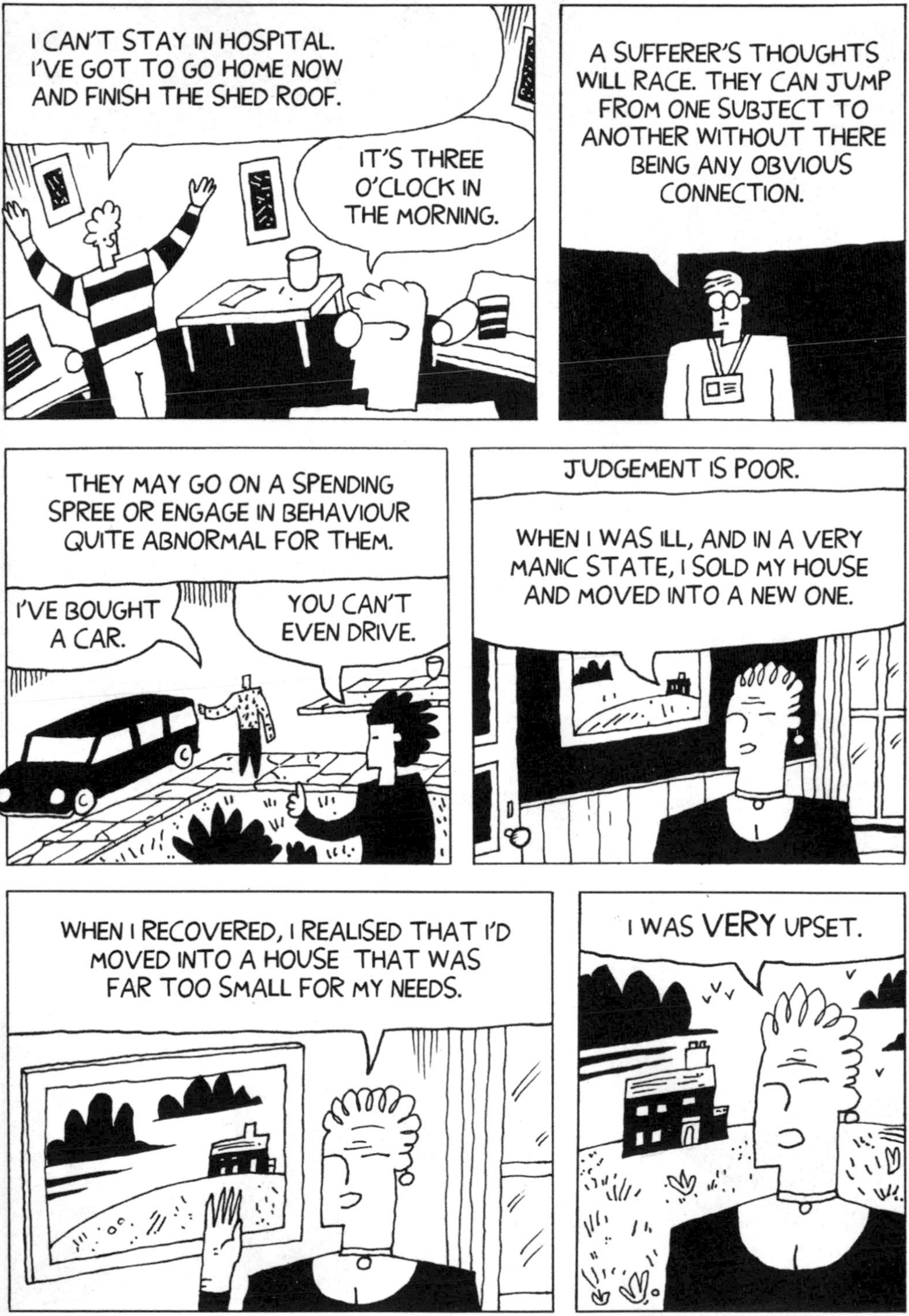
I CAN'T STAY IN HOSPITAL. I'VE GOT TO GO HOME NOW AND FINISH THE SHED ROOF.
IT'S THREE O'CLOCK IN THE MORNING.
A SUFFERER'S THOUGHTS WILL RACE. THEY CAN JUMP FROM ONE SUBJECT TO ANOTHER WITHOUT THERE BEING ANY OBVIOUS CONNECTION.
THEY MAY GO ON A SPENDING SPREE OR ENGAGE IN BEHAVIOUR QUITE ABNORMAL FOR THEM.
I'VE BOUGHT A CAR.
YOU CAN'T EVEN DRIVE.
JUDGEMENT IS POOR.
WHEN I WAS ILL, AND IN A VERY MANIC STATE, I SOLD MY HOUSE AND MOVED INTO A NEW ONE.
WHEN I RECOVERED, I REALISED THAT I'D MOVED INTO A HOUSE THAT WAS FAR TOO SMALL FOR MY NEEDS.
I WAS VERY UPSET.

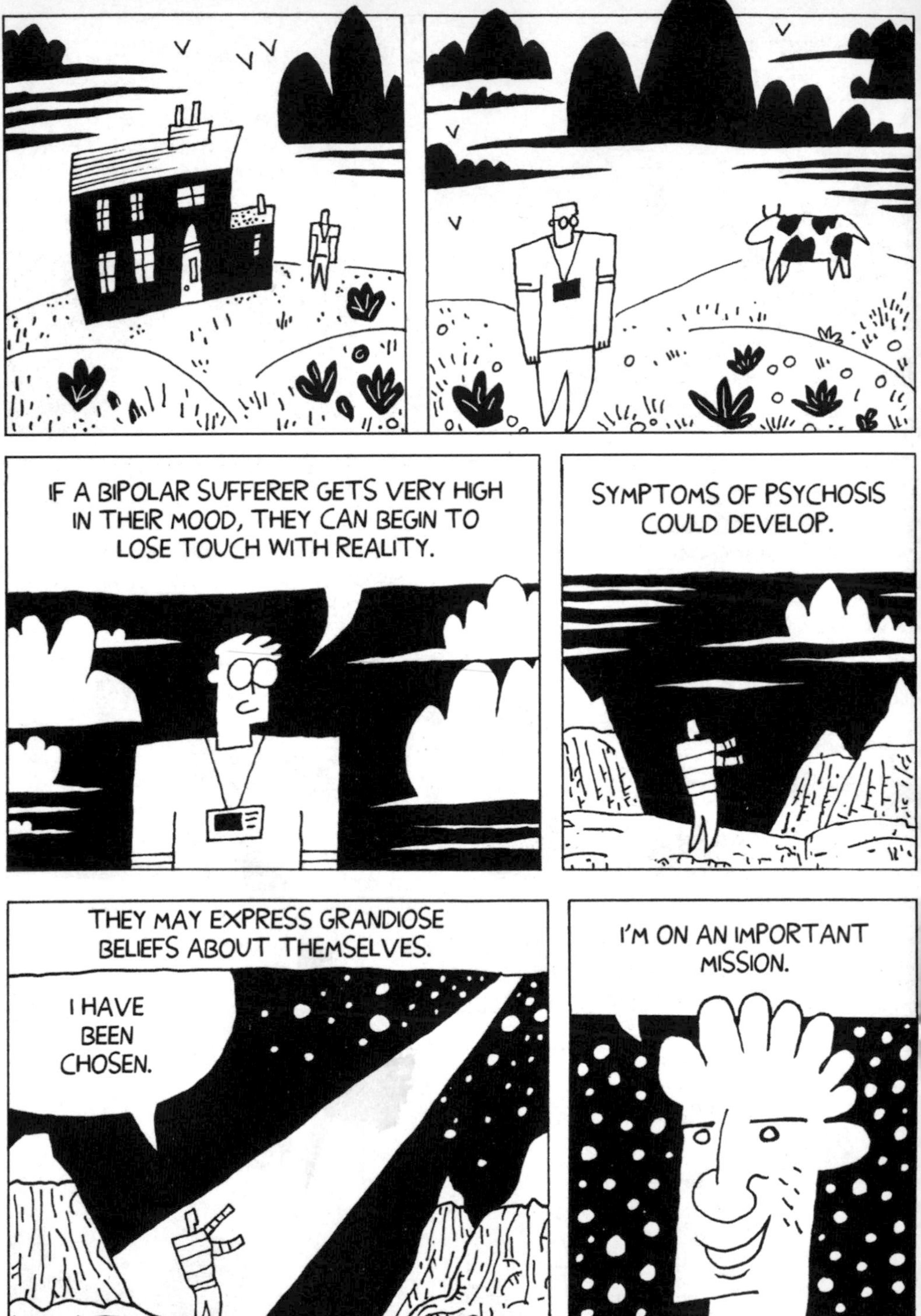

IF A BIPOLAR SUFFERER GETS VERY HIGH IN THEIR MOOD, THEY CAN BEGIN TO LOSE TOUCH WITH REALITY.
SYMPTOMS OF PSYCHOSIS COULD DEVELOP.
THEY MAY EXPRESS GRANDIOSE BELIEFS ABOUT THEMSELVES.
I HAVE BEEN CHOSEN.
I'M ON AN IMPORTANT MISSION.

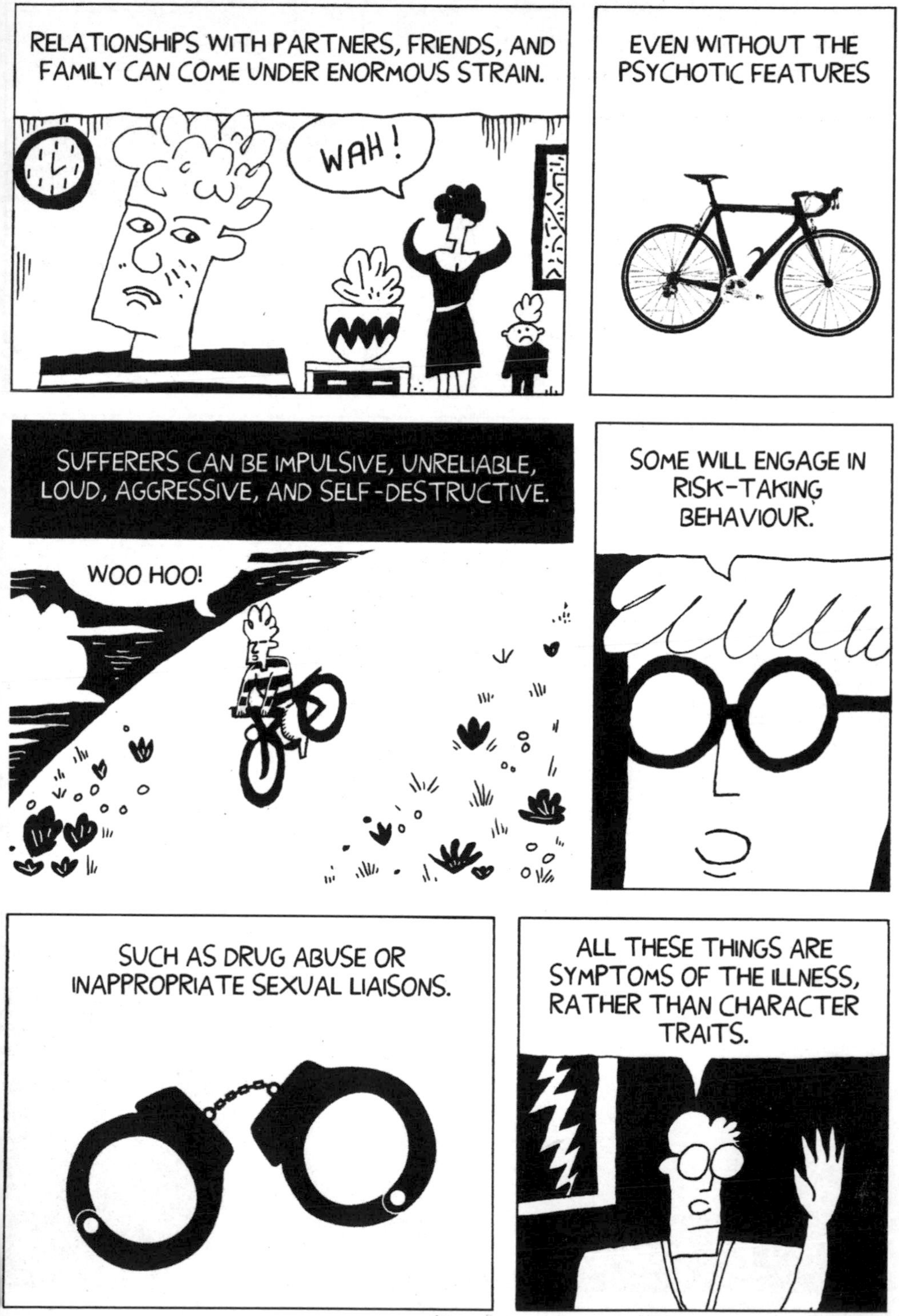
RELATIONSHIPS WITH PARTNERS, FRIENDS, AND FAMILY CAN COME UNDER ENORMOUS STRAIN.
WAH!
EVEN WITHOUT THE PSYCHOTIC FEATURES
SUFFERERS CAN BE IMPULSIVE, UNRELIABLE, LOUD, AGGRESSIVE, AND SELF-DESTRUCTIVE.
WOO HOO!
SOME WILL ENGAGE IN RISK-TAKING BEHAVIOUR.
SUCH AS DRUG ABUSE OR INAPPROPRIATE SEXUAL LIAISONS.
ALL THESE THINGS ARE SYMPTOMS OF THE ILLNESS, RATHER THAN CHARACTER TRAITS.

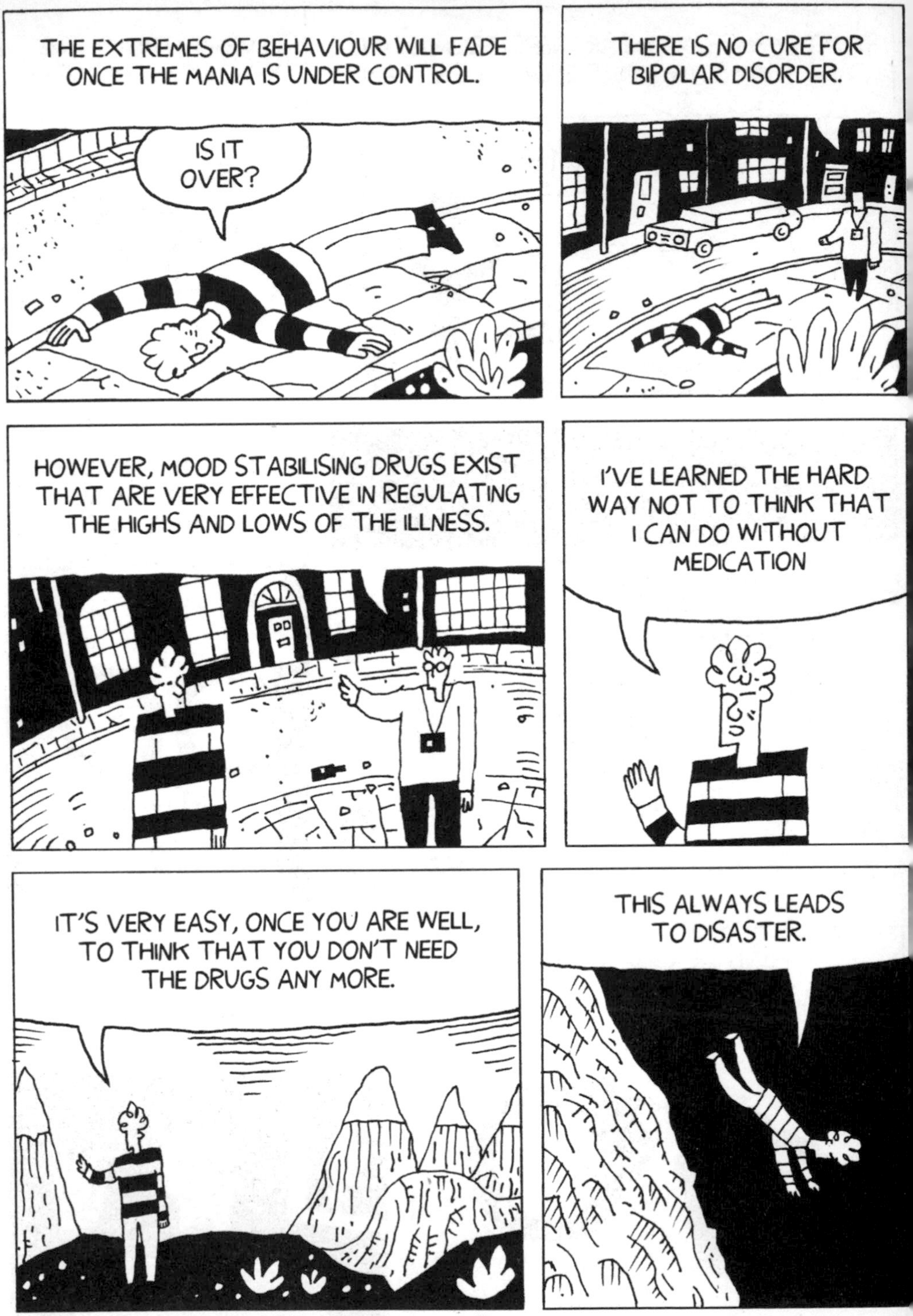
THE EXTREMES OF BEHAVIOUR WILL FADE ONCE THE MANIA IS UNDER CONTROL.
IS IT OVER?
THERE IS NO CURE FOR BIPOLAR DISORDER.
HOWEVER, MOOD STABILISING DRUGS EXIST THAT ARE VERY EFFECTIVE IN REGULATING THE HIGHS AND LOWS OF THE ILLNESS.
I'VE LEARNED THE HARD WAY NOT TO THINK THAT I CAN DO WITHOUT MEDICATION
IT'S VERY EASY, ONCE YOU ARE WELL, TO THINK THAT YOU DON'T NEED THE DRUGS ANY MORE.
THIS ALWAYS LEADS TO DISASTER.

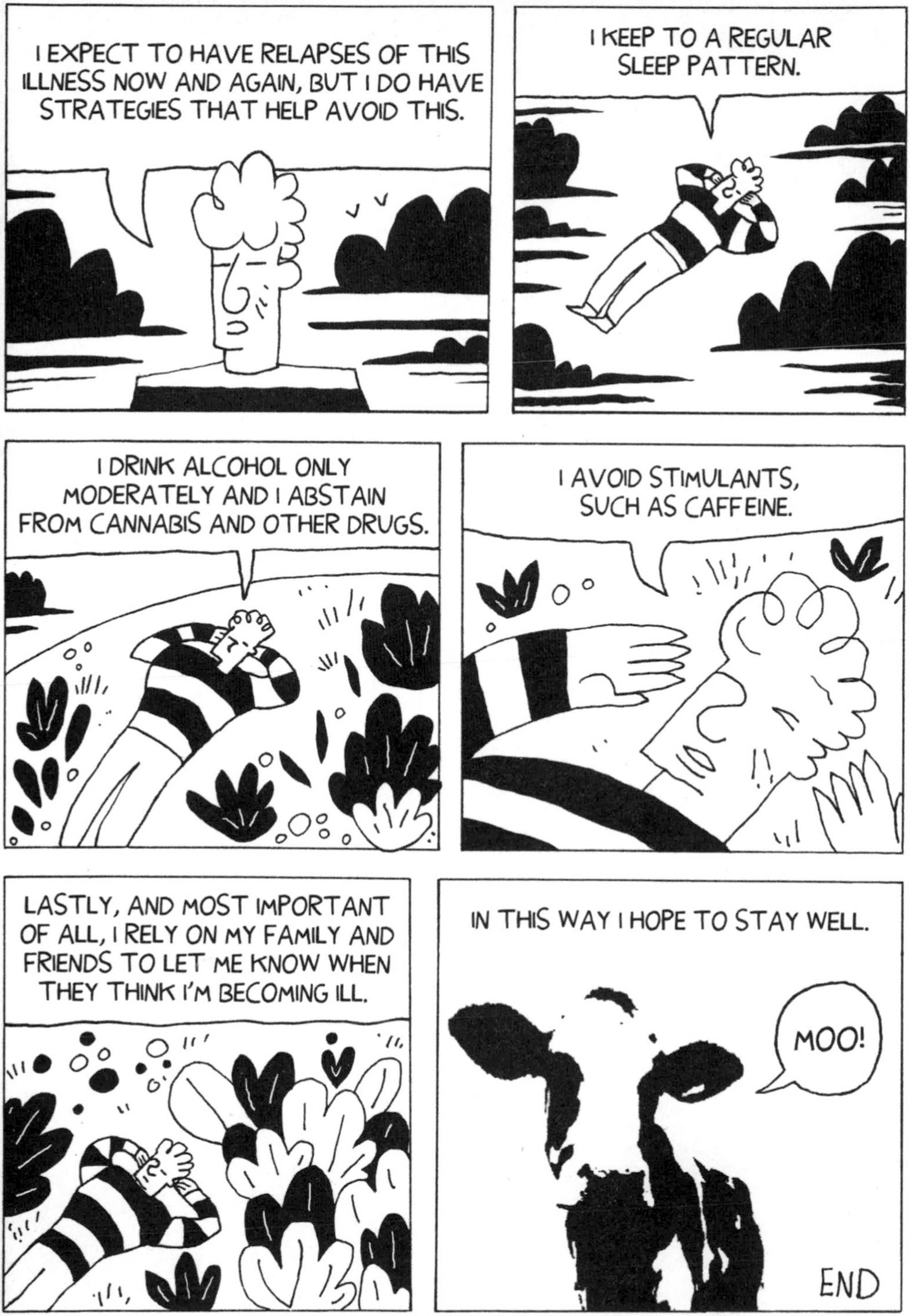
I EXPECT TO HAVE RELAPSES OF THIS ILLNESS NOW AND AGAIN, BUT I DO HAVE STRATEGIES THAT HELP AVOID THIS.
I KEEP TO A REGULAR SLEEP PATTERN.
I DRINK ALCOHOL ONLY MODERATELY AND I ABSTAIN FROM CANNABIS AND OTHER DRUGS.
I AVOID STIMULANTS, SUCH AS CAFFEINE.
LASTLY, AND MOST IMPORTANT OF ALL, I RELY ON MY FAMILY AND FRIENDS TO LET ME KNOW WHEN THEY THINK I'M BECOMING ILL.
IN THIS WAY I HOPE TO STAY WELL.
MOO!
END

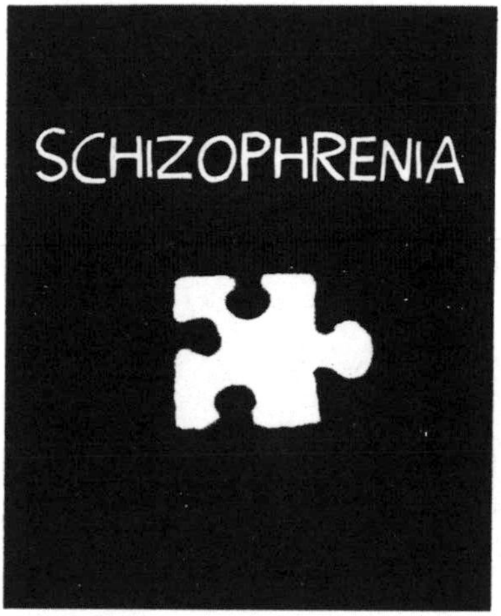
SCHIZOPHRENIA

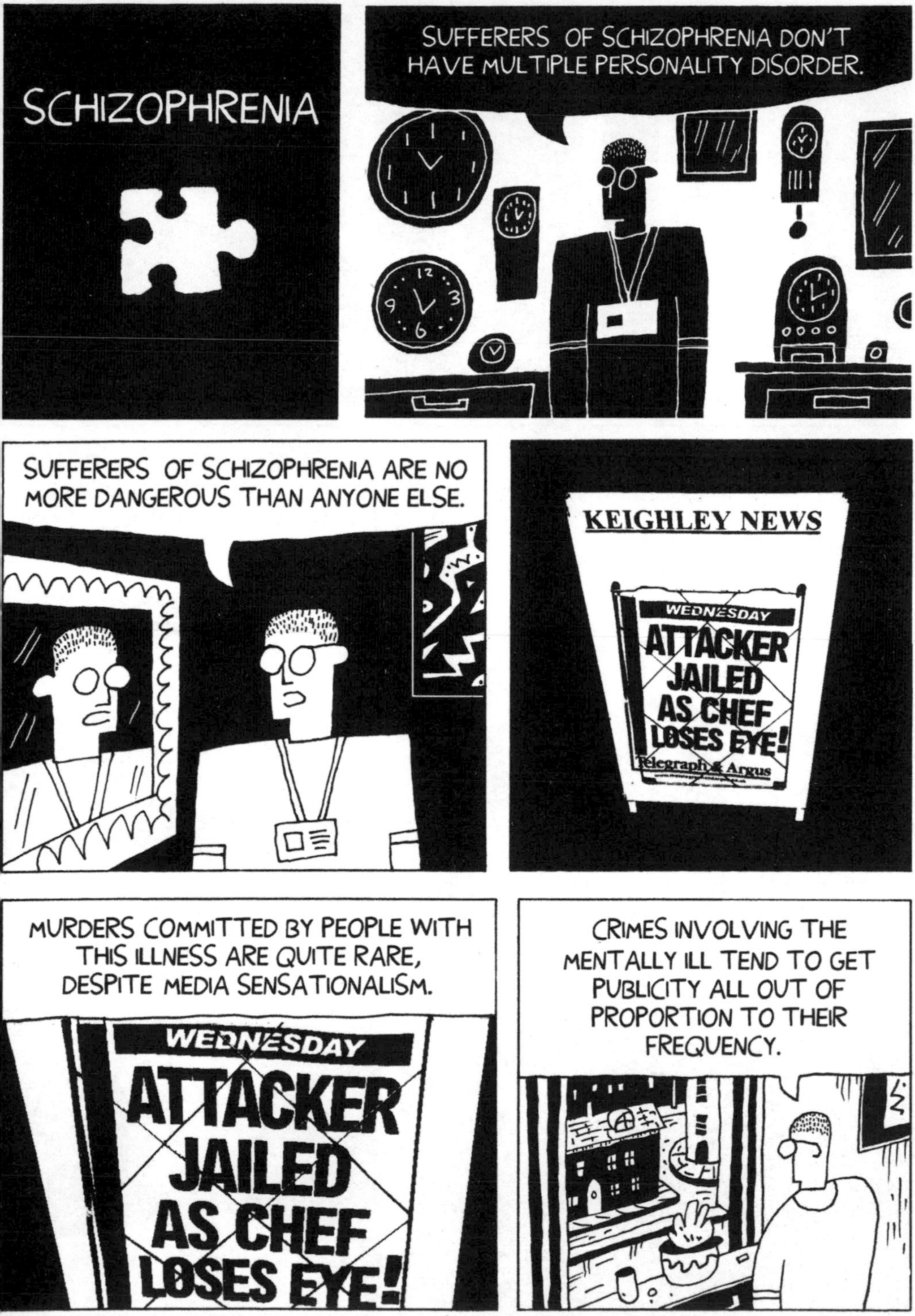
SCHIZOPHRENIA
SUFFERERS OF SCHIZOPHRENIA DON'T HAVE MULTIPLE PERSONALITY DISORDER.
SUFFERERS OF SCHIZOPHRENIA ARE NO MORE DANGEROUS THAN ANYONE ELSE.
KEIGHLEY NEWS
WEDNESDAY
ATTACKER JAILED AS CHEF LOSES EYE!
Telegraph & Argus
MURDERS COMMITTED BY PEOPLE WITH THIS ILLNESS ARE QUITE RARE, DESPITE MEDIA SENSATIONALISM.
WEDNESDAY
ATTACKER JAILED AS CHEF LOSES EYE!
CRIMES INVOLVING THE MENTALLY ILL TEND TO GET PUBLICITY ALL OUT OF PROPORTION TO THEIR FREQUENCY.

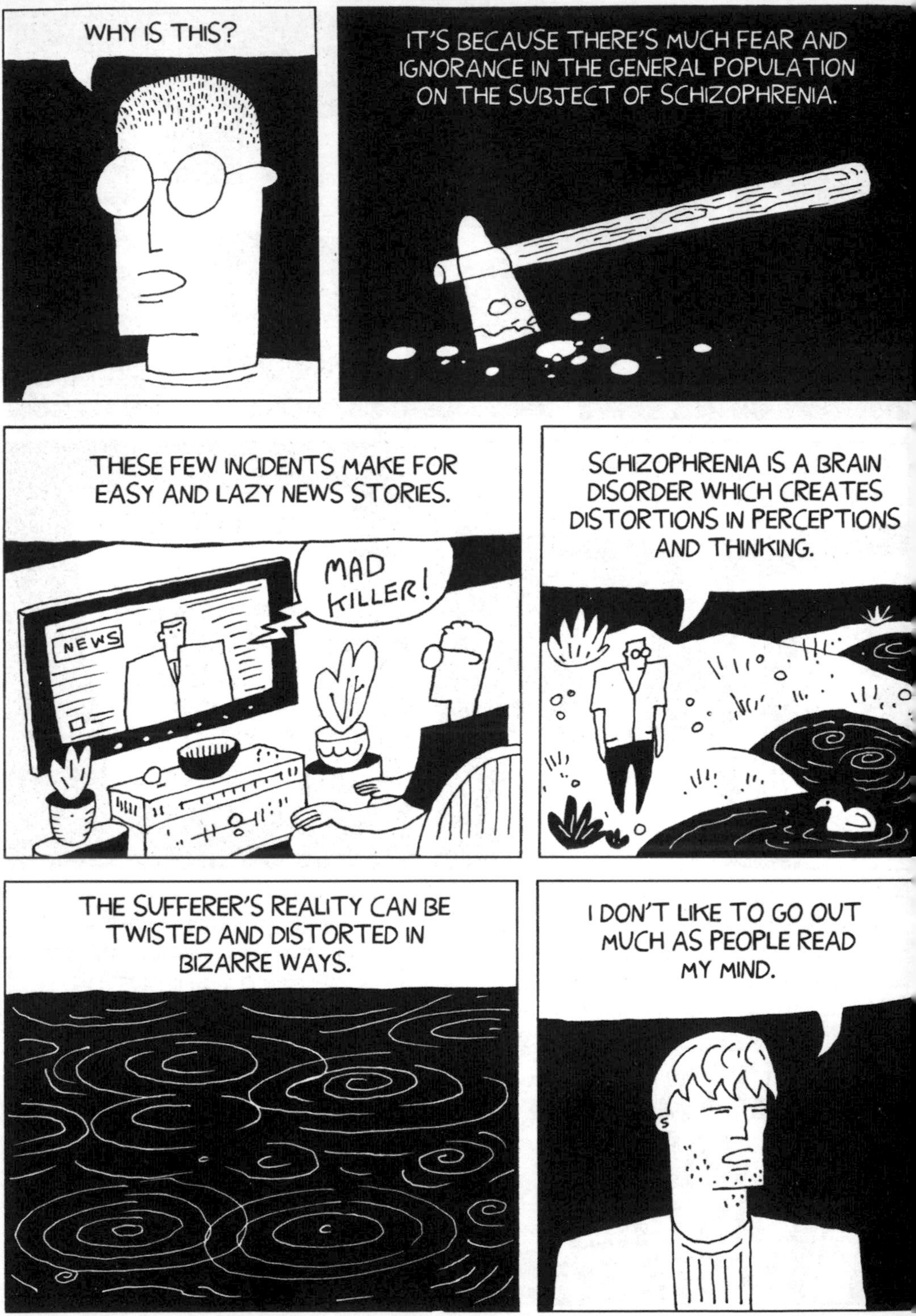
WHY IS THIS?
IT'S BECAUSE THERE'S MUCH FEAR AND IGNORANCE IN THE GENERAL POPULATION ON THE SUBJECT OF SCHIZOPHRENIA.
THESE FEW INCIDENTS MAKE FOR EASY AND LAZY NEWS STORIES.
NEWS
MAD KILLER!
SCHIZOPHRENIA IS A BRAIN DISORDER WHICH CREATES DISTORTIONS IN PERCEPTIONS AND THINKING.
THE SUFFERER'S REALITY CAN BE TWISTED AND DISTORTED IN BIZARRE WAYS.
I DON'T LIKE TO GO OUT MUCH AS PEOPLE READ MY MIND.

I HEAR HOSTILE AND CONTROLLING VOICES THAT COMMENT ON EVERYTHING I SAY AND DO.

LOOK AT WHAT SHE'S DOING NOW!

HA! HA!

PEOPLE KEEP INSERTING THEIR THOUGHTS INTO MY MIND, WHICH IS WHY I WEAR THIS HAT.

A WHITE VAN FOLLOWS ME AROUND. I SEE IT EVERYWHERE.

PSYCHOTIC SYMPTOMS FOR MEN USUALLY BEGIN IN THEIR LATE TEENS OR EARLY ADULTHOOD.

AND IN WOMEN, IN THEIR MID-TWENTIES TO EARLY THIRTIES

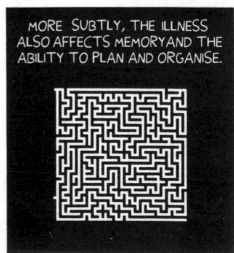

MORE SUBTLY, THE ILLNESS ALSO AFFECTS MEMORY AND THE ABILITY TO PLAN AND ORGANISE.

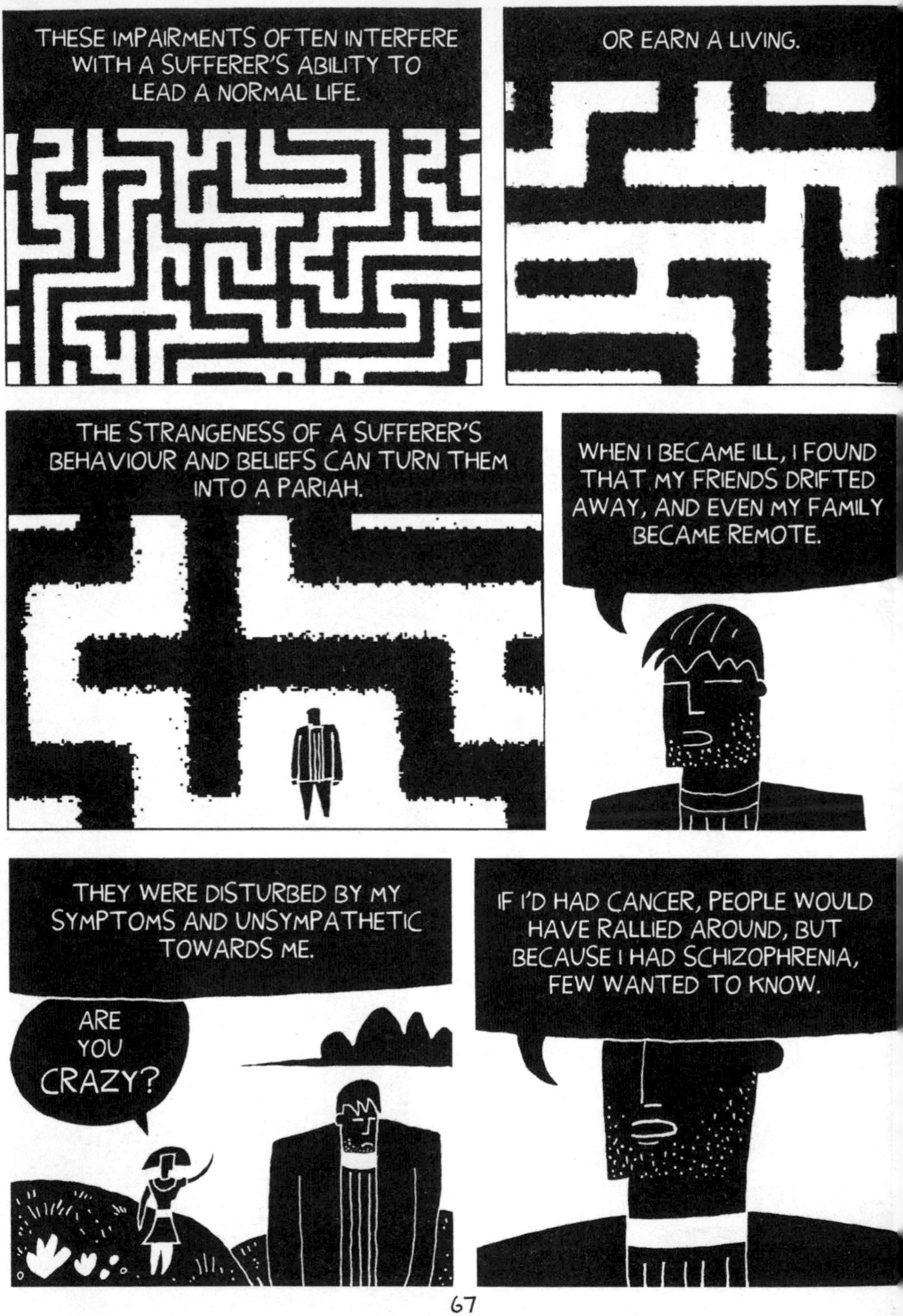
THESE IMPAIRMENTS OFTEN INTERFERE WITH A SUFFERER'S ABILITY TO LEAD A NORMAL LIFE.
OR EARN A LIVING.
THE STRANGENESS OF A SUFFERER'S BEHAVIOUR AND BELIEFS CAN TURN THEM INTO A PARIAH.
WHEN I BECAME ILL, I FOUND THAT MY FRIENDS DRIFTED AWAY, AND EVEN MY FAMILY BECAME REMOTE.
THEY WERE DISTURBED BY MY SYMPTOMS AND UNSYMPATHETIC TOWARDS ME.
ARE YOU CRAZY?
IF I'D HAD CANCER, PEOPLE WOULD HAVE RALLIED AROUND, BUT BECAUSE I HAD SCHIZOPHRENIA, FEW WANTED TO KNOW.

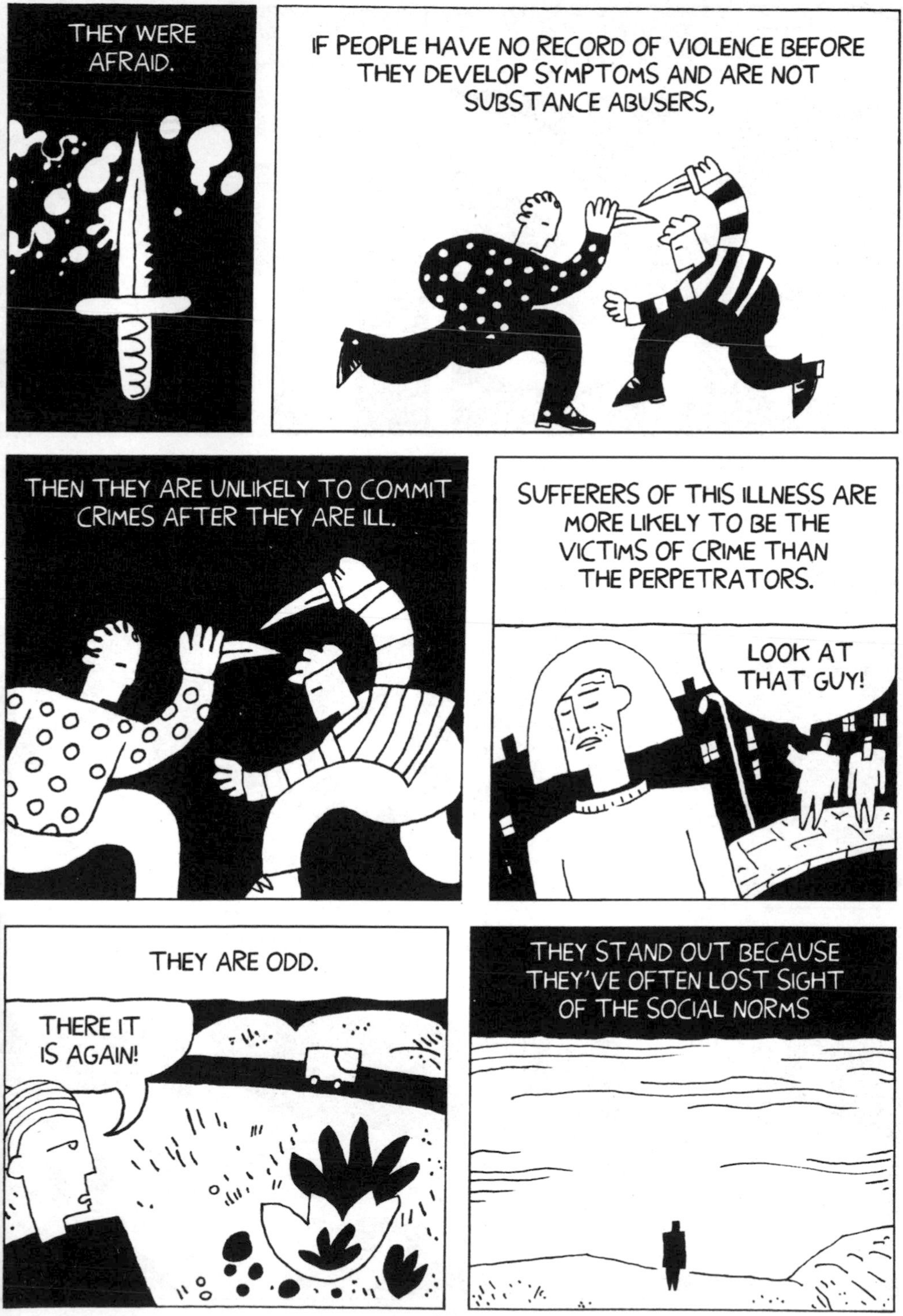
THEY WERE AFRAID.
IF PEOPLE HAVE NO RECORD OF VIOLENCE BEFORE THEY DEVELOP SYMPTOMS AND ARE NOT SUBSTANCE ABUSERS,
THEN THEY ARE UNLIKELY TO COMMIT CRIMES AFTER THEY ARE ILL.
SUFFERERS OF THIS ILLNESS ARE MORE LIKELY TO BE THE VICTIMS OF CRIME THAN THE PERPETRATORS.
LOOK AT THAT GUY!
THEY ARE ODD.
THERE IT IS AGAIN!
THEY STAND OUT BECAUSE THEY'VE OFTEN LOST SIGHT OF THE SOCIAL NORMS

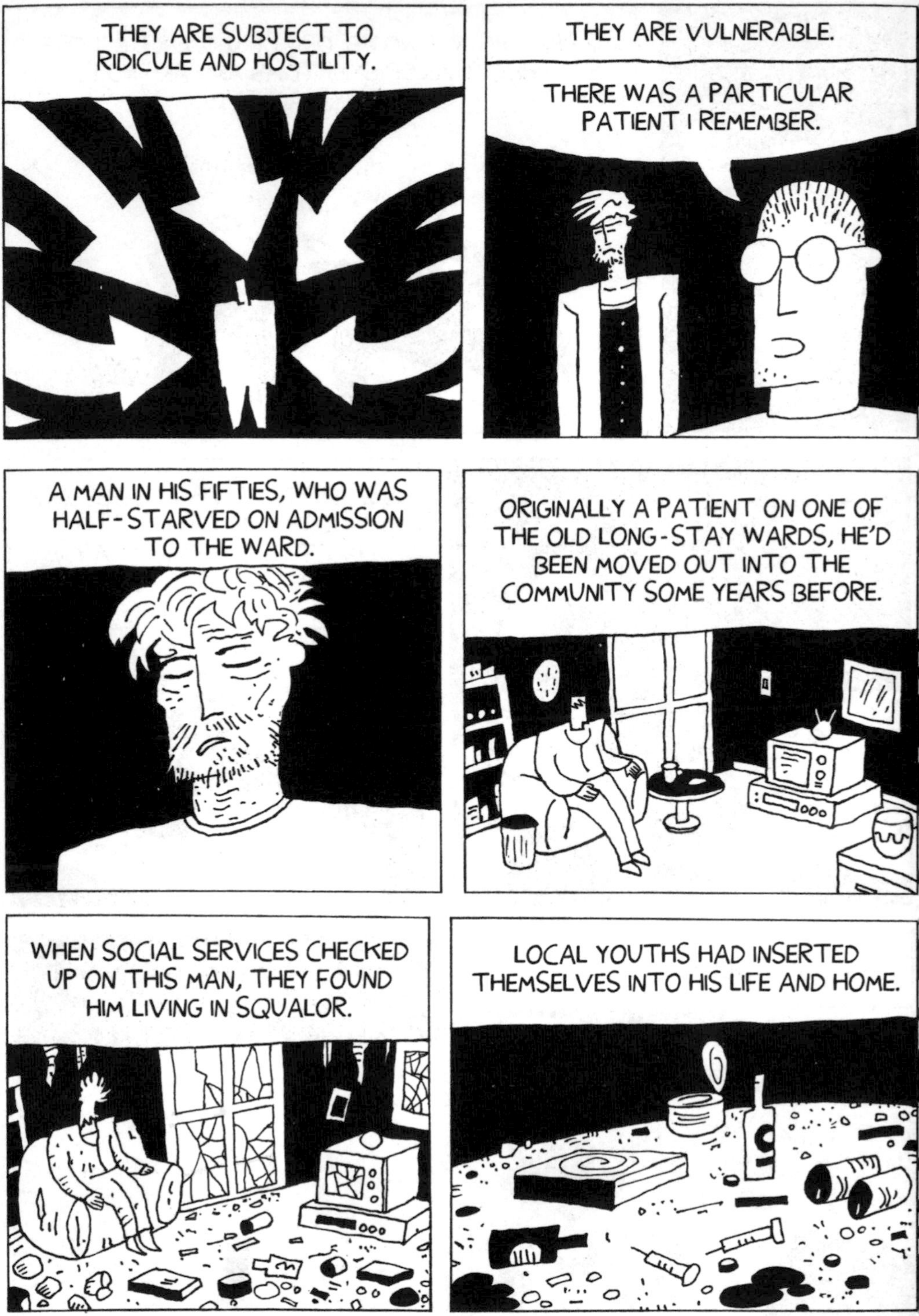
THEY ARE SUBJECT TO RIDICULE AND HOSTILITY.
THEY ARE VULNERABLE.
THERE WAS A PARTICULAR PATIENT I REMEMBER.
A MAN IN HIS FIFTIES, WHO WAS HALF-STARVED ON ADMISSION TO THE WARD.
ORIGINALLY A PATIENT ON ONE OF THE OLD LONG-STAY WARDS, HE'D BEEN MOVED OUT INTO THE COMMUNITY SOME YEARS BEFORE.
WHEN SOCIAL SERVICES CHECKED UP ON THIS MAN, THEY FOUND HIM LIVING IN SQUALOR.
LOCAL YOUTHS HAD INSERTED THEMSELVES INTO HIS LIFE AND HOME.

USING HIS FLAT TO HANG OUT IN AND TAKE DRUGS.

SYRINGES AND BEER CANS LITTERED THE FLOOR.

THEY'D EVEN TAKEN HIS BENEFIT BOOK AND TRIED TO CASH IT.

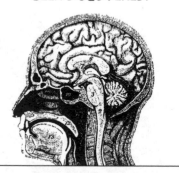

THIS GENTLEMAN STAYED ON THE WARD FOR SOME WEEKS UNTIL A RESIDENTIAL HOME COULD BE FOUND FOR HIM.

NO SINGLE CAUSE OF SCHIZOPHRENIA HAS BEEN DISCOVERED.

THE ILLNESS TENDS TO RUN IN FAMILIES, BUT IT IS THOUGHT THAT GENES ALONE CANNOT CAUSE THE DISORDER.

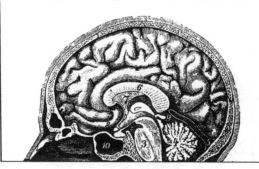

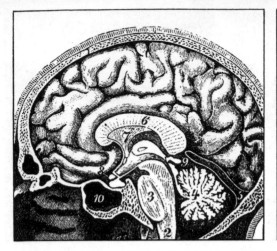

INTERACTION BETWEEN GENES AND THE ENVIRONMENT IS THOUGHT TO BE NECESSARY FOR SCHIZOPHRENIA TO DEVELOP.

MANY ENVIRONMENTAL FACTORS HAVE BEEN SUGGESTED AS RISK FACTORS.

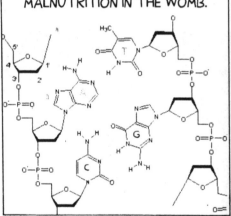

EXPOSURE TO VIRUSES OR MALNUTRITION IN THE WOMB.

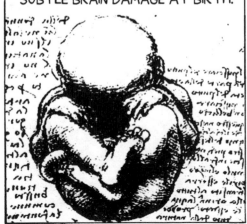

SUBTLE BRAIN DAMAGE AT BIRTH.

SOCIAL FACTORS SUCH AS STRESSFUL ENVIRONMENTAL CONDITIONS.

IN OTHER WORDS, ALMOST EVERYTHING IS IMPLICATED IN THE CAUSES OF SCHIZOPHRENIA

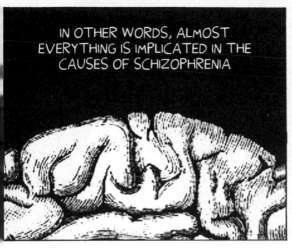

MAKING IT VERY DIFFICULT TO FOLLOW THE THREAD OF CAUSE AND EFFECT.

DO I HAVE TO TAKE ALL THESE?

YES, YOU DO.

THE OLD ANTI-PSYCHOTIC MEDICATIONS WHICH MANY STILL USE

CAN CAUSE MUSCLE RIGIDITY, TREMORS, AND AGITATION, OBLIGING PEOPLE TO TAKE FURTHER DRUGS IN ORDER TO COUNTER THESE SIDE-EFFECTS.

THE NEWER ANTI-PSYCHOTICS, WHICH WERE INTRODUCED IN THE NINETEEN-NINETIES, WORK WELL FOR THOSE WHOSE ILLNESS WAS PREVIOUSLY TREATMENT RESISTANT.

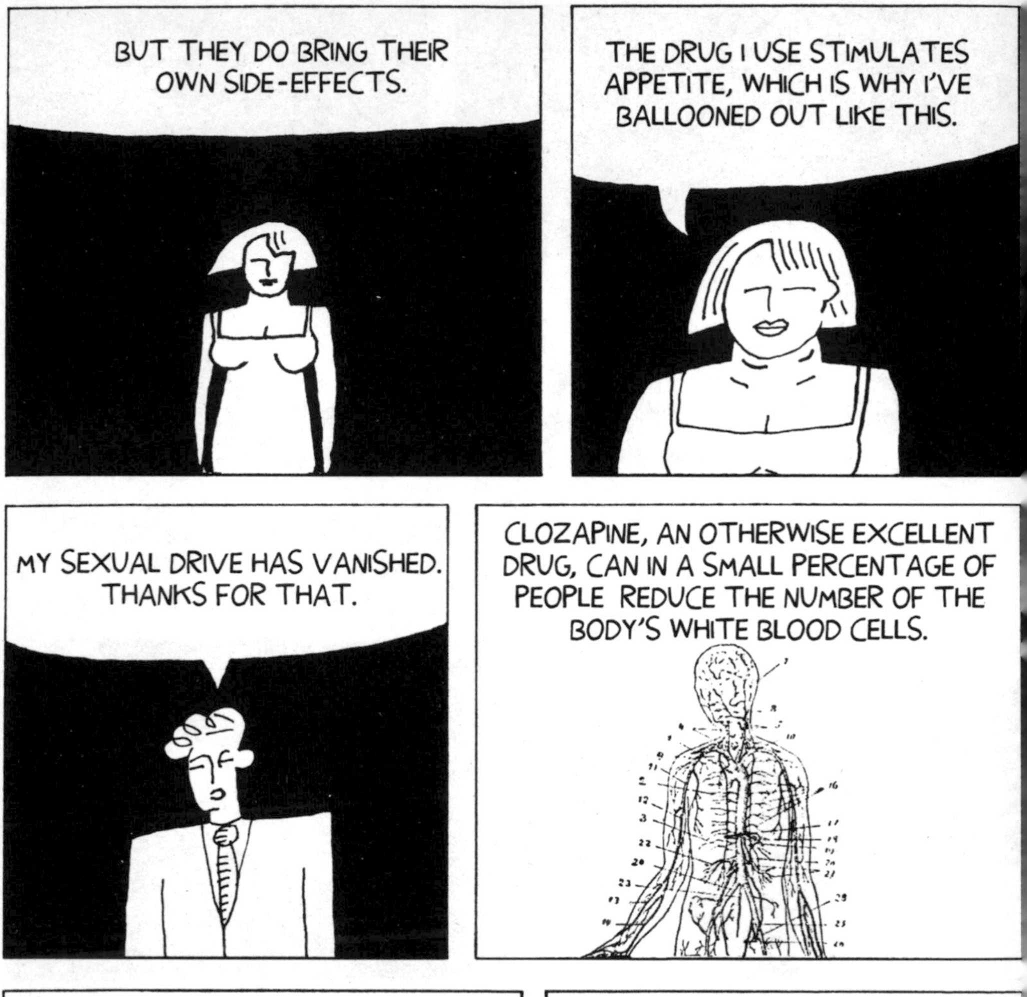

BUT THEY DO BRING THEIR OWN SIDE-EFFECTS.

THE DRUG I USE STIMULATES APPETITE, WHICH IS WHY I'VE BALLOONED OUT LIKE THIS.

MY SEXUAL DRIVE HAS VANISHED. THANKS FOR THAT.

CLOZAPINE, AN OTHERWISE EXCELLENT DRUG, CAN IN A SMALL PERCENTAGE OF PEOPLE REDUCE THE NUMBER OF THE BODY'S WHITE BLOOD CELLS.

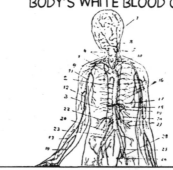

WHICH CAN COMPROMISE THE IMMUNE SYSTEM'S ABILITY TO FIGHT INFECTION.

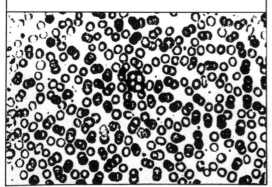

USERS NEED REGULAR BLOOD TESTS TO ENSURE THEIR WHITE BLOOD CELL COUNT IS NORMAL.

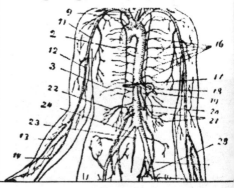

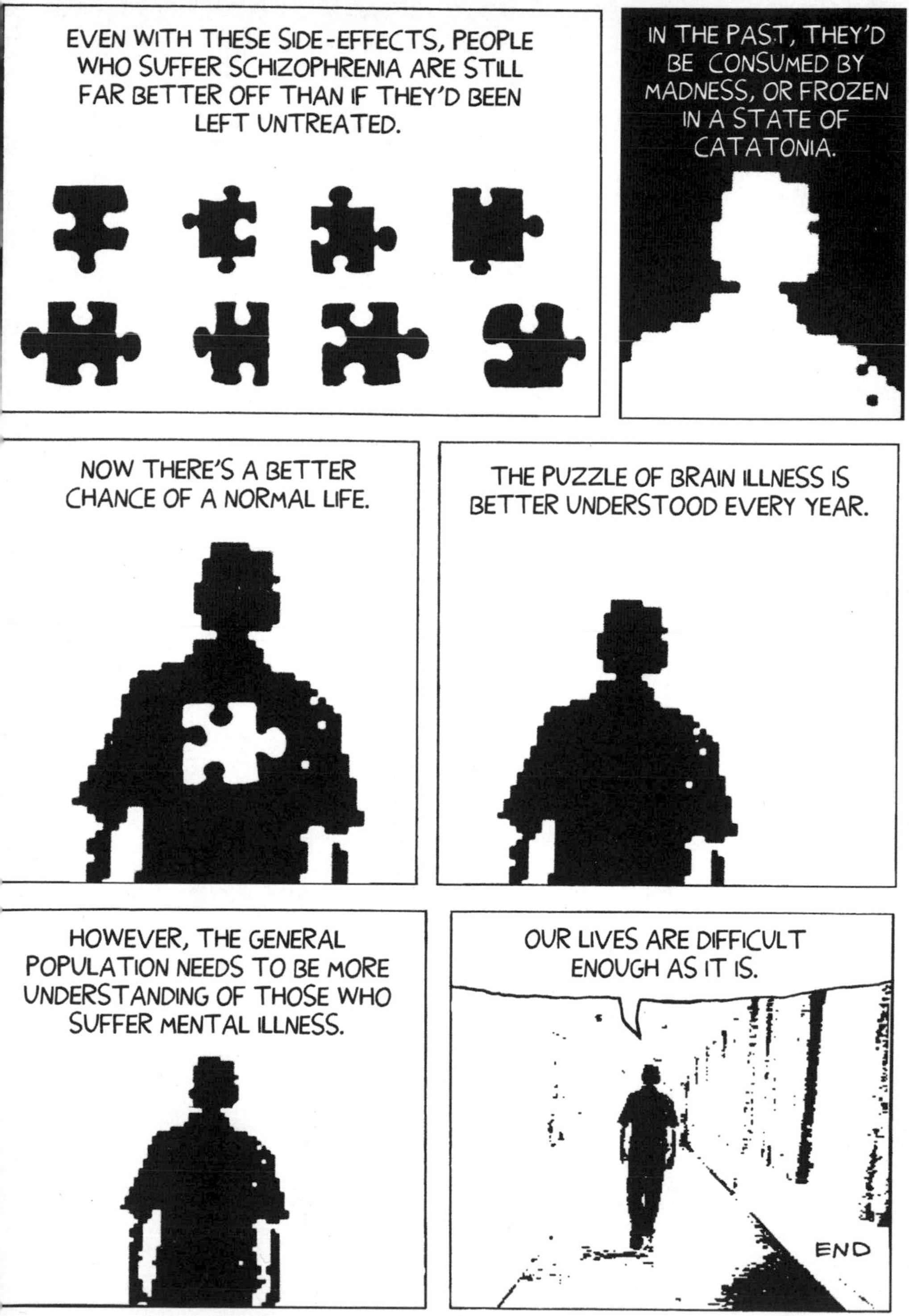
EVEN WITH THESE SIDE-EFFECTS, PEOPLE WHO SUFFER SCHIZOPHRENIA ARE STILL FAR BETTER OFF THAN IF THEY'D BEEN LEFT UNTREATED.
IN THE PAST, THEY'D BE CONSUMED BY MADNESS, OR FROZEN IN A STATE OF CATATONIA.
NOW THERE'S A BETTER CHANCE OF A NORMAL LIFE.
THE PUZZLE OF BRAIN ILLNESS IS BETTER UNDERSTOOD EVERY YEAR.
HOWEVER, THE GENERAL POPULATION NEEDS TO BE MORE UNDERSTANDING OF THOSE WHO SUFFER MENTAL ILLNESS.
OUR LIVES ARE DIFFICULT ENOUGH AS IT IS.
END

SUICIDE

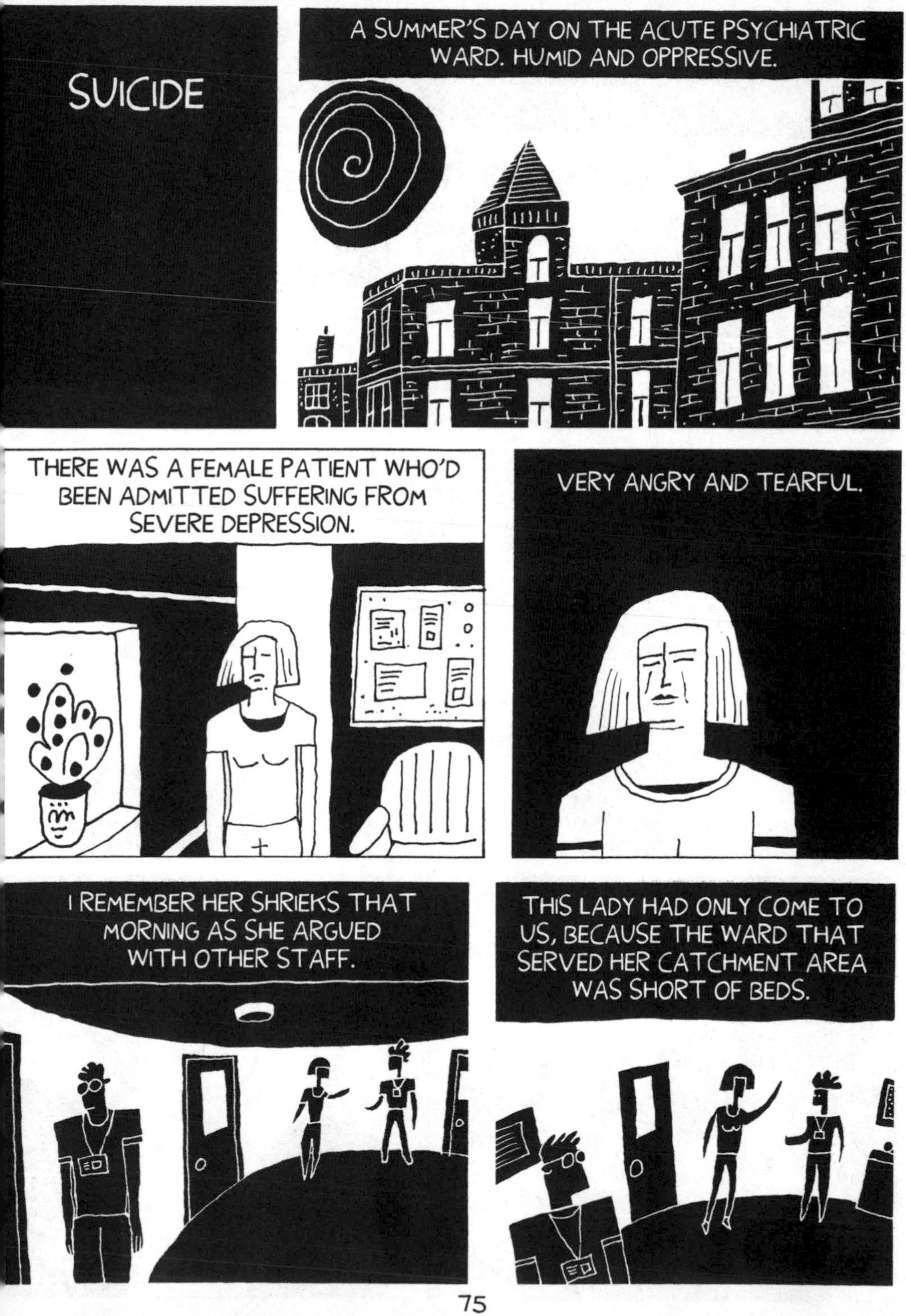
SUICIDE
A SUMMER'S DAY ON THE ACUTE PSYCHIATRIC WARD. HUMID AND OPPRESSIVE.
THERE WAS A FEMALE PATIENT WHO'D BEEN ADMITTED SUFFERING FROM SEVERE DEPRESSION.
VERY ANGRY AND TEARFUL.
I REMEMBER HER SHRIEKS THAT MORNING AS SHE ARGUED WITH OTHER STAFF.
THIS LADY HAD ONLY COME TO US, BECAUSE THE WARD THAT SERVED HER CATCHMENT AREA WAS SHORT OF BEDS.

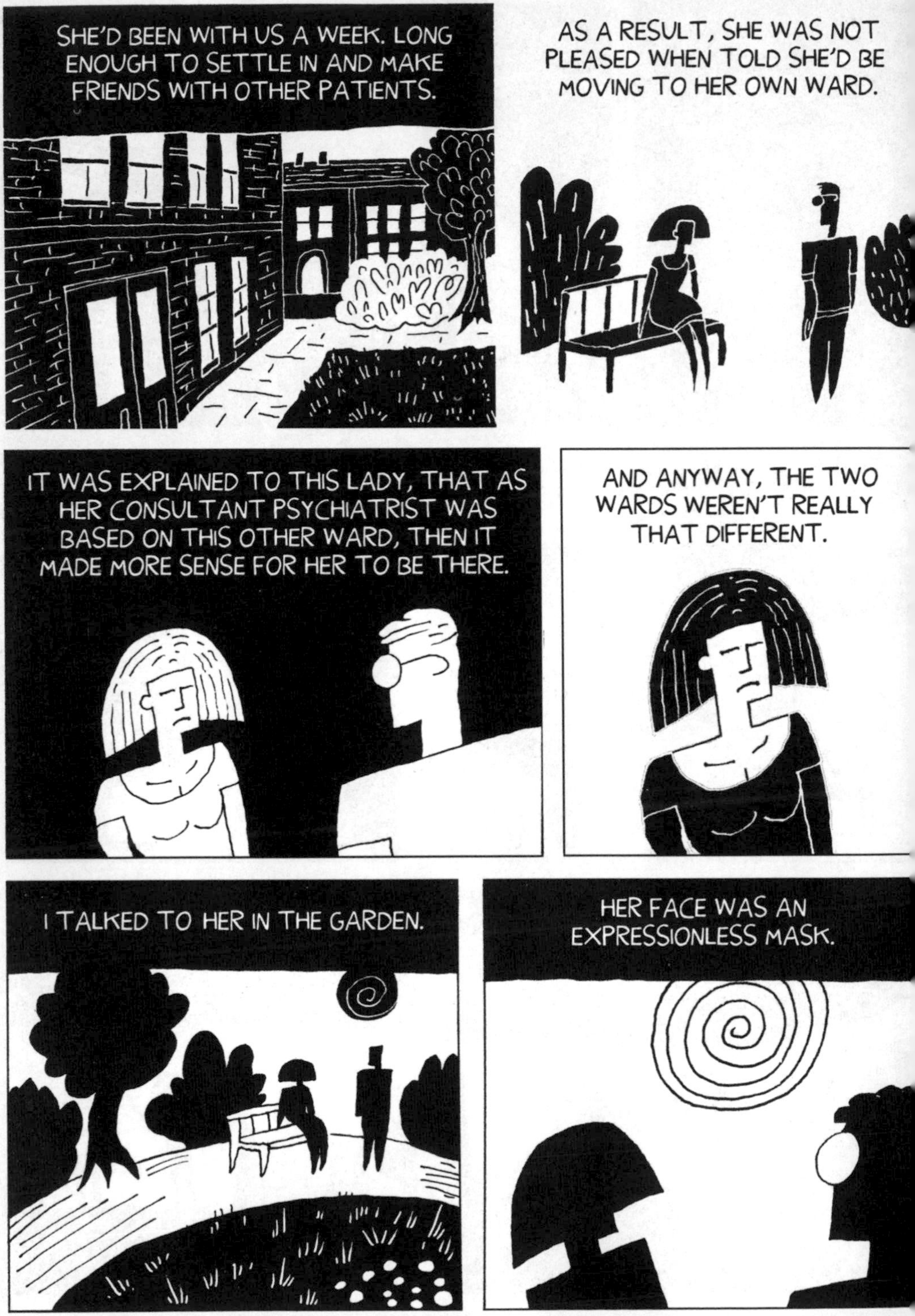
SHE'D BEEN WITH US A WEEK. LONG ENOUGH TO SETTLE IN AND MAKE FRIENDS WITH OTHER PATIENTS.
AS A RESULT, SHE WAS NOT PLEASED WHEN TOLD SHE'D BE MOVING TO HER OWN WARD.
IT WAS EXPLAINED TO THIS LADY, THAT AS HER CONSULTANT PSYCHIATRIST WAS BASED ON THIS OTHER WARD, THEN IT MADE MORE SENSE FOR HER TO BE THERE.
AND ANYWAY, THE TWO WARDS WEREN'T REALLY THAT DIFFERENT.
I TALKED TO HER IN THE GARDEN.
HER FACE WAS AN EXPRESSIONLESS MASK.

SHE APPEARED CALM, BUT I COULD SEE THAT JUST UNDER THE SURFACE THERE WAS STILL MUCH ANGER.

SHE WAS COLD IN HER ATTITUDE AND ALMOST HOSTILE.

MANY STAFF, INCLUDING THE DEPUTY WARD MANAGER, HAD SPOKEN TO HER THAT DAY, NOT JUST ME.

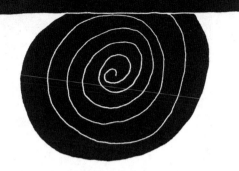

WE THOUGHT THAT OUR ATTEMPTS TO REASSURE THE PATIENT HAD GONE WELL, BUT WE WERE QUITE WRONG.

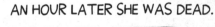

I LEFT HER IN THE GARDEN AND RETURNED TO THE WARD.

AN HOUR LATER SHE WAS DEAD.

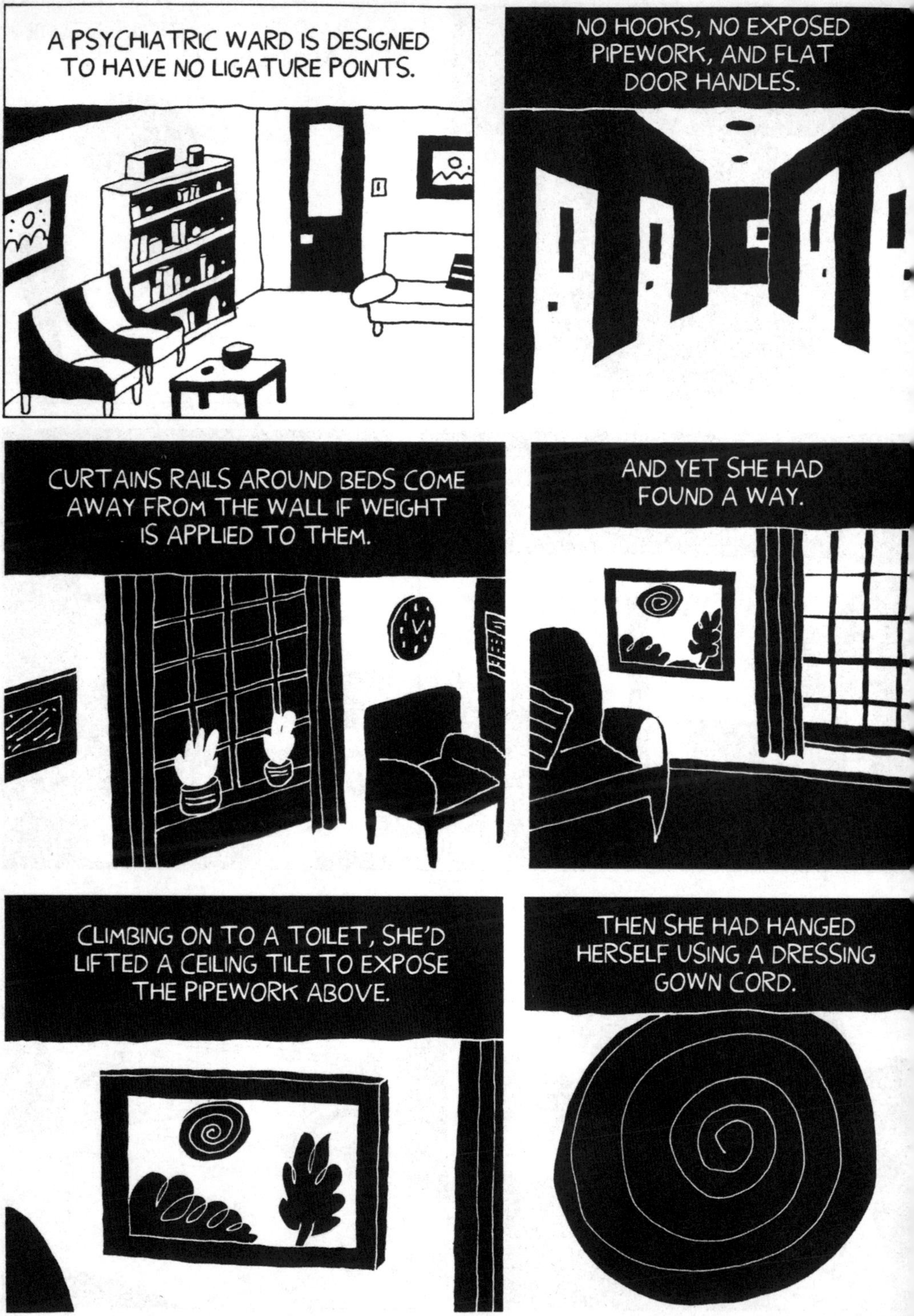
A PSYCHIATRIC WARD IS DESIGNED TO HAVE NO LIGATURE POINTS.
NO HOOKS, NO EXPOSED PIPEWORK, AND FLAT DOOR HANDLES.
CURTAINS RAILS AROUND BEDS COME AWAY FROM THE WALL IF WEIGHT IS APPLIED TO THEM.
AND YET SHE HAD FOUND A WAY.
CLIMBING ON TO A TOILET, SHE'D LIFTED A CEILING TILE TO EXPOSE THE PIPEWORK ABOVE.
THEN SHE HAD HANGED HERSELF USING A DRESSING GOWN CORD.

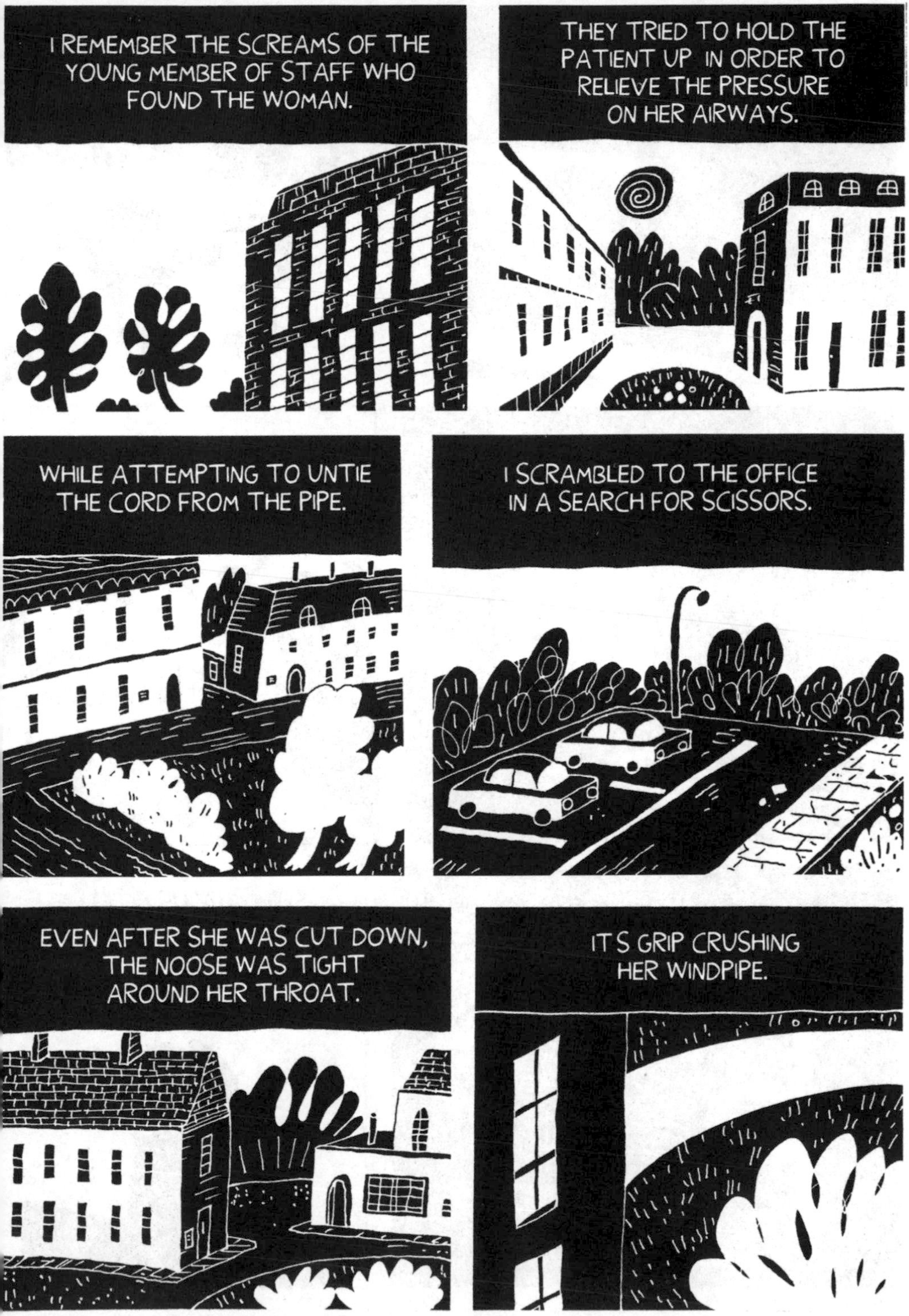
I REMEMBER THE SCREAMS OF THE YOUNG MEMBER OF STAFF WHO FOUND THE WOMAN.
THEY TRIED TO HOLD THE PATIENT UP IN ORDER TO RELIEVE THE PRESSURE ON HER AIRWAYS.
WHILE ATTEMPTING TO UNTIE THE CORD FROM THE PIPE.
I SCRAMBLED TO THE OFFICE IN A SEARCH FOR SCISSORS.
EVEN AFTER SHE WAS CUT DOWN, THE NOOSE WAS TIGHT AROUND HER THROAT.
ITS GRIP CRUSHING HER WINDPIPE.

THEY COULD NOT SAVE HER.

SHE DIED, LEAVING A YOUNG FAMILY BEHIND.

THE PATIENT HAD GIVEN US NO INDICATION THAT SHE WAS SUICIDAL.

NOT A HINT OF WHAT SHE HAD PLANNED WAS PICKED UP BY STAFF.

HER ANGER AND IMPASSIVITY HAD SUCCESSFULLY MASKED HER TRUE THOUGHTS.

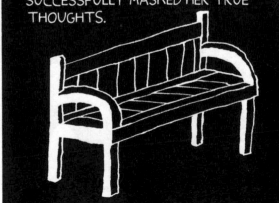

SHE GAVE US NO CLUE BECAUSE SHE DIDN'T WANT TO BE SAVED.

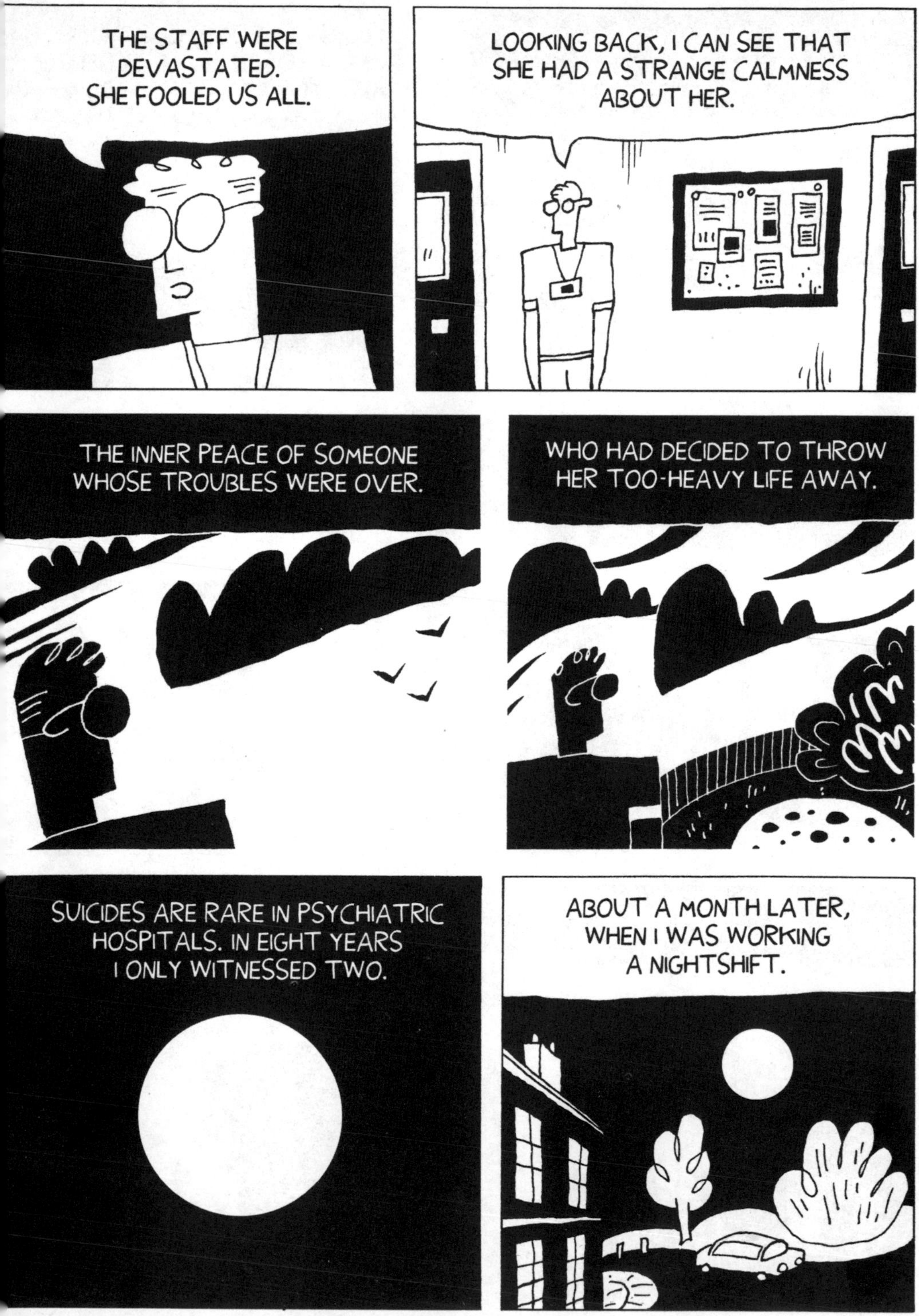
THE STAFF WERE DEVASTATED. SHE FOOLED US ALL.
LOOKING BACK, I CAN SEE THAT SHE HAD A STRANGE CALMNESS ABOUT HER.
THE INNER PEACE OF SOMEONE WHOSE TROUBLES WERE OVER.
WHO HAD DECIDED TO THROW HER TOO-HEAVY LIFE AWAY.
SUICIDES ARE RARE IN PSYCHIATRIC HOSPITALS. IN EIGHT YEARS I ONLY WITNESSED TWO.
ABOUT A MONTH LATER, WHEN I WAS WORKING A NIGHTSHIFT.

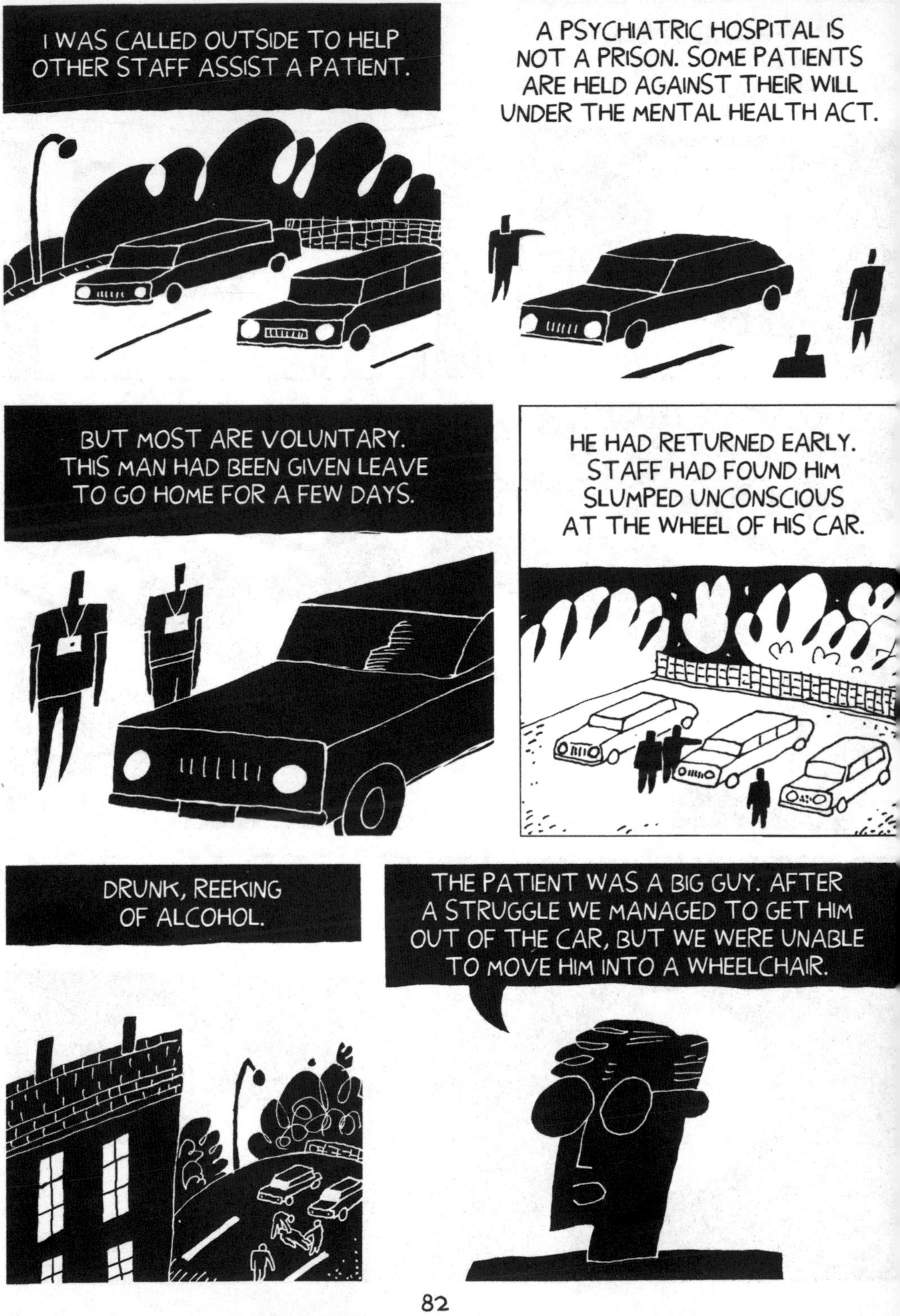
I WAS CALLED OUTSIDE TO HELP OTHER STAFF ASSIST A PATIENT.
A PSYCHIATRIC HOSPITAL IS NOT A PRISON. SOME PATIENTS ARE HELD AGAINST THEIR WILL UNDER THE MENTAL HEALTH ACT.
BUT MOST ARE VOLUNTARY. THIS MAN HAD BEEN GIVEN LEAVE TO GO HOME FOR A FEW DAYS.
HE HAD RETURNED EARLY. STAFF HAD FOUND HIM SLUMPED UNCONSCIOUS AT THE WHEEL OF HIS CAR.
DRUNK, REEKING OF ALCOHOL.
THE PATIENT WAS A BIG GUY. AFTER A STRUGGLE WE MANAGED TO GET HIM OUT OF THE CAR, BUT WE WERE UNABLE TO MOVE HIM INTO A WHEELCHAIR.

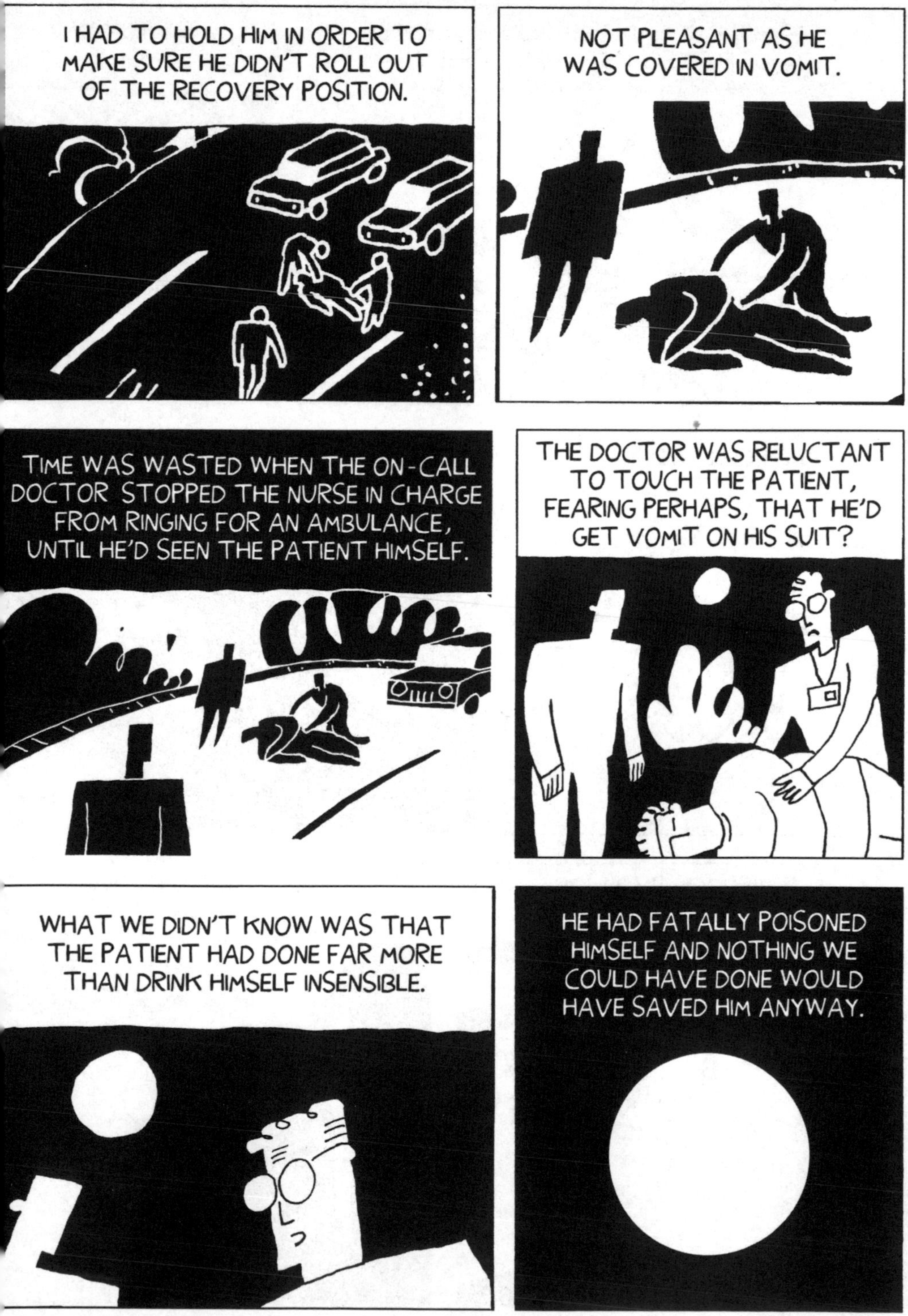
I HAD TO HOLD HIM IN ORDER TO MAKE SURE HE DIDN'T ROLL OUT OF THE RECOVERY POSITION.
NOT PLEASANT AS HE WAS COVERED IN VOMIT.
TIME WAS WASTED WHEN THE ON-CALL DOCTOR STOPPED THE NURSE IN CHARGE FROM RINGING FOR AN AMBULANCE, UNTIL HE'D SEEN THE PATIENT HIMSELF.
THE DOCTOR WAS RELUCTANT TO TOUCH THE PATIENT, FEARING PERHAPS, THAT HE'D GET VOMIT ON HIS SUIT?
WHAT WE DIDN'T KNOW WAS THAT THE PATIENT HAD DONE FAR MORE THAN DRINK HIMSELF INSENSIBLE.
HE HAD FATALLY POISONED HIMSELF AND NOTHING WE COULD HAVE DONE WOULD HAVE SAVED HIM ANYWAY.

AT HOME HE HAD TAKEN AN OVERDOSE OF FUROSEMIDE, A DRUG USED IN HEART FAILURE AND EDEMA.
Aorta
Pulmonary Artery
Pulmonary Artery
Left Atrium
THEN DRANK WHISKY.
AND FOLLOWED THAT WITH BLEACH.
Aorta
Pulmonary Artery
Pulmonary Artery
Pulmonary Veins
Pulmonary
Left Atrium
Right Atrium
Left Ventricle
Vena Cava
Right Ventricle
Aorta
WHEN THE AMBULANCE FINALLY ARRIVED, THE PARAMEDICS COULD DO LITTLE TO REVIVE HIM.
IN SHOCK I WALKED BACK TO THE WARD.
I DID THE REST OF THE SHIFT IN A DAZE.
YOU SHOULD STOP THINKING ABOUT IT.

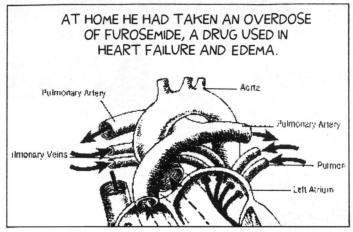

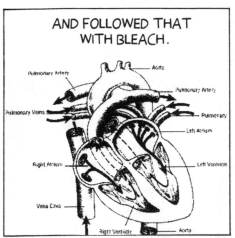

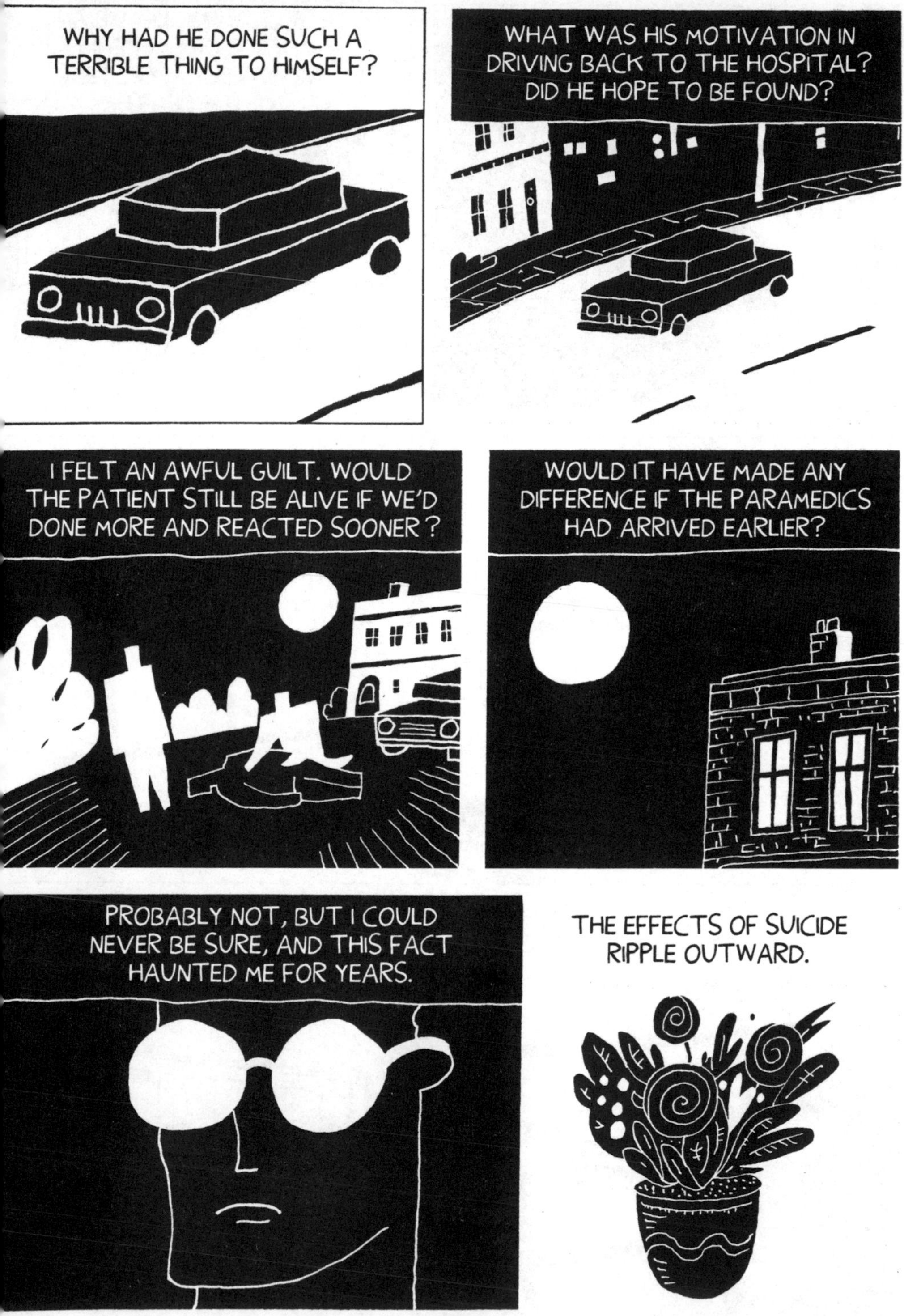
WHY HAD HE DONE SUCH A TERRIBLE THING TO HIMSELF?
WHAT WAS HIS MOTIVATION IN DRIVING BACK TO THE HOSPITAL? DID HE HOPE TO BE FOUND?
I FELT AN AWFUL GUILT. WOULD THE PATIENT STILL BE ALIVE IF WE'D DONE MORE AND REACTED SOONER?
WOULD IT HAVE MADE ANY DIFFERENCE IF THE PARAMEDICS HAD ARRIVED EARLIER?
PROBABLY NOT, BUT I COULD NEVER BE SURE, AND THIS FACT HAUNTED ME FOR YEARS.
THE EFFECTS OF SUICIDE RIPPLE OUTWARD.

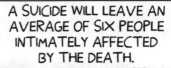

DAMAGING FAMILY, FRIENDS AND STRANGERS ALIKE.

A SUICIDE WILL LEAVE AN AVERAGE OF SIX PEOPLE INTIMATELY AFFECTED BY THE DEATH.

A PARENT, A SIGNIFICANT OTHER, A SIBLING, OR A CHILD OF THE DECEASED PERSON.

THESE PEOPLE ARE REFERRED TO AS THE SURVIVORS.

THESE ARE THE ONES LEFT TO SUFFER.

NEVER KNOWING WHY. ALWAYS WONDERING IF THEY COULD HAVE DONE MORE.

END

HOW I LIVED AGAIN

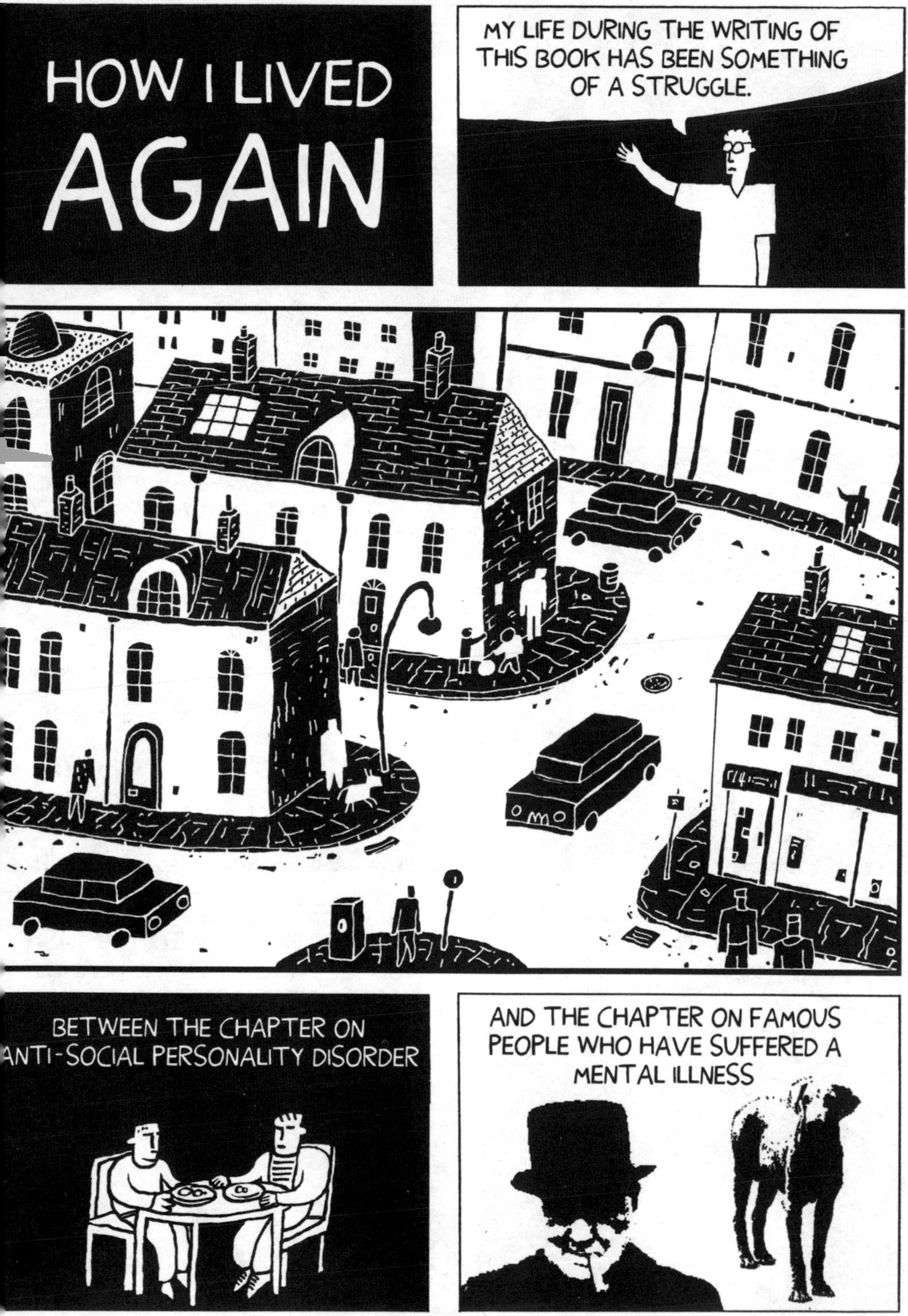
HOW I LIVED AGAIN
MY LIFE DURING THE WRITING OF THIS BOOK HAS BEEN SOMETHING OF A STRUGGLE.
BETWEEN THE CHAPTER ON ANTI-SOCIAL PERSONALITY DISORDER
AND THE CHAPTER ON FAMOUS PEOPLE WHO HAVE SUFFERED A MENTAL ILLNESS

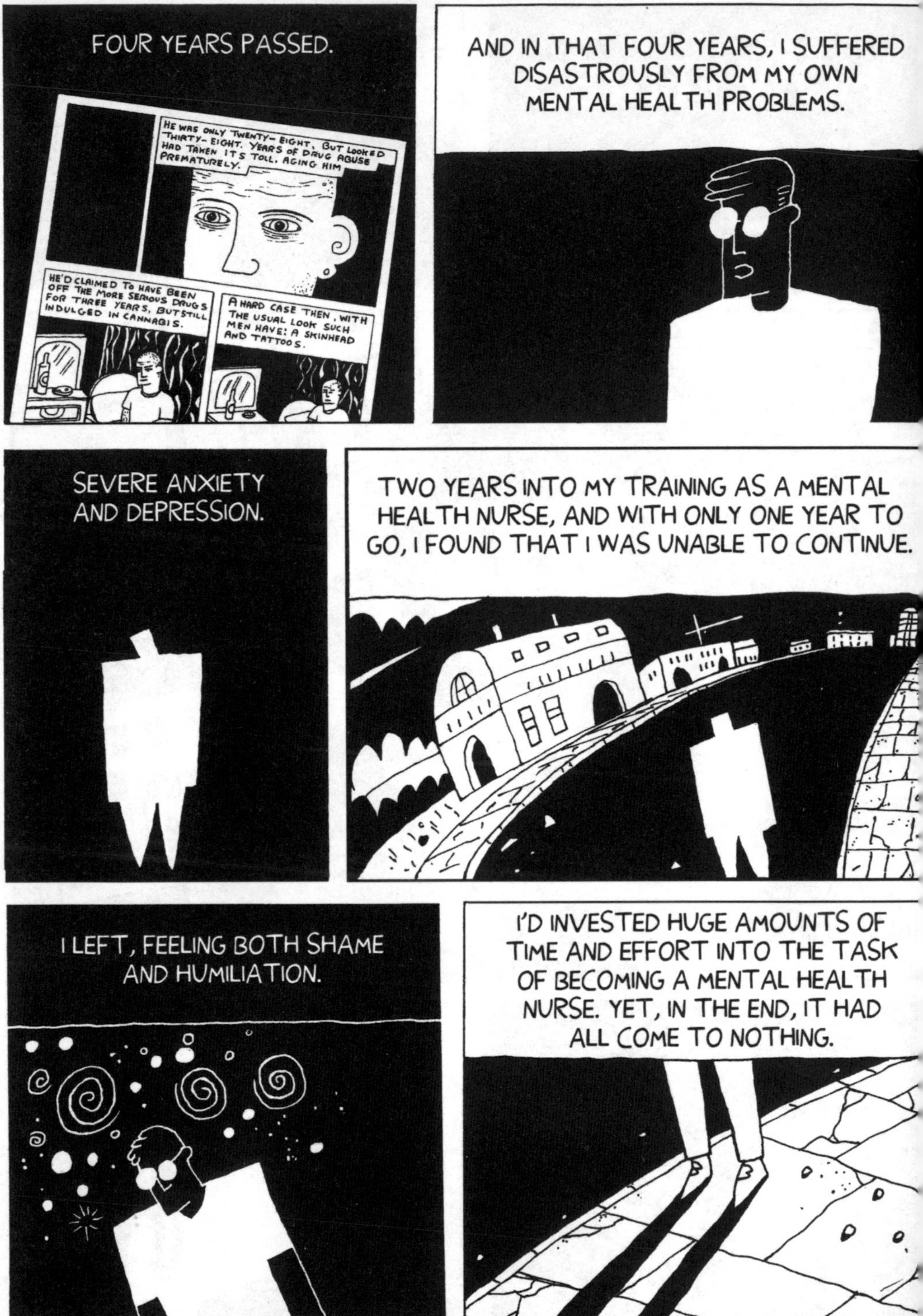
FOUR YEARS PASSED.
HE WAS ONLY TWENTY-EIGHT, BUT LOOKED THIRTY-EIGHT. YEARS OF DRUG ABUSE HAD TAKEN ITS TOLL, AGING HIM PREMATURELY.
HE'D CLAIMED TO HAVE BEEN OFF THE MORE SERIOUS DRUGS FOR THREE YEARS, BUT STILL INDULGED IN CANNABIS.
A HARD CASE THEN, WITH THE USUAL LOOK SUCH MEN HAVE: A SKINHEAD AND TATTOOS.
AND IN THAT FOUR YEARS, I SUFFERED DISASTROUSLY FROM MY OWN MENTAL HEALTH PROBLEMS.
SEVERE ANXIETY AND DEPRESSION.
TWO YEARS INTO MY TRAINING AS A MENTAL HEALTH NURSE, AND WITH ONLY ONE YEAR TO GO, I FOUND THAT I WAS UNABLE TO CONTINUE.
I LEFT, FEELING BOTH SHAME AND HUMILIATION.
I'D INVESTED HUGE AMOUNTS OF TIME AND EFFORT INTO THE TASK OF BECOMING A MENTAL HEALTH NURSE. YET, IN THE END, IT HAD ALL COME TO NOTHING.

I COULD NOT LOOK MY FELLOW STUDENTS IN THE EYE.

PRIOR TO STARTING THE COURSE, I'D BEEN A HEALTH CARE ASSISTANT

WORKING ON AN ACUTE PSYCHIATRIC WARD FOR SEVERAL YEARS.

HOSPITAL

MY BOSS ON THE WARD TOLD ME THAT MY PERSONALITY MIGHT NOT SUIT SUCH A TOUGH COURSE.

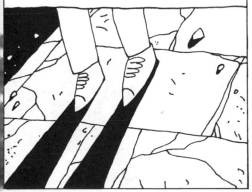

AND THAT I WOULD FIND IT EXTREMELY HARD.

ALTHOUGH SHE MEANT WELL, I WAS DETERMINED TO PROVE HER WRONG.

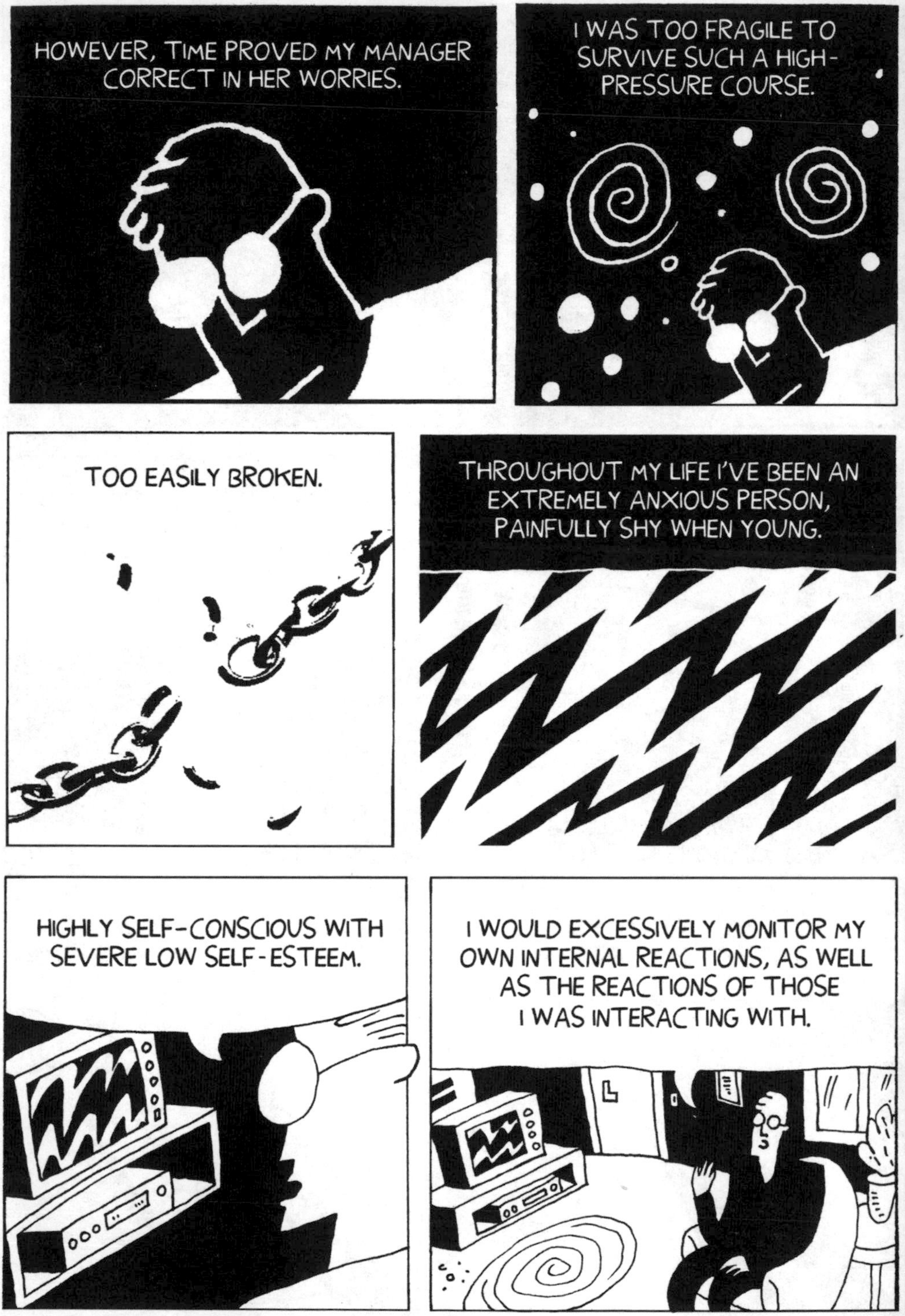
HOWEVER, TIME PROVED MY MANAGER CORRECT IN HER WORRIES.
I WAS TOO FRAGILE TO SURVIVE SUCH A HIGH-PRESSURE COURSE.
TOO EASILY BROKEN.
THROUGHOUT MY LIFE I'VE BEEN AN EXTREMELY ANXIOUS PERSON, PAINFULLY SHY WHEN YOUNG.
HIGHLY SELF-CONSCIOUS WITH SEVERE LOW SELF-ESTEEM.
I WOULD EXCESSIVELY MONITOR MY OWN INTERNAL REACTIONS, AS WELL AS THE REACTIONS OF THOSE I WAS INTERACTING WITH.

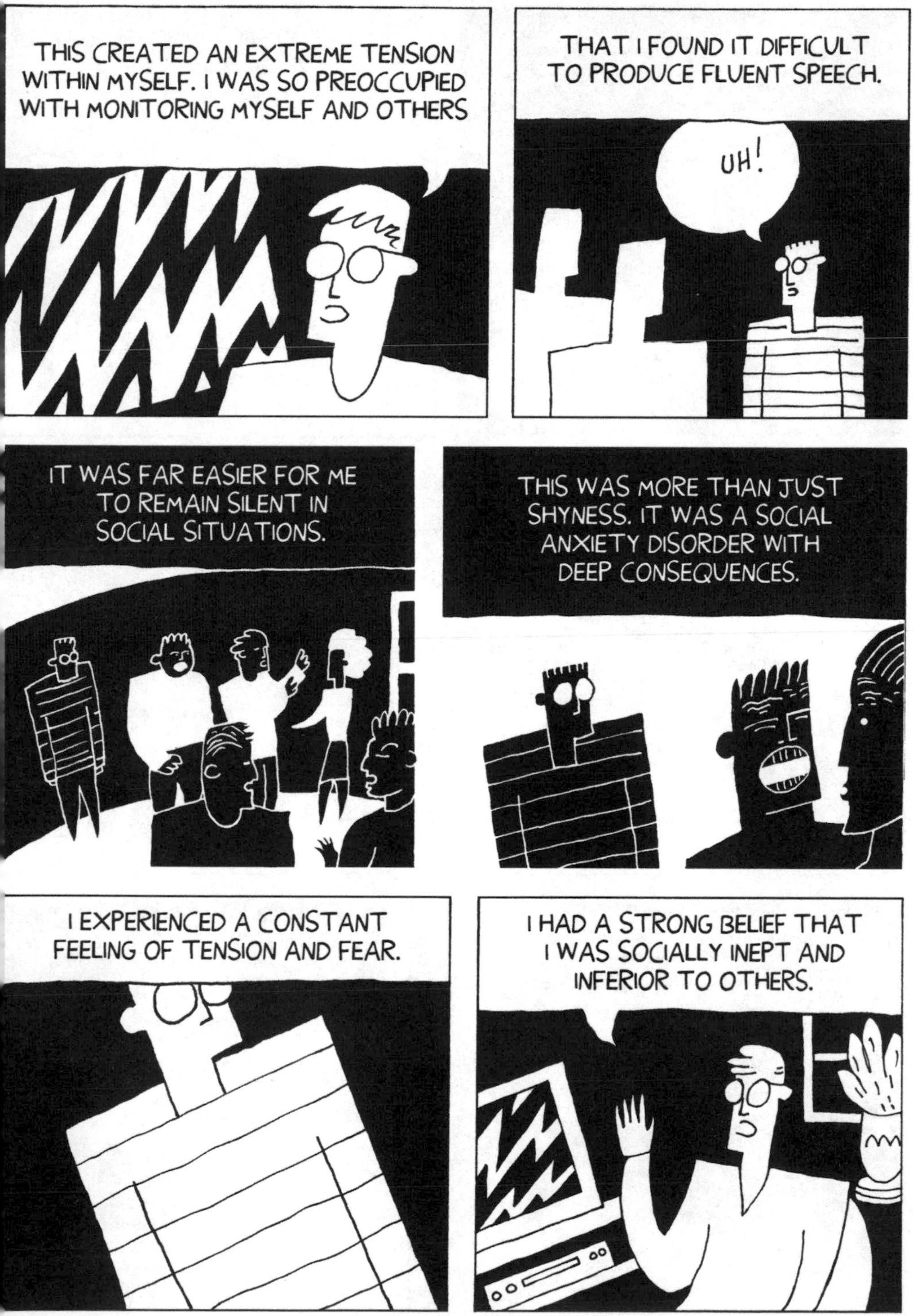
THIS CREATED AN EXTREME TENSION WITHIN MYSELF. I WAS SO PREOCCUPIED WITH MONITORING MYSELF AND OTHERS
THAT I FOUND IT DIFFICULT TO PRODUCE FLUENT SPEECH.
UH!
IT WAS FAR EASIER FOR ME TO REMAIN SILENT IN SOCIAL SITUATIONS.
THIS WAS MORE THAN JUST SHYNESS. IT WAS A SOCIAL ANXIETY DISORDER WITH DEEP CONSEQUENCES.
I EXPERIENCED A CONSTANT FEELING OF TENSION AND FEAR.
I HAD A STRONG BELIEF THAT I WAS SOCIALLY INEPT AND INFERIOR TO OTHERS.

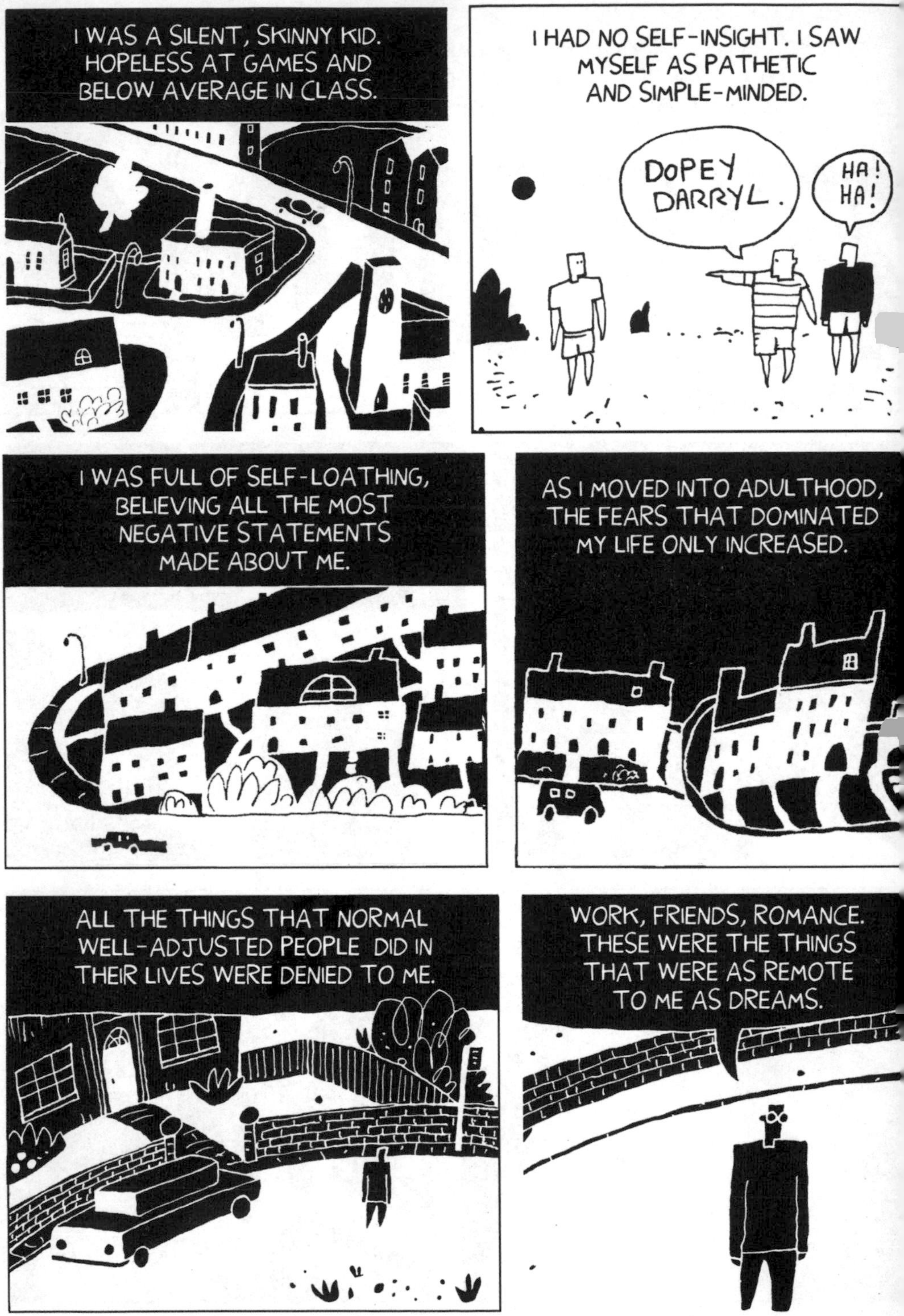
I WAS A SILENT, SKINNY KID. HOPELESS AT GAMES AND BELOW AVERAGE IN CLASS.
I HAD NO SELF-INSIGHT. I SAW MYSELF AS PATHETIC AND SIMPLE-MINDED.
DOPEY DARRYL.
HA! HA!
I WAS FULL OF SELF-LOATHING, BELIEVING ALL THE MOST NEGATIVE STATEMENTS MADE ABOUT ME.
AS I MOVED INTO ADULTHOOD, THE FEARS THAT DOMINATED MY LIFE ONLY INCREASED.
ALL THE THINGS THAT NORMAL WELL-ADJUSTED PEOPLE DID IN THEIR LIVES WERE DENIED TO ME.
WORK, FRIENDS, ROMANCE. THESE WERE THE THINGS THAT WERE AS REMOTE TO ME AS DREAMS.

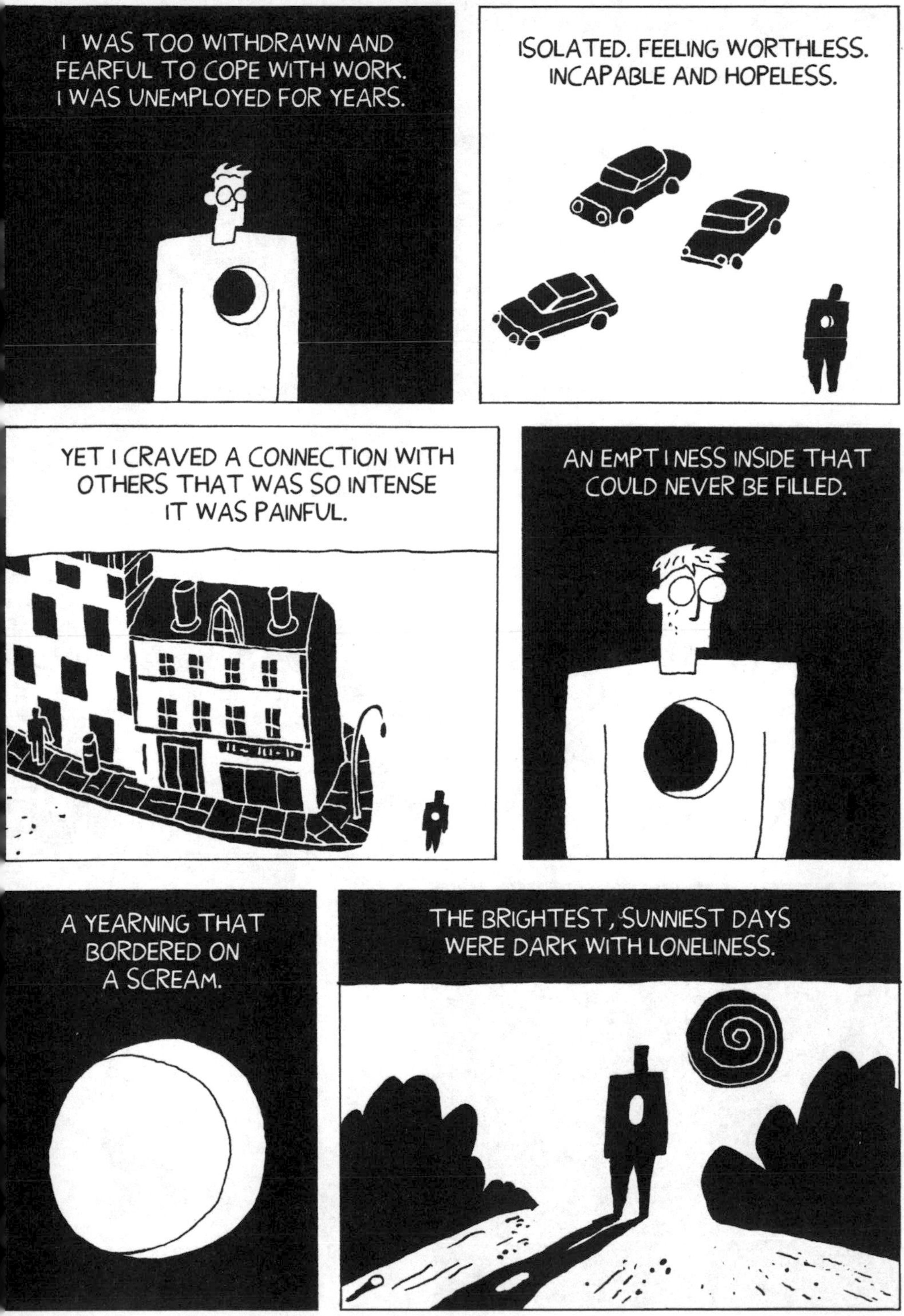
I WAS TOO WITHDRAWN AND FEARFUL TO COPE WITH WORK. I WAS UNEMPLOYED FOR YEARS.
ISOLATED. FEELING WORTHLESS. INCAPABLE AND HOPELESS.
YET I CRAVED A CONNECTION WITH OTHERS THAT WAS SO INTENSE IT WAS PAINFUL.
AN EMPTINESS INSIDE THAT COULD NEVER BE FILLED.
A YEARNING THAT BORDERED ON A SCREAM.
THE BRIGHTEST, SUNNIEST DAYS WERE DARK WITH LONELINESS.

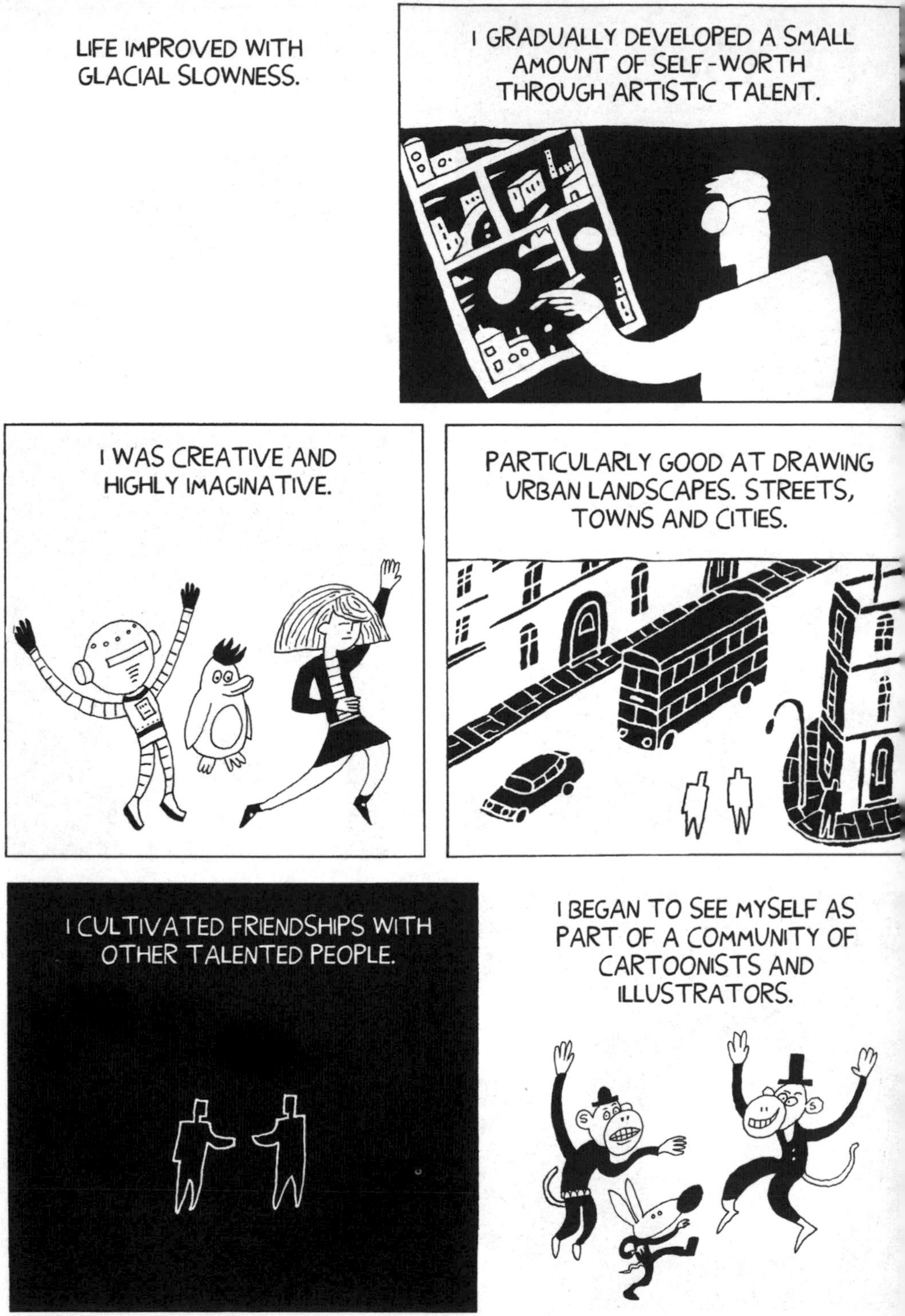
LIFE IMPROVED WITH GLACIAL SLOWNESS.
I GRADUALLY DEVELOPED A SMALL AMOUNT OF SELF-WORTH THROUGH ARTISTIC TALENT.
I WAS CREATIVE AND HIGHLY IMAGINATIVE.
PARTICULARLY GOOD AT DRAWING URBAN LANDSCAPES. STREETS, TOWNS AND CITIES.
I CULTIVATED FRIENDSHIPS WITH OTHER TALENTED PEOPLE.
I BEGAN TO SEE MYSELF AS PART OF A COMMUNITY OF CARTOONISTS AND ILLUSTRATORS.

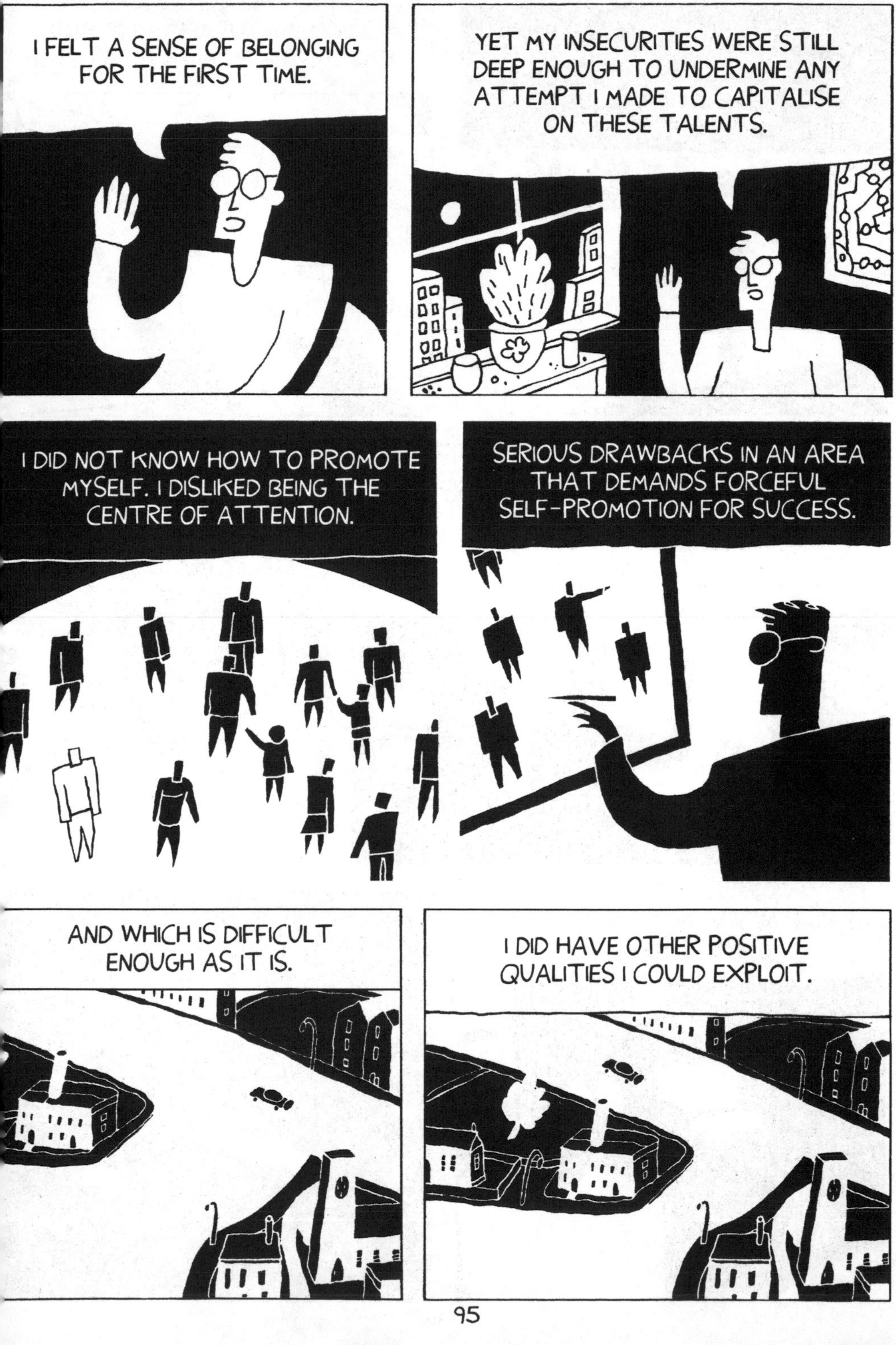

I FELT A SENSE OF BELONGING FOR THE FIRST TIME.
YET MY INSECURITIES WERE STILL DEEP ENOUGH TO UNDERMINE ANY ATTEMPT I MADE TO CAPITALISE ON THESE TALENTS.
I DID NOT KNOW HOW TO PROMOTE MYSELF. I DISLIKED BEING THE CENTRE OF ATTENTION.
SERIOUS DRAWBACKS IN AN AREA THAT DEMANDS FORCEFUL SELF-PROMOTION FOR SUCCESS.
AND WHICH IS DIFFICULT ENOUGH AS IT IS.
I DID HAVE OTHER POSITIVE QUALITIES I COULD EXPLOIT.

PERHAPS BECAUSE I WAS SO IMAGINATIVE, I FOUND IT EASY TO PLACE MYSELF IN ANOTHER'S SHOES.

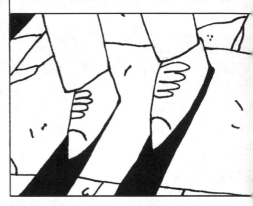

I WAS NATURALLY KIND AND HAD A GREAT DEAL OF PATIENCE.

MY INTEREST IN MENTAL HEALTH ISSUES, STEMMING FROM AN ATTEMPT TO UNDERSTAND MY OWN PROBLEMS

LED ME INTO MENTAL HEALTH WORK.

FIRST AS AN UNTRAINED HEALTH CARE ASSISTANT.

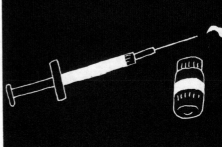

THEN AS A STUDENT ATTEMPTING TO QUALIFY AS A MENTAL HEALTH NURSE.

96

AND THIS IS WHEN I
OVERREACHED MYSELF.

THIS IS WHEN I BROKE.

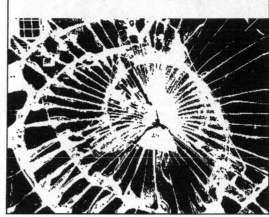

THE SITUATION BECAME
DESPERATE.

MY LIFE AS A NURSE WAS OVER
AND I WAS UNABLE TO MAKE
ANYTHING OF MYSELF AS
AN ILLUSTRATOR.

I SAW NOTHING IN THE FUTURE
EXCEPT MORE UNHAPPINESS

LONELINESS AND
GRIM POVERTY.

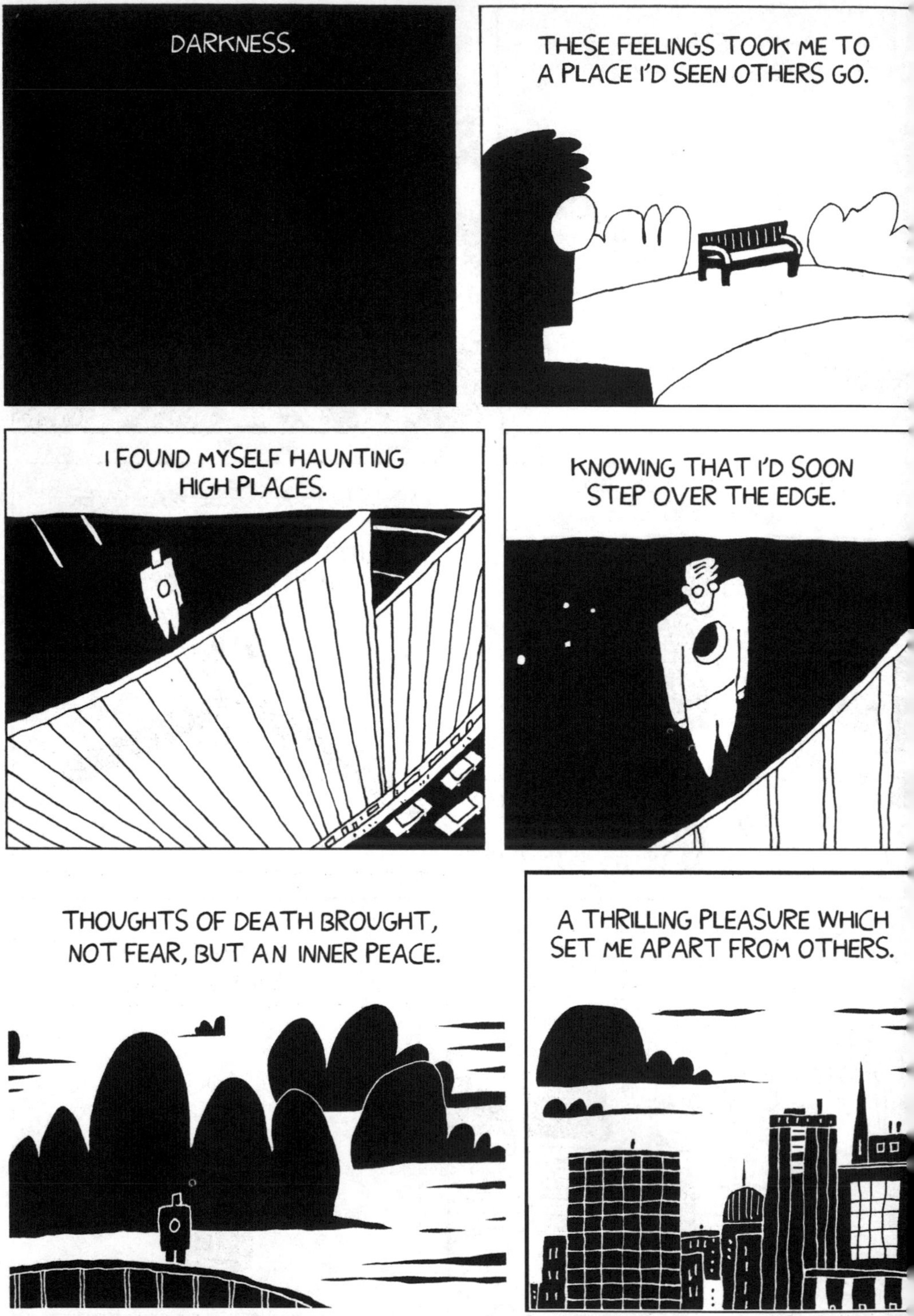
DARKNESS.
THESE FEELINGS TOOK ME TO A PLACE I'D SEEN OTHERS GO.
I FOUND MYSELF HAUNTING HIGH PLACES.
KNOWING THAT I'D SOON STEP OVER THE EDGE.
THOUGHTS OF DEATH BROUGHT, NOT FEAR, BUT AN INNER PEACE.
A THRILLING PLEASURE WHICH SET ME APART FROM OTHERS.

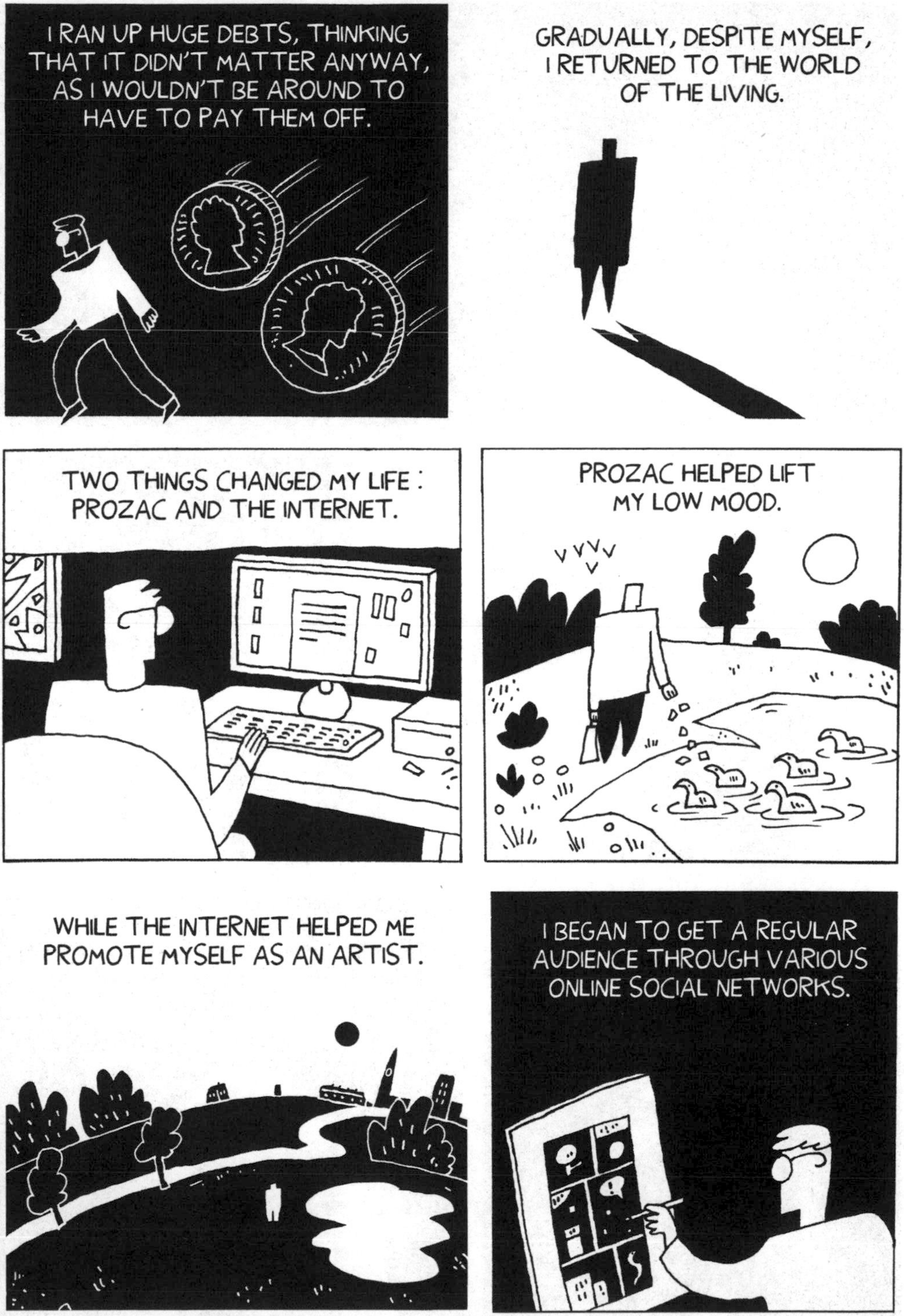
I RAN UP HUGE DEBTS, THINKING THAT IT DIDN'T MATTER ANYWAY, AS I WOULDN'T BE AROUND TO HAVE TO PAY THEM OFF.
GRADUALLY, DESPITE MYSELF, I RETURNED TO THE WORLD OF THE LIVING.
TWO THINGS CHANGED MY LIFE: PROZAC AND THE INTERNET.
PROZAC HELPED LIFT MY LOW MOOD.
WHILE THE INTERNET HELPED ME PROMOTE MYSELF AS AN ARTIST.
I BEGAN TO GET A REGULAR AUDIENCE THROUGH VARIOUS ONLINE SOCIAL NETWORKS.

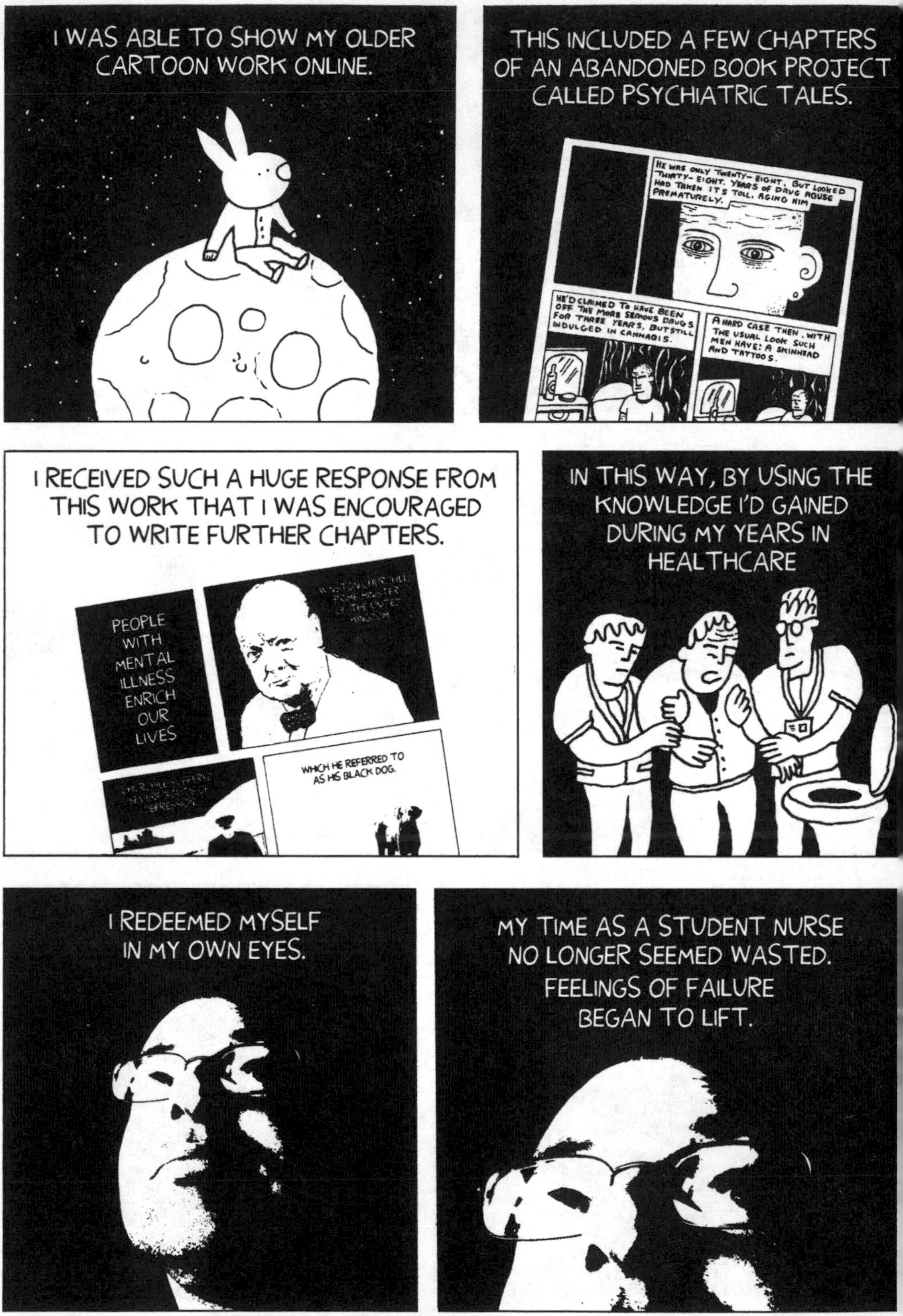
I WAS ABLE TO SHOW MY OLDER CARTOON WORK ONLINE.
THIS INCLUDED A FEW CHAPTERS OF AN ABANDONED BOOK PROJECT CALLED PSYCHIATRIC TALES.
HE WAS ONLY TWENTY-EIGHT, BUT LOOKED THIRTY-EIGHT. YEARS OF DRUG ABUSE HAD TAKEN IT'S TOLL, AGING HIM PREMATURELY.
HE'D CLAIMED TO HAVE BEEN OFF THE MORE SERIOUS DRUGS FOR THREE YEARS, BUTSTILL INDULGED IN CANNABIS.
A HARD CASE THEN, WITH THE USUAL LOOK SUCH MEN HAVE: A SKINHEAD AND TATTOOS.
I RECEIVED SUCH A HUGE RESPONSE FROM THIS WORK THAT I WAS ENCOURAGED TO WRITE FURTHER CHAPTERS.
PEOPLE WITH MENTAL ILLNESS ENRICH OUR LIVES
WHICH HE REFERRED TO AS HIS BLACK DOG.
IN THIS WAY, BY USING THE KNOWLEDGE I'D GAINED DURING MY YEARS IN HEALTHCARE
I REDEEMED MYSELF IN MY OWN EYES.
MY TIME AS A STUDENT NURSE NO LONGER SEEMED WASTED.
FEELINGS OF FAILURE BEGAN TO LIFT.

I'D FOUND ANOTHER WAY OF PUTTING ALL THAT HARD-EARNED KNOWLEDGE TO GOOD USE.

FUSING MY INTEREST IN MENTAL HEALTH WITH MY PASSION FOR DRAWING AND STORYTELLING.

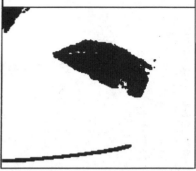

BEFORE THIS A BLACK WALL HAD STOOD WHERE THE FUTURE SHOULD HAVE BEEN.

BEYOND WHICH I COULD SEE NOTHING.

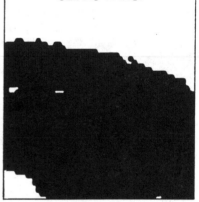

NOW A NEW LANDSCAPE HAD EMERGED.

FULL OF POSSIBILITIES.

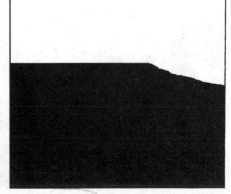

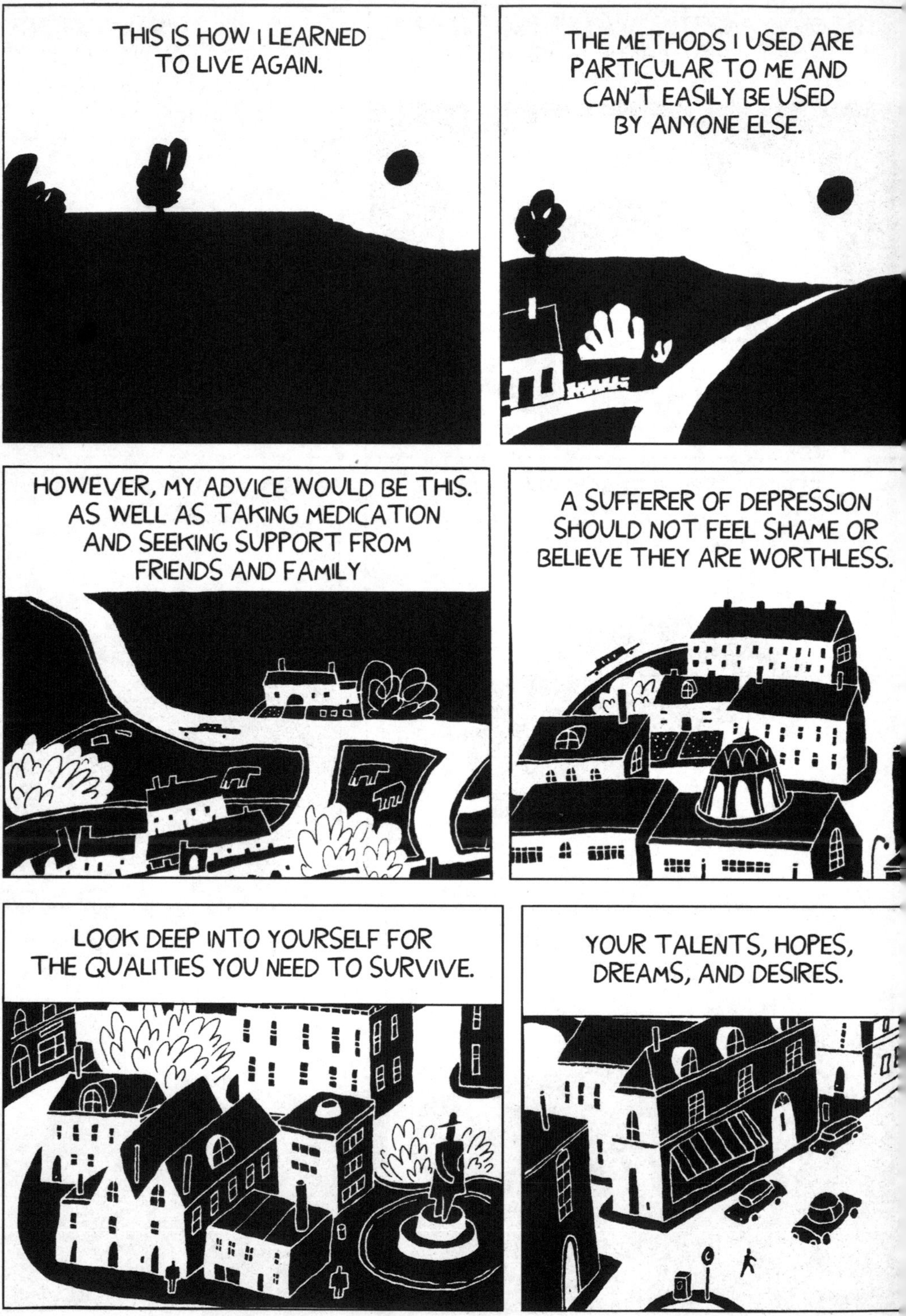
THIS IS HOW I LEARNED TO LIVE AGAIN.
THE METHODS I USED ARE PARTICULAR TO ME AND CAN'T EASILY BE USED BY ANYONE ELSE.
HOWEVER, MY ADVICE WOULD BE THIS. AS WELL AS TAKING MEDICATION AND SEEKING SUPPORT FROM FRIENDS AND FAMILY
A SUFFERER OF DEPRESSION SHOULD NOT FEEL SHAME OR BELIEVE THEY ARE WORTHLESS.
LOOK DEEP INTO YOURSELF FOR THE QUALITIES YOU NEED TO SURVIVE.
YOUR TALENTS, HOPES, DREAMS, AND DESIRES.

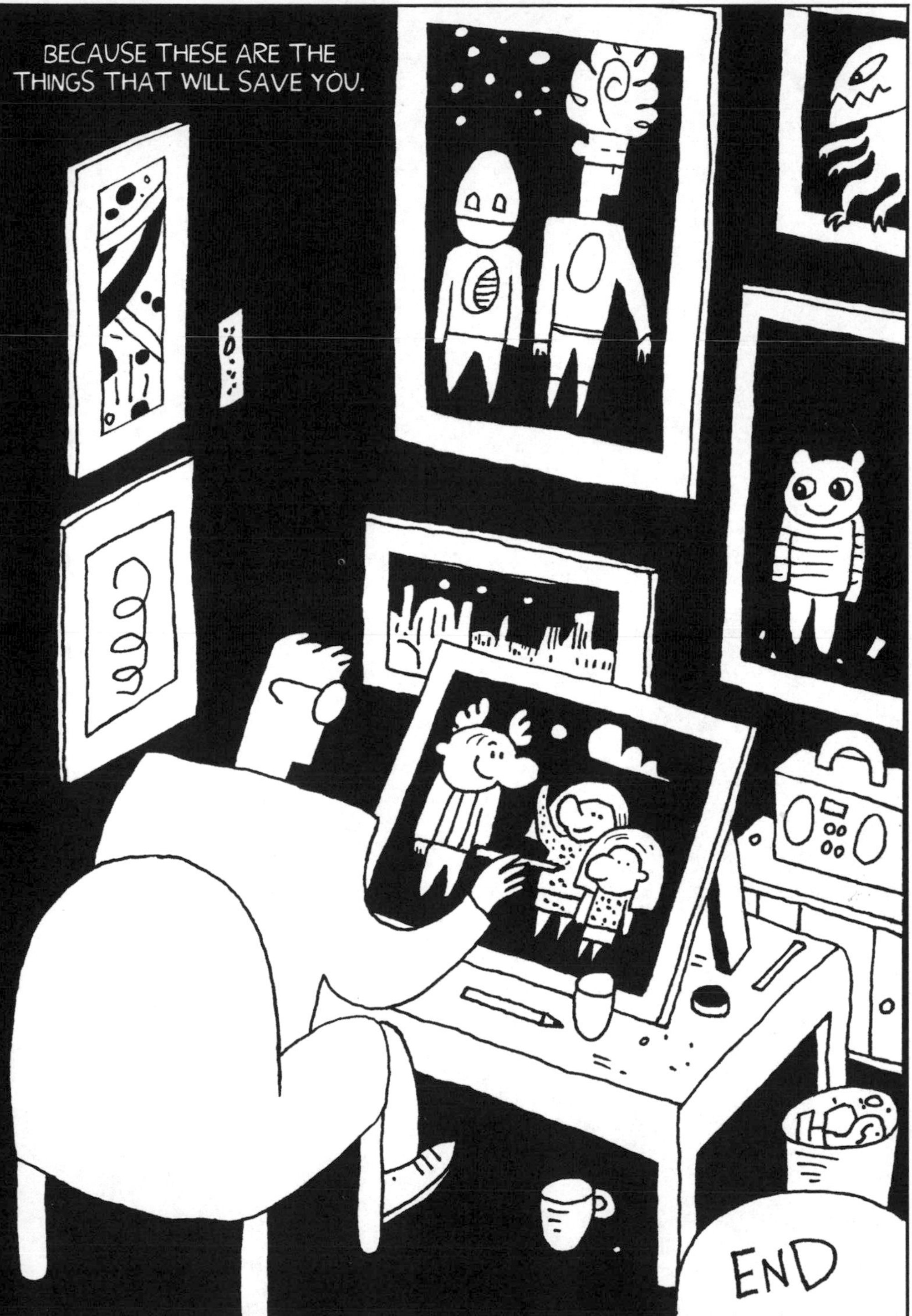
BECAUSE THESE ARE THE THINGS THAT WILL SAVE YOU.
END

Darryl Cunningham went to Leeds College of Art. He is a prolific cartoonist, sculptor and photographer. His long stint working as a health care assistant on an acute psychiatric ward was the inspiration for this book. He is the creator of the web-comics, 'Super-Sam and John-of-the-Night' and 'The Streets of San Diablo'.

He lives in Yorkshire.